LINCOLN and OHIO

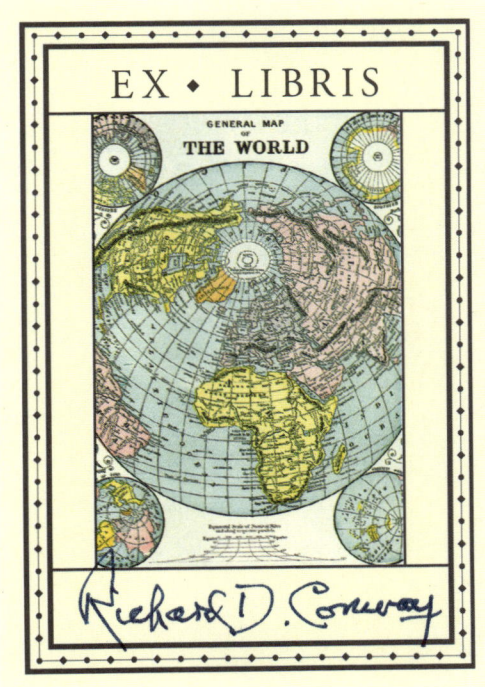

LINCOLN and OHIO

Daniel J. Ryan

Old Hundredth Press

ISBN 978-0-9793911-0-1

Original edition © 1923 by the Ohio Historical Society.

Additional material © 2008 by Old Hundredth Press.

Spelling, capitalization, and punctuation have been updated in Daniel J. Ryan's text, but no such changes have been made to letters, articles, and other excerpted materials, which are set in slightly smaller type.

Published by Old Hundredth Press, 2885 Gordon Road NW, Dover, Ohio 44622.

Proudly printed in the United States of America.

Contents

Preface 7

Introduction to the Original Edition 9

Chapter 1
Lincoln's First Contact with Ohio Statesmen 13

Chapter 2
Some Professional Associations in Ohio 17

Chapter 3
Lincoln in the Ohio Campaign of 1859;
His Speech at Columbus; At Dayton and Hamilton 25

Chapter 4
Lincoln's Speech at Cincinnati 63

Chapter 5
Ohio's Part in Lincoln's Nomination 91

Chapter 6
Lincoln in Ohio on His Way to Inauguration 113

Chapter 7
Lincoln's Relations with Ohio During the War;
The Case of Vallandigham; The Defection of Salmon P. Chase 143

Chapter 8
The Lincoln Obsequies in Ohio;
Ceremonies at Cleveland and Columbus 181

Notes 219

Index 233

Preface

When Abraham Lincoln was elected president of the United States in November 1860, the Union consisted of thirty-two states. While Ohio cannot claim to be the birthplace or home of the nation's sixteenth chief executive, it can, as readers of this interesting volume will discover, demonstrate that it played an important role in placing and keeping him in the White House.

Nearly six decades after the guns of the Civil War fell silent, officials of the Ohio Archaeological and Historical Society invested significant resources into properly documenting the state's part in the Lincoln story. In January 1923, a 274-page article entitled "Lincoln and Ohio" by state historian Daniel J. Ryan, accompanied with a brief introduction by Society Secretary Charles B. Galbreath, was published in the *Ohio Archaeological and Historical Quarterly*. Anticipating a larger market, the Society immediately reprinted it as a separate pamphlet.

In 2008, on the eve of the bicentennial of Lincoln's birth, the Society is pleased to have worked with Old Hundredth Press to again make this volume available to interested historians and collectors of Lincolniana. We trust you will find it as worthwhile as readers did in 1923.

William K. Laidlaw Jr.
Executive Director
Ohio Historical Society

Introduction to the Original Edition

A wide interest attaches to everything that is said or written of Abraham Lincoln. Ohioans will be pleased to review the authentic historic record that links his name and fame with the Buckeye State.

The monograph on the following pages presents for the first time in chronological order Lincoln's contact with Ohio and the relation of our state and its prominent public men to the crisis through which our nation passed in the Civil War, under the leadership of the martyr president whose fame, increasing with the passing years, has become to the civilized world a sacred heritage and hallowed memory. Abraham Lincoln is and will continue to be a beneficent, living influence in our republic.

Without the effective support given Lincoln by followers in Ohio, he could not have been nominated for the presidency. This will be the conclusion of those who read the chapter on the following pages entitled "Ohio's Part in Lincoln's Nomination." Especially interesting will be found the attitude of the Ohio delegation at the Chicago convention of 1860. With so able and deserving a candidate from their own state as Salmon P. Chase, it required on the part of delegates courage and pronounced preference to sway them from support of the home candidate.

The proceedings of that convention, to which attention is invited, exhibit contrasts with national political conventions of today. Sixty-three years ago political speeches and partisan contributions to newspapers as a rule were much longer than they are today. Nominating speeches in party conventions were then very brief, limited often to one sentence. Lincoln was fortunate in the statement with which his name was presented by a member of the Ohio delegation. The nominating speech of a single sentence by Columbus Delano, of Mt. Vernon, Ohio, was one of the most effective ever delivered in a party convention. Those who appreciate the "rare, strange virtue" of effective brevity in speech should read what Delano said in presenting the name of Lincoln.

It was left for another Ohio man—the leader of the delegation—at the critical moment to do the dramatic thing and throw to Lincoln the votes necessary to assure his nomination.

Not only did Ohio lend decisive aid in assuring his nomination, but it gave Lincoln a substantial majority in the November election.

It would be pleasing to record that our state never wavered in his support, but that in truth could not be said. The days that in a very special sense "tried the soul" of Abraham Lincoln were between September 22, 1862, and October 13, 1863. On the former of these two dates he issued what is generally called his "preliminary Emancipation Proclamation" in which he declared that if the southern states in rebellion did not lay down their arms, he would, by virtue of the war power vested in him by the constitution, liberate all their slaves.

Lincoln was elected on a platform pledge to oppose the extension of slavery into the territories. The proposal to end that institution where it already existed was new and at first encountered with violent opposition, even in the loyal North. At the fall elections following the issue of the "preliminary proclamation," New York, Pennsylvania, the president's state, Illinois, and our own Ohio registered their votes against his party, and of course inferentially against his emancipation policy.

Think of the position of Abraham Lincoln then. The South in arms against him and winning victories on the field of battle; the North arrayed against him at the ballot box and organizing in secret societies to destroy his administration and aid the enemies of the Republic. With threatening clouds on every hand growing darker with each passing day; with foes exulting in his discomfiture; with faltering friends advising that the promised Emancipation Proclamation be postponed, Abraham Lincoln moved onward in his course with conscience uncompromised and courage sublime to the accomplishment of his mission. On the first day of January, 1863, he issued his Emancipation Proclamation and linked his name with the immortals. The closing lines express the spirit and unfaltering faith with which this instrument was written:

And upon this act, sincerely believed to be an act of justice, warranted by the constitution upon military necessity, I invoke the considerate judgment of mankind and the gracious favor of Almighty God.

The proclamation was issued, and upon his broad shoulders fell heavily the responsibility to make it good. Dark days were ahead. Mr. Ryan has graphically described the Vallandigham campaign of the summer and autumn following. It is difficult for us at this day to understand how thoroughly the people of Ohio were aroused and how bitterly the contending parties hurled denunciation at each other. A single stanza from a popular song of the followers of Vallandigham gives but an inadequate glimpse of the spirit of the time:

> We are coming, Abraham Lincoln,
>   From mountain, wood and glen;
> We are coming, Abraham Lincoln,
>   With the ghosts of murdered men.
> Yes! we're coming, Abraham Lincoln,
>   With curses loud and deep,
> That will haunt you in your waking,
>   And disturb you in your sleep.

The fate of the nation turned upon the result of this election in Ohio. Lincoln and his followers felt this. The result at times seemed involved in doubt. The description of that campaign on the following pages will grip the interest of the reader. No one can without a thrill picture Abraham Lincoln in Washington anxiously receiving from John Brough, candidate for governor in Ohio, the telegraphic returns of that fateful election. Early in the evening following the close of the polls the president was cheered with the assurance that Ohio has sustained him. At midnight he was further encouraged on learning that the majority was a substantial one. At five o'clock in the morning following, on receiving word from Brough that the majority was more than one hundred thousand, Abraham Lincoln poured forth his soul in that famous telegram: *"Glory to God in the highest; Ohio has saved the Nation."*

Ohio indeed had redeemed herself and by a decisive majority had rallied to the support of Abraham Lincoln and universal liberty in America.

Today every Ohioan must read with pride the record of our state, in this fateful test, for liberty and union.

Most appropriately has the writer of this monograph given generous space to the obsequies of Lincoln within the borders of our state. It was James G. Blaine who said in describing the funeral ceremonies in which Ohio had a conspicuous part:

> For seventeen hundred miles, through eight states of the Union whose population was not less than fifteen millions, an almost continuous procession of mourners attended the remains of the beloved President. There was no pageantry save their presence. There was no tribute but their tears.... A countless multitude of men, with music and banner and cheer and the inspiration of a great cause, presents a spectacle that engages the eye, fills the mind, appeals to the imagination. But the deepest sympathy of the soul is touched, the height of human sublimity is reached, when the same multitude, stricken with a common sorrow, stands with uncovered head, reverent and silent.

The Ohio State Archaeological and Historical Society is fortunate in having as its vice president one so peculiarly qualified to make the contribution in these pages. Daniel J. Ryan, from his boyhood days, has been deeply interested in everything relating to the history of his native state. He served two terms as Secretary of State of Ohio and his reports bear testimony to this interest. They include, in addition to the routine matters relating to his office, a number of papers of distinct historic value. He was at the head of the Ohio commission that gave our state honorable and conspicuous representation at the Columbian Exposition in Chicago in 1893. Later he was one of the tax commissioners of Ohio, and he has for forty years been an officer in the Ohio State Archaeological and Historical Society. He has contributed not only to the publication of that society but to magazines and periodicals a number of valuable monographs. He is the author of books on Ohio history. Of the well-known standard work, *History of Ohio, The Rise and Progress of an American State,* by Randall and Ryan, Mr. Ryan is the author of volumes 3 and 4 and joint author of one of the remaining volumes. Those interested in the history of our state are his debtors. No future history of Ohio can be written without frequent reference to his fundamental work. *Lincoln and Ohio* has occupied his spare moments for some time past and the thoroughness with which he has collected and used his materials is attested in the following pages.

C. B. GALBREATH

CHAPTER 1

LINCOLN'S FIRST CONTACT WITH OHIO STATESMEN

Lincoln's first contact with Ohio men and influences began with his entrance into the Thirtieth Congress, December 6, 1847. The Mexican War was in full tilt, and the Whig party was opposing it. Two Ohioans—one in the Senate and one in the House—were conspicuous leaders in a bitter antagonism that was combating war legislation on every hand. They were representing the antislavery Whigs, who saw in the war a Democratic move to add slave territory to the Union. These leaders were Senator Thomas Corwin[1] and Representative Joshua R. Giddings.[2] The former had delivered in the Senate a passionate philippic, which will forever rank among the classics of American eloquence, against the Polk administration and the war. Giddings maintained the same attitude in the house, opposing appropriations and war measures. This opposition of Corwin and Giddings was heartily approved by the ultra antislavery Whigs, but it was received rather coldly by the party at large. It was not a patriotic position and was not sanctioned by the American people. They had their sons in a foreign land fighting a foreign foe, and a refusal to pay for their services, munitions, and food was an insupportable position. Besides, the Americans were winning victories; a militant spirit was throughout the land, and the people were exultant in the triumph of our arms at Palo Alto, Monterey, and the City of Mexico.

Under the influence of these events and the pressure of resultant public sentiment, the Whig party was silenced, and Senator Corwin found himself deserted by his colleagues who had pledged him their support in the Senate. The most powerful of these deserters from his cause were Webster of Massachusetts and Crittenden of Kentucky. In the House Giddings found himself in the same position. The indifference of the Whig party to the Mexican War was its death knell, as was the conduct of the Federal party in the War of 1812; for no party which fails its country in a foreign war can live.

Congressman Lincoln was an ardent admirer of Corwin—"Tom" Corwin, as his friends lovingly called him—and they frequently met at the Whig breakfasts which Senator Webster had made famous in Washington. But neither the influence of the powerful Webster, nor the charms of the companionship and eloquence of Corwin, radical fellow Whigs though they were, could induce him to oppose the war. He believed it to be unjustly initiated, and thus far agreed with his Whig associates, but he voted in every way to sustain its prosecution. Notwithstanding his disagreement with Corwin, they were fast friends, and continued so, and in after years when power came to the obscure congressman from Illinois, he made Corwin minister to Mexico.

His relations with Giddings were more intimate. Both "messed" at Mrs. Spriggs' boarding house on Capitol Hill, and many an evening and walk were filled with discussion on their respective positions, and for the first time Lincoln got a graphic view of Ohio politics from one of its most courageous characters. A friendship grew between the two that lasted until Giddings' death, and, as with Corwin, Lincoln remembered his old messmate when the opportunity came, for he appointed him consul general to Canada.

While both were Whigs, they differed radically on the slavery question. Their relationship continued when both became associated with the subsequently formed Republican Party. Lincoln was opposed to slavery; he believed it to be a great moral wrong. But he was firmly convinced that there was no power in Congress, under the Constitution, to interfere with its existence in the states. He was opposed to its extension, and he believed Congress had no power for that purpose. His stand was that while Congress was powerless to free the slaves in the states, it was equally so to make slaves in the territories. As he afterwards said, "this government cannot endure half slave and half free"; he was satisfied it would not last under the blazing rays of a fierce public opinion, and he felt that it would rot where it lay. His own words were, "let us draw a cordon, so to speak, around the slave states, and the hateful institution, like a reptile poisoning itself, will perish by its infamy." He was even willing to destroy it by purchase or colonization, but never by unconstitutional action. These were his opinions to his death, and he never veered from them for a moment.

Giddings on the other hand was an uncompromising abolitionist. To him slavery was such a monstrous evil that he was for its riddance regardless of law or constitution. Every method, lawful or unlawful, was to him justifiable, whether it was the Underground Railroad or the John Brown raid. The Whig Party was too slow for him, likewise was the Republican. But he recognized that they were the best practical antislavery agencies of their time. Notwithstanding that Lincoln could not follow him in his abolitionism, Giddings had a high regard for his integrity of mind and purpose. Sometimes he seemed that he bent his vigorous abolitionism for him. Lincoln's bill for the gradual abolition of slavery in the District of Columbia, which he introduced January 16, 1849, provided for full compensation to the owners of the slaves, but provided that the law should not go into effect until it had been favorably voted upon by the inhabitants of the district. Queerly enough, Giddings approved this, and had evidently talked it over with Lincoln before he introduced it. In his journal of January 11, 1849, Giddings gives his reasons for his support: "This evening our whole mess remained in the dining-room after tea and conversed upon the subject of Mr. Lincoln's bill to abolish slavery. It was approved by all; I believe it is as good a bill as we could get at this time, and I was willing to pay for slaves in order to save them from the southern market, as I suppose every man in the district would sell his slaves if he saw that slavery was to be abolished."

After Lincoln was nominated for president there came to him many letters; there was one that may be anticipated here as indicating an estimate formed in congressional days:

> DEAR LINCOLN: You're nominated. You will be elected. After your election, thousands will crowd around, claiming rewards for services rendered. I, too, have my claims upon you. I have not worked for your nomination, nor for that of any other man. I have labored for the establishment of principles; and when men came to me asking my opinion of you, I only told them "Lincoln is an honest man." All I ask of you in return for my services is, *make my statement good through your administration.*
>
> Yours,
> GIDDINGS.

Lincoln's short congressional career, although he had no realization of it at the time, was the climacteric of his political life. If he had followed any other course on the Mexican War he would have made his future impossible. As it was, some of his friends at home regretted his attitude. But he followed his own counsel, and time demonstrated the wisdom of his judgment. Ten years later in his first debate with Senator Douglas, he had the satisfaction of presenting his record. Douglas charged him with "opposition to the Mexican War, taking the side of the common enemy against his own country." Lincoln's reply was thorough:

> The judge charges me with having, while in Congress, opposed our soldiers who were fighting in the Mexican War. I will tell you what I can prove by referring to the record. You remember I was an old Whig; and whenever the Democratic party tried to get me to vote that *the war had been righteously begun* by the President I would not do it. But whenever they asked for any money or landwarrants, or anything to pay the soldiers, I gave *the same vote that Douglas did*. Such is the truth, and the Judge has a right to make all he can out of it.

If Abraham Lincoln had agreed and associated politically with Corwin and Giddings on the Mexican War, he would never have been able to make such a reply to Douglas. Neither would he have been nominated for senator, nor would he have been heard of for the presidency.

CHAPTER 2

SOME PROFESSIONAL ASSOCIATIONS IN OHIO

When Congress adjourned March 3, 1849, Lincoln returned to his home to resume the practice of law. He was a successful lawyer, for he had a mind calculated to bring him success. He was analytical, thorough, logical, and industrious. Added to these mental qualities, he was a good talker before a jury. When he attained the presidency he ranked among the leading lawyers of his state. His business extended beyond Illinois.

On Christmas Eve, 1849, he was in Cincinnati, and wrote to the chief justice of the Supreme Court of Ohio the following letter:

MR. PETER HITCHCOCK, *Esq.*, [3]
    Judge at Columbus.

DEAR SIR:—
Mr. Fox informed me this morning that I had better write to you in reference to the case of Linus Logan and the Steamboat Clipper now on the docket. We have been ready at any time to take up the case but have waited for the brief of the other side. We have not yet received it, but it is promised us today.

    Judge Coffin left here yesterday saying that he would have the case put down for Friday. If I get the brief today or tomorrow we can be ready to hear it then and will be in Columbus for that purpose.

    We are very anxious to have it heard on account of our clients in this case and because the same question presented in the record is now before

the courts of this country in several cases. Some cause, I am not fully aware what, has prevented counsel from furnishing the brief, etc. I hope the case will not be continued.
Yours respectfully,
A. LINCOLN.

The case to which Lincoln referred was, in itself, of not unusual importance, but because it marks his first professional association with the Ohio courts, it becomes of more than passing interest.

The original action was for trespass brought by Logan, who was Lincoln's client, against the steamboat *Clipper* for wrongfully running into and damaging the steamboat *Mail* while navigating the Ohio River near Manchester, Ohio, on the 20th day of March, 1844. The case was tried at the June term, 1848, of the Superior Court of Cincinnati, when Logan got a verdict for $3,760; it was taken in error to the Supreme Court of Ohio, in bank, at Columbus, on the question of certain testimony, and was again decided in favor of Lincoln's client. The case—Steamboat *Clipper* vs. Linus Logan—will be found in the 18th Ohio Reports, pages 375–399, reported in full. We are deprived of further and more definite knowledge of Lincoln's connection with this case for the reason that the records of the Superior Court of Cincinnati and the Supreme Court at Columbus were destroyed by fire, the former in the riots of 1884. Whether he tried the case in the Superior Court, or argued it in the Supreme Court we have no means of knowing. The brief for his client in the Ohio Reports is signed by T. D. Lincoln[4] of Cincinnati, one of the leading lawyers of the Ohio Valley in his generation, and the Mr. Fox referred to in Lincoln's letters was T. D.'s partner. He was known as an expert in admiralty law, and there was little litigation concerning disputes on the western waters that he was not counsel on one side or the other. He was always employed by nonresident lawyers in their suits before Ohio courts. As Lincoln was not eligible to practice in Ohio it may be taken as a fact that the case was argued by "Tim" Lincoln, as he was popularly called, and it is equally certain that Abraham Lincoln, judging from his letter, was present.

Eight years later these two Lincolns were opposing counsel in the United States courts at Chicago in an admiralty case of great importance, and which at the time was viewed with almost sensational interest throughout the West. It was known as the Rock Island Bridge Company case, growing out of the construction of a bridge over the

Mississippi River. It was the day of intense rivalry between steamboat and railroad, and in the narrow view of pioneer progress, was regarded as involving the commercial supremacy of St. Louis or Chicago. In this litigation Lincoln of Ohio and Lincoln of Illinois were strenuous antagonists, with the latter as the victor.

Lincoln was sensitive over his professional honor, as his experience with an Ohio client demonstrates. In 1859 the Columbus Machine Manufacturing Company, owned by a Mr. Ambos of Columbus, had forwarded to Lincoln through Samuel Galloway,[5] attorney, certain claims for collection against parties, purchasers of machinery, at Springfield, Illinois. The collection was slow, and complaint was made against Lincoln for his apparent negligence. Thereupon came the following letter to the Columbus attorney:

SPRINGFIELD, ILL., July 27, 1859.

HON. SAMUEL GALLOWAY.
MY DEAR SIRS: Your letter in relation to the claim of Mr. Ambos for the Columbus Machine Manufacturing Company against Barret and others received. This has been a somewhat disagreeable matter to me. As I remember, you first wrote me on the general subject, Barret then having had a credit of four or five hundred dollars, and there was some question about his taking the machinery. I think you inquired as to Barret's responsibility; and that I answered I considered him an honest and honorable man, having a great deal of property, owing a good many debts, and hard pressed for ready cash. I was a little surprised soon after to learn that they had enlarged the credit to near ten thousand dollars, more or less. They wrote me to take notes and a mortgage, and to hold on to the notes awhile to fix amounts. I inferred the notes and mortgage were both to be held up for a time, and did so; Barret gave a second mortgage on part of the premises, which was first recorded, and I was blamed some for not having recorded the other mortgage when first executed. My chief annoyance with the case now is that the parties at Columbus seem to think it is by my neglect that they do not get their money. There is an older mortgage on the real estate mortgaged, though not on the machinery. I got a decree of foreclosure in the present month; but I consented to delay advertising for sale till September, on a reasonable prospect that something will then be paid on a collateral Barret has put in my hands. When we come to sell on the decree, what will we do about the older mortgage? Barret has offered one or two other good notes—that is, notes on good men—if we would take them, *pro tanto*, as payment, but I notified Mr. Ambos, and he declined.

My impression is that the whole of the money cannot be got very soon, anyway, but that it all will be ultimately collected, and that it could be got faster by turning in every little parcel we can, than by trying to force it through by the law in a lump. There are no special personal relations between Barret and myself. We are personal friends in a general way—no business transactions between us—not akin, and opposed on politics.
Yours truly, A. LINCOLN.

Whatever the fault of Lincoln may have been, whether negligence or lack of confidence, he brought suit to enforce his liens, and the litigation was pending when he was elected president.

Lincoln's second visit to Cincinnati was in September, 1855, and out of it grew a professional disappointment which he felt very keenly, and which he did not attempt to conceal. In addition to being an important event in his life as a lawyer, it was an interesting fact in connection with his subsequent history. It resulted from his engagement as one of the leading counsel in the patent case of McCormick vs. Manny. John H. Manny was sued by Cyrus H. McCormick in the Circuit Court of the United States for the Northern District of Illinois. The plaintiff sought an injunction to prevent Manny from infringing on certain patents and to recover four hundred thousand dollars as damages. Lincoln represented Manny; afterwards Edwin M. Stanton[6] was employed as cocounsel together with a Mr. Harding of Philadelphia as a patent expert. Reverdy Johnson of Baltimore represented the plaintiff; and he ranked among the greatest of American lawyers; he had served in the United States Senate and as attorney general in President Taylor's cabinet. Lincoln looked forward with pardonable pride to this forensic debate and prepared his brief with studious care. It was a professional opportunity which would add to his already high standing at the Illinois bar. He knew that Mr. Harding was to make the technical argument, but he was not aware of Mr. Stanton's employment until he reached Cincinnati; it was done by his client without his knowledge. This was a keen disappointment, but Lincoln silently acquiesced. At a meeting of the three counsel Messrs. Harding and Stanton determined that but two should argue their side. By all rules of professional courtesy, Lincoln, as the original counsel, should of course speak. Mr. Stanton therefore suggested to Lincoln that he should argue the law of the case, whereupon he answered, "No, do you speak." To which Mr. Stanton snapped, "I will," and immediately left for preparation. Thus Lincoln by his personal and professional courtesy brought upon himself one of the greatest disappointments of his life. He expected, of course, either a declination on Stanton's part or a rearrangement of the program. Neither occurred, and he was humiliated and chagrined, and the expected glory vanished.

This is without doubt the true story of Lincoln's rebuff in this celebrated case, as told by William M. Dickson[7] of Cincinnati, nearly forty years after, in *Harper's Monthly* for June 1884. He was in a position to learn the facts. Mrs. Dickson and Mrs. Lincoln were cousins, and Lincoln was a guest at the Dickson home during his stay in Cincinnati.

Several of his biographers have added other features, very sensational if true, to this episode of his life. The most striking of these is that Stanton expressed contempt of Lincoln's appearance and professional ability. There is no satisfying evidence of this statement. Stanton himself was a lawyer of high standing, and he knew that Lincoln ranked likewise at the Illinois bar, that he was the original counsel in the case, and had appeared before Judge McLean at Chicago. His employment in this important case alone was evidence of his professional standing. As a matter of fact, Lincoln had attained high position at the bar of his state. Up to this time he had argued more than one hundred and fifty cases in its Supreme Court; he was engaged in most of the important and lucrative litigation in the federal courts at Chicago and in the state courts of his circuit. Some of the cases, such as the Rock Island Bridge case, involved federal constitutional questions of national importance. Stanton's conduct on this occasion was in full keeping with his disposition. He was cold-blooded, selfish, and domineering, but he was a gentleman, and it was not in his nature to insult, with the methods of a boor, a brother lawyer, much less Lincoln. He simply displayed those traits of character that the country witnessed daily while he was secretary of war, and which at that time were invaluable to the Union cause.

With Lincoln's disappearance from the case he left his brief with Mr. Harding. It is interesting to know that he kept his retainer (five hundred dollars), received two thousand dollars as an additional fee, and that his client won his case, the court dismissing the action at the costs of the plaintiff.

He was in the city a week viewing the various places of interest. He was unknown and sought the acquaintance of nobody, but met about twenty persons. For the time he was moody and depressed. He was attracted in his solitary rambles to the gardens and conservatory of Nicholas Longworth.[8] Here is an interesting picture by Judge Dickson:

> The meeting of these remarkable men is worthy of a passing note. Nor can it be given without allusion to their dress and bearing. Mr. Lincoln entered the open yard, with towering form and ungainly gait, dressed in plain clothing cut too small. His hands and feet seemed to be growing out of their environment, conspicuously seen from their uncommon size. Mr. Longworth happened at the time to be near the entrance, engaged in weeding the shrubbery by the walk. His alert eye quickly observed the coming of a person of unusual appearance. He rose and confronted him.
> "Will a stranger be permitted to walk through your grounds and conservatories?" inquired Mr. Lincoln.
> "Y-e-s," haltingly, half unconsciously, was the reply, so fixed was the gaze of Mr. Longworth.
> As they stood thus face to face, the contrast was striking, so short in stature was the one that he seemed scarcely to reach the elbow of the other. If the dress of Mr. Lincoln seemed too small for him, the other seemed lost in the baggy bulkiness of his costume; the overflowing sleeves concealed his hands, and the extremities of the pantaloons were piled in heavy folds upon the open ears of the untied shoes. His survey of Mr. Lincoln was searching; beginning with the feet, he slowly raised his head, closely observing, until his upturned face met the eye of Mr. Lincoln. Thus for a moment gazed at each other in mutual and mute astonishment the millionaire pioneer and the now forever famous President. Mr. Lincoln passed on, nor did Mr. Longworth ever become aware that he had seen Mr. Lincoln.

Afterward came trips to the suburbs—Walnut Hills, Mount Auburn, Clifton, and then to Spring Grove Cemetery. He spent a morning in Room No. 1 of the Superior Court presided over by Judge Bellamy Storer—very odd and very able. Between motions and demurrers, he joked, told stories, and lambasted the lawyers, while the court room was in a roar. Lincoln enjoyed it hugely, remarking to Judge Dickson, "I wish we had that judge in Illinois. I think he would share with me the fatherhood of the legal jokes of the Illinois bar. As it is now, they put them all on me, while I am not the author of one-half of them."

When this visit was ended, he took the hand of his hostess cordially and said: "You have made my stay here most agreeable, and I am a thousand times obliged to you; but in reply to your request for me to come again, I must say to you, I never expect to be in Cincinnati again.

I have nothing against the city, but things have so happened here as to make it undesirable for me ever to return here."

"Man proposes and God disposes." Little did he realize that he was an unforged bolt in the arsenal of Fate, and that within a few years this same city, from which he departed so dejectedly, would hail him with great acclaim and demonstration on his way to immortal fame.

CHAPTER 3

LINCOLN IN THE OHIO CAMPAIGN OF 1859; HIS SPEECH AT COLUMBUS; AT DAYTON AND HAMILTON

Lincoln's first potential relationship with Ohio began with the campaign in the fall of 1859, when he formed political associations that had great influence in determining his future. We shall be better able to assess the value of these, as well as the important part he played in the canvass of that year, by reviewing the political situation.

The personnel of the candidates for governor was beyond reproach. Hon. William Dennison[9] was the nominee of the Republican Party, and Judge Rufus P. Ranney[10] of the Democratic. Both were men of distinction and great ability but of different types. Mr. Dennison, although a lawyer by profession, had acquired his reputation by reason of his business standing and financial ability. He had, it is true, served a term in the United States Senate, but on the whole he was a newcomer in state politics. His opponent, Judge Ranney, was the Nestor of the Ohio Bar when it numbered among its ranks such distinguished lawyers as Allen G. Thurman,[11] Thomas Ewing,[12] and Henry Stanberry.[13] His career as a great judge on the Supreme Bench, and his ability as a profound and learned lawyer justified his reputation. In the campaign the candidates met frequently in joint debates. Mr. Dennison developed unexpected powers as a political orator. Judge Ranney, whose judicial opinions were quoted as authority in every state in the Union, and whose powerful arguments and legal knowledge before the courts placed him at the head of his profession, was unimpressive in the forum of the people. In fact the contest was not as to who should be governor of Ohio, but the controlling question was whether this nation should be "half slave and half free." Men and their attainments were not considered in the overwhelming issue of the nationalization of slavery.

This was the question involved in the Lincoln–Douglas debates of the year before. It grew out of the passage of the Kansas–Nebraska Act in 1854, which repealed the Missouri Compromise of 1820, thus opening to the extension of slavery the vast public domain included in the Louisiana Purchase, and reaching from the Rio Grande River to the Canadian line. By this legislation was broken the pact by which it was agreed between the North and South to forever prohibit slavery north of 36 degrees, 30 minutes; and for thirty-four years this line between slavery and freedom was faithfully accepted, and it was supposed generally to have settled that sensitive question.

The man who was responsible for this radical and unexpected move was Senator Stephen A. Douglas[14] of Illinois, a Democratic statesman of great courage and force and unequalled among his fellow senators as a parliamentarian and debater. He embodied in his law what he called the principle of "popular sovereignty," by which he conferred upon the people of a territory the right to have slavery or not, as they voted. It was a specious and plausible plan, but by it the whole West became the legitimate quarry of the slave power; before, they could occupy less than one-third. Douglas was proud of his work and did not hesitate to take full credit to himself: "I passed the Kansas–Nebraska Act myself. I had the authority and power of a dictator, through the whole controversy, in both houses."

Douglas really believed that he was solving the question in a democratic way and that his law would be popular and would make him president. In the end it pleased neither the North nor the South, and resulted in his own political ruin, in the disruption of his party, and in the doom of slavery. In the North it was received as a "fire-bell in the night." Press, pulpit, mass meetings, and legislatures protested. The author was denounced as a Judas Iscariot; a society of Ohio women sent him thirty pieces of silver; attention was called to his middle name, recalling the traitor of the Revolution; he was hooted off the stage when he attempted to speak in his home city of Chicago; to use his own words, he "could travel from Boston to Chicago by the light of his own effigies."[15]

The immediate effect of Douglas' work was the organization of the Republican Party. It was a motley crowd composed of nearly the entire Whig Party of the North, hundreds of thousands of Democrats, most of the American Party, all of the Free Soilers, and the practical Abolitionists, but unanimous, earnest, and uncompromising in its opposition to the extension of slavery. This proposition was the cohesive principle that held it together, and its leaders showed wisdom by confining its object and declarations to this. There were some in the new party that sought for the abolition of slavery and the repeal of the Fugitive Slave Law, but their ideas were rejected. When the first national convention of the Republican Party was held, it declared against slavery extension; it confined its declaration on slavery to denying "the authority of Congress, of a territorial legislature, of any individuals or association of individuals, to give legal existence to slavery in any territory of the United States, while the present Constitution shall be maintained," and it declared it to be the "imperative duty of Congress" to prohibit slavery in the territories.

Representing these principles the Republicans of Ohio met in state convention June 2 at Columbus. It was a notable gathering and assembled at a time of great public agitation, which grew out of what was known as the "Oberlin–Wellington Rescue Case." There was an arrest of a fugitive slave who had lived near Oberlin for two years; this was resisted by a body of Oberlin students led by one of the professors. Two of the rescuers were arrested, tried, convicted, and imprisoned in the Cleveland jail under the Fugitive Slave Act. These proceedings aroused great interest throughout the country and inflamed to the highest pitch the indignation of the people in northern Ohio. An appeal for relief was made to the state courts, and a writ of *habeas corpus* was granted by one of the judges of the Supreme Court, commanding the sheriff of Cuyahoga County to bring his prisoners before the court for inquiry as to his right to detain them. The Supreme Court heard the case and passed upon the issue with great deliberation.[16] It was of political and historical importance. The question raised was whether the Fugitive Slave Act was constitutional, and could the Supreme Court of Ohio nullify the judgment of the United States Court for the Northern District of Ohio?

The story of the decision and its results was a vital element in the campaign of 1859, and its most tragic incident. It is a glaring example of flagrantly contemptible politics on one hand, and on the other a display of heroic fidelity to duty, which attained a lofty idealism. The situation has been described as follows:[17]

> The excitement was intense, and it was an occasion which called for the coolest judgment, the highest official independence, and indomitable judicial integrity. A bare majority of the Supreme Court of five members sustained the United States District Court, and the prisoners were therefore remanded to the custody of the Federal authorities. Judge Joseph R. Swan, as Chief Justice of the Court, prepared and delivered the opinion, in which he held that a state court could not interfere with the orderly action of the United States court within its constitutional limit. A more courageous opinion from an honest judge was never given. Judge Swan had been elected in 1854 by the anti-slavery sentiment of Ohio. It was the opposition to the Democratic party that eventually developed into the Republican party. The Fugitive Slave Law was extremely odious from a political standpoint to Judge Swan and his party associates. Notwithstanding that the law had been held constitutional by the Supreme Court of the United States, there was a deep seated hostility to it in Ohio. The opposition to it was one of the cardinal points of the new Republican party, of which Judge Swan was a distinguished member. It was in the face of these facts that he adhered to his judicial integrity and conscience and held the law as authoritative, whether he personally or politically approved its spirit and terms or not. For his firmness and independence in adhering to the principle which should always control the fearless judge, he accepted a retirement from public life and even alienated the best of his political friends.
>
> In the opinion of the Court, the majority of which was represented by Judge Swan, he takes occasion in his final words to indicate that his personal feelings and his judicial findings are not in accord. His closing words are:
>
>> As a citizen, I would not deliberately violate the Constitution or the law by interference with fugitives from service; but if a weary, frightened slave should appeal to me to protect him from his pursuers, it is possible that I might momentarily forget my allegiance to the law and Constitution, and give him a covert from those who were upon his track. There are, no doubt, many slave holders who would thus follow the impulses of human sympathy; and if I did it, and were prosecuted, condemned and imprisoned, and brought by my counsel before this tribunal on a *habeas corpus,* and were there permitted to pronounce judgment in my own case, I trust I should have the moral courage to say, before God and the country, as I am now compelled to say, under the solemn duties of a

judge, bound by my official oath to sustain the supremacy of the Constitution and the law, *the prisoner must be remanded.*

On June 2, 1859, the Republican State Convention assembled at Columbus; on the Monday morning previous Chief Justice Swan had rendered his famous opinion. Judge Swan was one of the founders of the Republican Party; he was a Democratic antislavery man, and joined with all others of that manner of thinking in order to form a party consecrated to freedom. He had been nominated and elected as judge of the Supreme Court in 1854 by a majority exceeding seventy-seven thousand. His fine career as a jurist, his high character, his decided views against the extension of slavery, all called for a nomination to the high office which he held, but his opinion had aroused the indignation of the radical element of the Republican Party, and under the leadership of Wade, Chase, and Giddings, a renomination was refused him.

It is difficult in moments of deliberation to conceive how men well versed in the law and having high ideals of citizenship could take this attitude. Judge Swan's position was such as any just and honorable judge, who had due regard for his oath of office and who honored his conscience, would take, but the intolerance of the abolitionists was exercised against him. Judge Rufus P. Spaulding, one of the attorneys in the famous case growing out of the Oberlin–Wellington Rescue, wrote concerning the defeat of Judge Swan for renomination: "He was dropped for the reason that he, as a judicial officer, recognized the Fugitive Slave enactment of 1850 to be of binding force in Ohio, and the two judges who were with him in opinion will be dropped in the same way as soon as they are reached in the order of time. We do not recognize them as Republicans here in northern Ohio who will for a moment sustain this miserable enactment."

In other words, the proposition was, that a judge of the Supreme Court should ignore a law that was duly passed by the Congress of the United States and declared constitutional by the highest tribunal of the land; and this should be done because the judgment of the majority of citizens of Ohio was opposed to the law in principle and for that reason would decline to obey it.

The influence of the radical or abolition element of the party was further evidenced by the adoption of a resolution in the platform declaring for the "repeal of the Fugitive Slave Act of 1850 as subversive of both the rights of the states and the liberties of the people, and as contrary to the plainest duties of humanity and justice, and as abhorrent to the moral sense of the civilized world." To the conservative Republicans these actions were looked upon with concern and regret. They had abandoned their lifelong political affiliations to join this new party for the single purpose of checking slavery, and they disapproved injecting the byproducts of abolitionism into this new association. They knew that it would hurt nationally. The mass of Republicans, while they were opposed to the principle of the Fugitive Slave Law, felt that it was one of the evil results of slavery. Such a law was required by the Constitution as one of the compromise measures of the Fathers. A similar law had been on the statute books of the government almost since its foundation. Washington signed the first fugitive slave law in 1793, and it was, as all such laws must be, one-sided and unjust. But the Constitution recognized slavery and made it the duty of Congress to protect it.

Lincoln was bitterly opposed to the principle of the law, but he favored obedience because it was the law. When he learned of the actions of the Ohio convention he did not hesitate to express his dissent. In a letter to Hon. Samuel Galloway (on another subject which we will read hereafter) he said: "Two things done by the Ohio Republican convention—the repudiation of Judge Swan and the 'plank' for a repeal of the Fugitive Slave Law—I very much regretted. These two things are of a piece; and they are viewed by many good men, sincerely opposed to slavery, as a struggle against, and in disregard of, the Constitution itself. And it is the very thing that will greatly endanger our cause, if it be not kept out of our national convention."

More deliberately did he write on the subject to Governor Chase. In a letter remarkable for its clarity of expression and soundness of opinion, he gave his construction of the Constitution:

SPRINGFIELD, ILL., June 20, 1859.

HON. S. P. CHASE,[18]
MY DEAR SIR: Yours of the 13th inst. is received. You say you would be glad to have my views. Although I think Congress has constitutional authority to enact a Fugitive Slave law, I have never elaborated an opinion upon the subject. My view has been, and is, simply this: The U. S. Constitution says the fugitive slave *"shall be delivered up,"* but it does not expressly say *who* shall deliver him up. Whatever the Constitution says *"shall be done"* and

has omitted saying who shall do it, the government established by the Constitution, *ex vi termini,* is vested with the power of doing; and Congress is, by the Constitution expressly empowered to make all laws which shall be necessary and proper for carrying into execution all powers vested by the Constitution in the government of the United States. This would be my view, on a simple reading of the Constitution; and it is greatly strengthened by the historical fact that the Constitution was adopted, in great part in order to get a government which could execute its own behests, in contradiction to that under the Articles of Confederation, which depended in many respects, upon the States, for its execution; and the other fact that one of the earliest Congresses under the Constitution, did enact a Fugitive Slave law.

But I did not write you on this subject, with any view of discussing the Constitutional question. My only object was to impress you with what I believe is true, that the introduction of a proposition for repeal of the Fugitive Slave law, into the next Republican National Convention, will explode the Convention and the party. Having turned your attention to the point, I wish to do no more.

Yours very truly,
A. LINCOLN.

This was the calm judgment of a man who hated the principles of this law, and who, in his debates with Douglas declared it bore all the marks of a design to maintain and perpetuate slavery, yet who favored its enforcement and so declared even after he was elected president.

The campaign opened immediately after the convention and waxed in intensity as the summer passed; in every section of the state great interest was aroused by the joint debates of the candidates for governor. The leaders of their respective parties were appealing day and night to the people. For the Republicans there were Governor Chase, Senator Wade, John Sherman,[19] "Tom" Corwin, Joshua R. Giddings, and a hundred lesser lights, while the Democrats in equal force were led by Senator Pugh,[20] Judge Thurman, S. S. Cox,[21] George H. Pendleton,[22] and William Allen.[23] At first the sacrificing of Judge Swan and the Fugitive Slave Law were sought by the Democrats to be made the paramount issues; in the Western Reserve the challenge was accepted.[24] But it was not long until it became apparent that the overwhelming one of slave extension was the question in the minds of the people. This was emphasized when Senator Douglas entered the campaign in September, which at once gave it a national character.

The newspapers of the time plainly indicate that the campaign had reached the passionate and unreasoning stage. The excited people were further inflamed by a press that seemed to have no other purpose than to abuse the opposite party, ridicule their political opponents, and misrepresent the occurrences of the canvass. For this reason the contemporary journals furnish little real information to one seeking the facts of this period. The actual condition as to public meetings, their size, conduct, and a fair report of the speeches find no place in their columns. In sharp contrast is the fair and newsbearing journalism of today; even in party organs opposing principles and men are discussed with a spirit of fair play. Illustrative of this comparison is the reception of Douglas on the occasion of his speech at Columbus on September 7. There is a dearth of real news concerning him; both party organs from the opposite viewpoints treat him with unfair ridicule on one side and lavish laudation on the other. The opposition paper writes him down as a "great knave," "trickster," "gigantic dwarf," "compound of cunning and impudence," "charlatan," "famous hypocrite"; his own party organ so extravagantly records everything concerning him that few facts are reported.[25] Douglas also spoke in Cincinnati on the 13th of September.

At the first announcement of Douglas' appointments to speak in Columbus and Cincinnati, the Republicans instinctively turned to Lincoln. The State Central Committee, and also that of Hamilton County, invited him to Ohio to reply to Douglas, and to the chairman of the latter he wrote:

SPRINGFIELD, ILL., Sept. 6, 1859.

Peter Zinn, *Esq.,*
DEAR SIR: Yours of the 2nd in relation to my appearing at Cincinnati in behalf of the Opposition is received. I already had a similar letter from Mr. W. T. Bascom, Secretary of the Republican State Central Committee at Columbus, which I answer today. You are in correspondence with him and will learn all from him. I shall try to speak at Columbus and Cincinnati; but cannot do more.
Yours truly,
A. LINCOLN.

On Friday, September 16, he spoke twice in Columbus, in the afternoon at two o'clock on the east terrace of the Statehouse, and in the evening before the Young Men's Republican Club at the city hall. During the day he also visited the county fair.

The principal speech was that of the afternoon; Lincoln was introduced by George M. Parsons, chairman of the Republican County Committee, and his speech as written and revised by him is as follows:[26]

Fellow Citizens of the State of Ohio: I cannot fail to remember that I appear for the first time before an audience in this now great State,—an audience that is accustomed to hear such speakers as Corwin, and Chase, and Wade, and many other renowned men; and, remembering this, I feel that it will be well for you, as for me, that you should not raise your expectations to that standard to which you would have been justified in raising them had one of these distinguished men appeared before you. You would perhaps be only preparing a disappointment for yourselves, and, as a consequence of your disappointment, mortification to me. I hope, therefore, that you will commence with very moderate expectations; and perhaps, if you will give me your attention, I shall be able to interest you to a moderate degree.

Appearing here for the first time in my life, I have been somewhat embarrassed for a topic by way of introduction to my speech; but I have been relieved from that embarrassment by an introduction which the *Ohio Statesman* newspaper gave me this morning. In this paper I have read an article, in which, among other statements, I find the following:

> In debating with Senator Douglas during the memorable contest of last fall, Mr. Lincoln declared in favor of negro suffrage, and attempted to defend that vile conception against the Little Giant.

I mention this now, at the opening of my remarks, for the purpose of making three comments upon it. The first I have already announced,—it furnishes me an introductory topic; the second is to show that the gentleman is mistaken; thirdly, to give him an opportunity to correct it.

In the first place, in regard to this matter being a mistake. I have found that it is not entirely safe, when one is misrepresented under his very nose, to allow the misrepresentation to go uncontradicted. I therefore propose, here at the outset, not only to say this is a misrepresentation, but to show conclusively that it is so; and you will bear with me while I read a couple of extracts from the very "memorable" debate with Judge Douglas last year, to which this newspaper refers. In the first pitched battle which Senator Douglas and myself had, at the town of Ottawa, I used the language which I will now read. Having been previously reading an extract, I continued as follows:

> Now, gentlemen, I don't want to read at any greater length, but this is the true complexion of all I have ever said in regard to the institution of slavery and the

black race. This is the whole of it, and anything that argues me into his idea of perfect social and political equality with the negro, is but a specious and fantastic arrangement of words, by which a man can prove a horse-chestnut to be a chestnut horse. I will say here, while upon this subject, that I have no purpose directly or indirectly to interfere with the institution of slavery in the States where it exists. I believe I have no lawful right to do so, and I have no inclination to do so. I have no purpose to introduce political and social equality between the white and black races. There is a physical difference between the two which, in my judgment, will probably forbid their ever living together upon the footing of perfect equality; and inasmuch as it becomes a necessity that there must be a difference, I, as well as Judge Douglas, am in favor of the race to which I belong having the superior position. I have never said anything to the contrary, but I hold that, notwithstanding all this, there is no reason in the world why the negro is not entitled to all the natural rights enumerated in the Declaration of Independence,—the right to life, liberty, and the pursuit of happiness. I hold that he is as much entitled to these as the white man. I agree with Judge Douglas, he is not my equal in many respects—certainly not in color, perhaps not in moral or intellectual endowments. But in the right to eat the bread, without leave of anybody else, which his own hand earns, *he is my equal, and the equal of Judge Douglas, and the equal of every living man.*

Upon a subsequent occasion, when the reason for making a statement like this recurred, I said:

While I was at the hotel today an elderly gentleman called upon me to know whether I was really in favor of producing perfect equality between the negroes and white people. While I had not proposed to myself on this occasion to say much on that subject, yet, as the question was asked me I thought I would occupy perhaps five minutes in saying something in regard to it. I will say, then, that I am not, nor ever have been, in favor of bringing about in any way the social and political equality of the white and black races—that I am not, nor ever have been, in favor of making voters or jurors of negroes, not of qualifying them to hold office, or intermarry with white people; and I will say in addition to this that there is a physical difference between the white and black races which I believe will forever forbid the two races living together on terms of social and political equality. And inasmuch as they cannot so live, while they do remain together there must be the position of superior and inferior, and I, as much as any other man, am in favor of having the superior position assigned to the white race. I say upon this occasion that I do not perceive that because the white man is to have the superior position, the negro should be denied everything. I do not understand that because I do not want a negro woman for a slave, I must necessarily want her for my wife. My understanding is that I can just let her alone. I am now in my fiftieth year, and I certainly never had a black woman for either a slave or a wife. So it seems to me quite possible for us to get along without making either slaves or wives of negroes. I will add to this that I have never seen, to my knowledge, a man, woman or child, who was in favor of producing perfect equality, social and political, between negroes and white men. I recollect of but one distinguished instance that I ever heard of so frequently as to be satisfied of its correctness—and that is the case of Judge Douglas's old friend, Col. Richard M. Johnson. I will also add to the remarks that I have made (for I am not going to enter at large upon this subject), that I have never had the least apprehension that I or my friends would marry negroes, if there was no law to keep them from it; but as Judge Douglas and his friends seem to be in great apprehension that they might, if there was no law to keep them from it, I give him the most solemn pledge that I will to the very last stand by the law of the State, which forbids the marrying of white people with negroes.

There, my friends, you have briefly what I have, upon former occasions, said upon the subject to which this newspaper, to the extent of its ability, has drawn the public attention. In it you not only perceive as a probability, that in that contest I did not at any time say I was in favor of negro suffrage; but the absolute proof that twice—once substantially and once expressly—I declared against it. Having shown you this, there remains but a word of comment upon that newspaper article. It is this: that I presume the editor of that paper is an honest and truth-loving man, and that he will be greatly obliged to me for furnishing him thus early an opportunity to correct the misrepresentation he has made, before it has run so long that malicious people can call him a liar.

The Giant himself has been here recently. I have seen a brief report of his speech. If it were otherwise unpleasant to me to introduce the subject of the negro as a topic for discussion, I might be somewhat relieved by the fact that he dealt exclusively in that subject while he was here. I shall, therefore, without much hesitation or diffidence, enter upon this subject.

The American people, on the first day of January, 1854, found the African slave-trade prohibited by a law of Congress. In a majority of the States of this Union, they found African slavery, or any other sort of slavery, prohibited by State constitutions. They also found a law existing, supposed to be valid, by which slavery was excluded from almost all the territory the United States then owned. This was the condition of the country, with reference to the institution of slavery, on the first of January, 1854. A few days after that, a bill was introduced into Congress, which ran through its regular course in the two branches of the National Legislature, and finally passed into a law in the month of May, by which the act of Congress prohibiting slavery from going into the Territories of the United States was repealed. In connection with the law itself, and, in fact, in the terms of the law, the then existing prohibition was not only repealed, but there was a declaration of a purpose on the part of Congress never thereafter to exercise any power that they might have, real or supposed, to prohibit the extension or spread of slavery. This was a very great change; for the law thus repealed was of more than thirty years' standing. Following rapidly upon the heels of this action of Congress, a decision of the Supreme Court is made, by which it is declared that Congress, if it desires to prohibit the spread of slavery into the Territories, has no constitutional power to do so. Not only so, but that decision lays down the principles, which, if pushed to their logical conclusion,—I say pushed to their logical conclusion,—would decide that the constitutions of free States, forbidding slavery, are themselves unconstitutional. Mark me, I do not say the Judges said this, and let no man say I affirm the Judges used these words; but I only say it is my opinion that what they did say, if pressed to its logical conclusion, will inevitably result thus.

Looking at these things, the Republican party, as I understand its principles and policy, believe that there is great danger of the institution of slavery being spread out and extended, until it is ultimately made alike lawful in all the States of this Union; so believing, to prevent that incidental and ultimate consummation is the original and chief purpose of the Republican organization. I say "chief purpose" of the Republican organization; for it is certainly true that if the National House shall fall into the hands of the Republicans, they will have to attend to all the other matters of national house-keeping, as well as this. The chief and real purpose of the Republican party is eminently conservative. It proposes nothing save and except to restore this government to its original tone in regard to this element of slavery, and there to maintain it, looking for no further change in reference to it, than that which the original framers of the government themselves expected and looked forward to.

The chief danger to this purpose of the Republican party is not just now the revival of the African slave trade, or the passage of a Congressional slave code, or the declaring of a second Dred Scott decision, making slavery lawful in all the states. These are not pressing us just now. They are not quite ready yet. The authors of these measures know that we are too strong for them; but they will be upon us in due time, and we will be grappling with them hand to hand, if they are not now headed off. They are not now the chief danger to the purpose of the Republican organization; but the most imminent danger that now threatens that purpose is that insidious Douglas popular sovereignty. This is the miner and sapper. While it does not propose to revive the African slave trade, nor to pass a slave code, nor to make a second Dred Scott decision, it is preparing us for the onslaught and charge of these ultimate enemies when they shall be ready to come on and the word of command for them to advance shall be given. I say this "Douglas popular sovereignty"—for there is a broad distinction, as I now understand it, between that article and a genuine popular sovereignty.

I believe there is a genuine popular sovereignty. I think a definition of "genuine popular sovereignty," in the abstract, would be about this: That each man shall do precisely as he pleases with himself, and with all those things which exclusively concern him. Applied to government, this principle would be, that a general government shall do all those things which pertain to it, and all the local governments shall do precisely as they please in respect to those matters which exclusively concern them. I understand that this government of the United States, under which we live, is based upon this principle; and I am misunderstood if it is supposed that I have any war to make upon that principle.

Now, what is Judge Douglas's popular sovereignty? It is, as a principle, no other than that, if one man chooses to make a slave of another man, neither that other man nor anybody else has a right to object. Applied in government, as he seeks to apply it, it is this: If, in a new territory into which a few people are beginning to enter for the purpose of making their homes, they choose to either exclude slavery from their limits, or to establish it there, however one or the other may affect the persons to be enslaved, or the infinitely greater number of persons who are afterward to inhabit that Territory, or the other members of the families of communities, of which they are but an incipient member, of the general head of the family of States as parent of all—however their action may affect one or the other of these, there is no power or right to interfere. That is Douglas's popular sovereignty applied.

He has a good deal of trouble with popular sovereignty. His explanations explanatory of explanations explained are interminable. The most lengthy, and, as I suppose, the most maturely considered of his long series of explanations, is his great essay in *Harper's Magazine*. I will not attempt to enter on any very thorough investigation of his argument, as there made and presented. I will nevertheless occupy a good portion of your time here in drawing your attention to certain points in it. Such of you as may have read this document will have perceived that the Judge, early in the document, quotes from two persons as belonging to the Republican party, without naming them, but who can readily be recognized as being Governor Seward of New York and myself. It is true that exactly fifteen months ago this day, I believe, I for the first time expressed a sentiment upon this subject, and in such a manner that it should get into print, that the public might see it beyond the circle of my hearers; and my expression of it at that time is the quotation that Judge Douglas makes. He has not made the quotation with accuracy, but justice to him requires me to say that it is sufficiently accurate not to change its sense.

The sense of that quotation condensed is this—that this slavery element is a durable element of discord among us, and that we shall probably not have perfect peace in this country with it until it either masters the free principle in our government, or is so far mastered by the free principle as for the public mind to rest in the belief that it is going to its end. This sentiment, which I now express in this way, was, at no great distance of time, perhaps in different language, and in connection some collateral ideas, expressed by Governor Seward. Judge Douglas has been so much annoyed by the expression of that sentiment that he has constantly, I believe, in almost all his speeches since it was uttered, been referring to it. I find he alluded to it in his speech here, as well as in the copyright essay. I do not now enter upon this for the purpose of making an elaborate argument to show that we are right in the expression of that sentiment. In other words, I shall not stop to say all that might properly be said upon this point; but I only ask your attention to it for the purpose of making one or two points upon it.

If you will read the copyright essay, you will discover that Judge Douglas himself says a controversy between the American Colonies and the Government of Great Britain began on the slavery question in 1699, and continued from that time until the Revolution; and, where he did not say so, we all know that it has continued with more or less violence ever since the Revolution.

Then we need to appeal to history, to the declarations of the framers of the government, but we know from Judge Douglas himself that slavery began to be an element of discord among the white people of this country as far back as 1699, or one hundred and sixty years ago, or five generations of men,—counting thirty years to a generation. Now, it would seem to me that it might have occurred to Judge Douglas, or anybody who had turned his attention to these facts, that there was something in the nature of that thing, slavery, somewhat durable for mischief and discord.

There is another point I desire to make in regard to this matter, before I leave it. From the adoption of the Constitution down to 1820 is the precise period of our history when we had comparative peace upon this question,—the precise period of time when we came nearer to having peace about it than any other time of that entire one hundred and sixty years, in which he says it began, or of the eighty years of our own Constitution. Then it would be worth our while to stop and examine into the probable reason of our coming nearer to having peace then than at any other time. This was the precise period of time in which our fathers adopted, and during which they followed, a policy restricting the spread of slavery, and the whole Union was acquiescing in it. The whole country looked forward to the ultimate extinction of the institution. It was when a policy had been adopted and was prevailing, which led all just and right-minded men to suppose that slavery was gradually coming to an end, and that they might be quiet about it, watching it as it expired. I think Judge Douglas might have perceived that too; and whether he did or not, it is worth the attention of fair-minded men, here and elsewhere, to consider whether that is not the truth of the case. If he had looked at these two facts,—that this matter has been an element of discord for one hundred and sixty years among this people, and that the only comparative peace we have had about it was when that policy prevailed in this Government, which he now wars upon,—he might then, perhaps, have been brought to a more just appreciation of what I said fifteen months ago,—that "a house divided against itself cannot stand. I believe that this Government cannot endure permanently half slave and half free. I do not expect the house to fall; I do not expect the Union to dissolve; but I do expect it will cease to be divided. It will become all one thing or all the other. Either the opponents of slavery will arrest the further spread of it, and place it where the public mind will rest in the belief that it is in the course of ultimate extinction, or its advocates will push it forward, until it shall become alike lawful in all the States, old as well as new, north as well as south." That was my sentiment at that time. In connection with it, I said: "We are now far into the fifth year since a policy was inaugurated with the avowed object and confident promise of putting an end to slavery agitation. Under the operation of the policy that agitation has not only not ceased, but has constantly augmented." I now say to you here that we are advanced still farther into the sixth year since that policy of Judge Douglas—that popular sovereignty of his, for quieting the slavery question—was made the national policy. Fifteen months more have been added since I uttered that sentiment; and I call upon you and all other right-minded men to say whether that fifteen months have belied or corroborated my words.

While I am here upon this subject, I cannot but express gratitude that this true view of the element of discord among us—as I believe it is—is attracting more and more attention. I do not believe that Governor Seward uttered that sentiment because I had done so before, but because he reflected upon this subject and saw the truth of it. No do I believe, because Governor Seward or I uttered it, that Mr. Hickman of Pennsylvania, in different language, since that time, has declared his belief in the utter antagonism which exists between the principles of liberty and slavery. You see we are multiplying. Now, while I am speaking of Hickman, let me say, I know but little about him. I have never seen him, and know scarcely any thing about the man; but I will say this much of him: Of all the anti-Lecompton Democracy that have been brought to my notice, he alone has the true, genuine ring of the metal. And now, without indorsing any thing else he has said, I will ask this audience to give three cheers for Hickman. (The audience responded with three rousing cheers for Hickman.)

Another point in the copyright essay to which I would ask your attention is rather a feature to be extracted from the whole thing, than from any express declaration of it at any point. It is a general feature of that document, and, indeed, of all of Judge Douglas's discussion of this question, that the Territories of the United States and the States of this Union are exactly alike—that there is no difference between them at all—that the Constitution applies to the Territories precisely as it does to the

States—and that the United States Government, under the Constitution, may not do in a State what it may not do in a Territory, and what it must do in a State it must do in a Territory. Gentlemen, is that a true view of the case? It is necessary for this squatter sovereignty, but is it true?

Let us consider. What does it depend upon? It depends altogether upon the proposition that the states must, without the interference of the General Government, do all those things that pertain *exclusively* to themselves,—that are local in their nature, that have no connection with the General Government. After Judge Douglas had established this proposition, which nobody disputes or ever has disputed, he proceeds to assume, without proving it, that slavery is one of those little, unimportant, trivial matters which are of just about as much consequence as the question would be to me, whether my neighbor should raise horned cattle or plant tobacco; that there is no moral question about it, but that it is altogether a matter of dollars and cents; that when a new Territory is opened for settlement, the first man who goes into it may plant there a thing which, like the Canada thistle or some other of those pests of the soil, cannot be dug out by the millions of men who will come thereafter; that it is one of those little things that is so trivial in its nature that it has no effect upon anybody save the few men who first plant upon the soil; that it is not a thing which in any way affects the family of communities composing these States, nor any way endangers the General Government. Judge Douglas ignores altogether the very well known fact that we have never had a serious menace to our political existence, except it sprang from this thing, which he chooses to regard as only upon a par with onions and potatoes.

Turn it, and contemplate it in another view. He says, that according to his popular sovereignty, the General Government may give to the Territories governors, judges, marshals, secretaries, and all the other chief men to govern them, but they must not touch upon this other question. Why? The question of who shall be governor of a Territory for a year or two, and pass away, without his track being left upon the soil, or an act which he did for good or for evil being left behind, is a question of vast national magnitude. It is so much opposed in its nature to locality, that the Nation itself must decide it; while this other matter of planting slavery upon a soil—a thing which once planted cannot be eradicated by the succeeding millions who have as much right here as the first comers, or if eradicated, not without infinite difficulty and a long struggle—he considers the power to prohibit it, as one of these little, local, trivial things that the Nation ought not to say a word about; that it affects nobody save the few men who are there.

Take these two things and consider them together, present the question of planting a State with the institution of slavery by the side of a question of who shall be the Governor of Kansas for a year or two, and is there a man here,—is there a man on earth, who would not say the governor question is the little one, and the slavery question is the great one? I ask any honest Democrat if the small, the local, and the trivial and temporary question is not, who shall be governor? While the durable, the important and the mischievous one is, Shall this soil be planted with slavery?

This is an idea, I suppose, which has arisen in Judge Douglas's mind from his peculiar structure. I suppose the institution of slavery really looks small to him. He is so put up by nature that a lash upon his back would hurt him, but a lash upon anybody else's back does not hurt him. That is the build of the man, and consequently he looks upon the matter of slavery in this unimportant light.

Judge Douglas ought to remember, when he is endeavoring to force this policy upon the American people, that while he is put up in that way a good many are not. He ought to remember that there was once in this country a man by the name of Thomas Jefferson, supposed to be a Democrat—a man whose principles and policies are not very prevalent amongst Democrats today, it is true; but that man did not take exactly this view of the insignificance of the element of slavery which our friend Judge Douglas does. In contemplation of this thing, we all know he was led to exclaim "I tremble for my country when I remember that God is just!" We know how he looked upon it when he thus expressed himself. There was danger to this country—danger in the avenging justice of God in that little unimportant Popular Sovereignty question of Judge Douglas. He supposed there was a question of God's eternal justice wrapped up in the enslaving of any race of men, or any man, and that those who did so braved the arm of Jehovah—that when a nation thus dared the Almighty, every friend of that nation had cause to dread his wrath. Choose ye between Jefferson and Douglas as to what is the true view of this element among us.

There is another little difficulty about this matter of treating the Territories and States alike in all things, to which I ask your attention, and I shall leave this branch of the case. If there is no difference between them, why not make the Territories States at once? What is the reason that Kansas was not fit to come into the Union when it was organized into a Territory, in Judge Douglas's view? Can any of you tell any reason why it should not have come into the Union at once? They are fit, as he thinks, to decide upon the slavery question—the largest and most important with which they could possibly deal—what could they do by coming into the Union that they are not fit to do, according to his view, by staying out of it? Oh, they are not fit to sit in Congress and decide upon the rates of postage, or question of ad valorem or specific duties on foreign goods, or live oak timber contracts; they are not fit to decide these vastly important matters, which are national in their import, but they are fit "from the jump" to decide this little negro question. But, gentlemen, the case is too plain;

I occupy too much time on this head, and I pass on.

Near the close of the copyright essay, the Judge, I think, comes very near kicking his own fat into the fire. I did not think, when I commenced these remarks, that I would read from that article, but I now believe I will:

> This exposition of the history of these measures, shows conclusively that the authors of the Compromise Measure of 1850 and of the Kansas–Nebraska Act of 1854, as well as the members of the Continental Congress of 1774, and the founders of our system of government subsequent to the Revolution, regarded the people of the Territories and Colonies as political communities which were entitled to a free and exclusive power of legislation in their provisional legislatures, where their representation could alone be preserved, in all cases of taxation and internal polity.

When the Judge saw that putting in the word "slavery" would contradict his own history, he put in what he knew would pass as synonymous with it: "internal polity." Whenever we find *that* in one of his speeches, the substitute is used in this manner: and I can tell you the reason. It would be too bald a contradiction to say slavery; but "internal polity" is a general phrase, which would pass in some quarters, and which he hopes will pass with the reading community for the same thing:

"This right pertains to the people collectively, as a law-abiding and peaceful community, and not in the isolated individuals who may wander upon the public domain in violation of the law. It can only be exercised where there are inhabitants sufficient to constitute a government, and capable of performing its various functions and duties, a fact to be ascertained and determined by"—who do you think? Judge Douglas says, "By Congress!"

"Whether the number shall be fixed at ten, fifteen or twenty thousand inhabitants, does not affect the principle."

Now I have only a few comments to make. Popular Sovereignty, by his own words, does not pertain to the few persons who wander upon the public domain in violation of the law. We have his words for that. When it does pertain to them, is when they are sufficient to be formed into an organized political community, and he fixes the minimum for that at 10,000 and the maximum at 20,000. Now, I would like to know what is to be done with the 9,000? Are they all to be treated, until they are large enough to be organized into a political community, as wanderers upon the public land in violation of law? And if so treated and driven out, at what point of time would there ever be ten thousand? If they were not driven out, but remained there as trespassers upon the public land in violation of the law, can they establish slavery there? No,—the Judge says popular sovereignty don't pertain to them then. Can they exclude it then? No, popular sovereignty don't pertain to them then. I would like to know, in the case covered by the essay, what condition the people of the Territory are in before they reach the number of ten thousand?

But the main point I wish to ask attention to is, that the question as to when they shall have reached a sufficient number to be formed into a regular organized community is to be decided "by Congress." Judge Douglas says so. Well, gentlemen, that is about all we want. No, that is all the Southerners want. That is what all those who are for slavery want. They do not want congress to prohibit slavery from coming into the new Territories, and they do not want popular sovereignty to hinder it; and as Congress is to say when they are ready to be organized, all that the South has to do is to get Congress to hold off. Let Congress hold off until they are ready to be admitted as a State, and the South has all it wants in taking slavery into and planting it in all the Territories that we now have, or hereafter may have. In a word, the whole thing, at a dash of the pen, is at last put in the power of Congress; for if they do not have this popular sovereignty until Congress organizes them, I ask if it at last does not come from Congress. If, at last, it amounts to anything at all, Congress gives it to them. I submit this rather for your reflection than for comment. After all that is said, at last by the dash of a pen, everything that has gone before is undone, and he puts the whole thing under the control of Congress. After fighting through more than three hours, if you undertake to read it, he at last places the whole matter under the control of that power which he had been contending against, and arrives at a result directly contrary to what he had been laboring to do. He at last leaves the whole matter to the control of Congress.

There are two main objects, as I understand it, of this *Harper's Magazine* essay. One was to show, if possible, that the men of our revolutionary times were in favor of his popular sovereignty; and the other was to show that the Dred Scott decision had not entirely squelched out this popular sovereignty. I do not propose, in regard to this argument drawn from the history of former times, to enter into a detailed examination of the historical statements he has made. I have the impression that they are inaccurate in a great many instances,—sometimes in a positive statement, but very much more inaccurate by the suppression of statements that really belong to the history. But I do not propose to affirm that this is so to any very great extent; or to enter into a very minute examination of his historical statements. I avoid doing so upon this principle—that if it were important for me to pass out of this lot in the least period of time possible, and I came to that fence and saw by a calculation of my known strength and agility that I could clear it at a bound, it would be folly for me to stop and consider whether I could or not crawl through a crack. So I say of the whole history, contained in his essay, where he endeavored to link the men of the Revolution to popular sovereignty. It only requires an effort to leap out of it—a single bound to be entirely successful. If you read it over you will find that he quotes here and there from documents of the revolutionary times, tending to show that the people of the colonies were desirous of regulating their own concerns in their own way, that the British Government should not interfere; that at one time they struggled with the British Government to be permitted to exclude the African slave trade; if not directly, to be permitted to exclude it indirectly by taxation sufficient to discourage and destroy it. From these and many things of this sort, Judge Douglas argues that they were in favor of the people of our own Territories excluding slavery if they wanted to, or planting it there if they wanted to, doing just as they pleased from the time they settled upon the Territory. Now, however, his history may apply, and whatever of his argument there may be that is sound and accurate or unsound and inaccurate, if we can find out what these men did themselves do upon this very question of slavery in the Territories, does it not end the whole thing? If, after all this labor and effort to show that the men of the Revolution were in favor of his popular sovereignty and his mode of dealing with slavery in the Territories, we can show that these very men took hold of that subject, and dealt with it, we can see for ourselves, *how* they dealt with it. It is not a matter of argument or inference, but we know what they thought about it.

It is precisely upon that part of the history of the country that one important omission is made by Judge Douglas. He selects parts of the history of the United States upon the subject of slavery, and treats it as the whole, omitting from his historical sketch the legislation of Congress in regard to the admission of Missouri, by which the Missouri Compromise was established and slavery excluded from a country half as large as the present United States. All this is left out of his history, and in nowise alluded to by him, so far as I can remember, save once, when he makes a remark, that upon his principle the Supreme Court was authorized to pronounce a decision that the act called the Missouri Compromise was unconstitutional. All that history has been left out. But this part of the history of the country was not made by the men of the Revolution.

There was another part of our political history, made by the very men who were the actors in the Revolution, which has taken the name of the Ordinance of '87. Let me bring that history to your attention. In 1784, I believe, this same Mr. Jefferson drew up an ordinance for the government of the country upon which we now stand; or, rather, a frame or draft of an ordinance for the government of this country, here in Ohio, our neighbors in Indiana, us who live in Illinois, our neighbors in Wisconsin and Michigan. In that ordinance, drawn up not only for the government of that Territory, but for the Territories south of the Ohio River, Mr. Jefferson expressly provided for the prohibition of slavery. Judge Douglas says, and perhaps is right, that that provision was lost from that ordinance. I believe that is true. When the vote was taken upon it, a majority of all present in the Congress of the Confederation voted for it; but there were so many absentees that those voting for it did not make the clear majority necessary, and it was lost. But three years after that, the Congress of the Confederation were together again, and they adopted a new ordinance for the government of this Northwest Territory, not contemplating territory south of the river, for the States owning that territory had hitherto refrained from giving it to the General Government; hence they made the ordinance apply only to what the Government owned. In fact, the provision excluding slavery *was inserted and passed unanimously,* or at any rate it passed and became a part of the law of the land. Under the ordinance we live. First here in Ohio you were a Territory; then an enabling act was passed, authorizing you to form a Constitution and State Government, provided it was republican and not in conflict with the Ordinance of '87.

When you framed your constitution and presented it for admission, I think you will find the legislation upon the subject will show that, whereas you had formed a constitution that was republican, and not in conflict with the Ordinance of '87, therefore, you were admitted upon equal footing with the original States. The same process in a few years was gone through with in Indiana, and so with Illinois, and the same substantially with Michigan and Wisconsin.

Not only did that Ordinance prevail, but it was constantly looked to whenever a step was taken by a new Territory to become a State. Congress always turned their attention to it, and in all their movements upon this subject they traced their course by that Ordinance of '87. When they admitted new States, they advised them of this Ordinance, as a part of the legislation of the country. They did so because they had traced the Ordinance of '87 throughout the history of this country. Begin with the men of the Revolution, and go down for sixty entire years, and until the last scrap of that Territory comes into the Union in the form of the State of Wisconsin—everything was made to conform with the Ordinance of '87, excluding slavery from that vast extent of country.

I omitted to mention in the right place that the Constitution of the United States was in process of being framed when that Ordinance was made by the Congress of the Confederation; and one of the first acts of Congress itself, under the new Constitution itself, was to give force to that Ordinance by putting power to carry it out in the hands of the new officers under the Constitution, in the place of the old ones, who had been legislated out of existence by the change in the government from the Confederation to the Constitution. Not only so, but I believe Indiana once or twice, if not Ohio, petitioned the General Government for the privilege of suspending that provision and allowing them to have slaves. A report made by Mr. Randolph of Virginia, himself a slaveholder, was directly against it, and the action was to refuse them the privilege of violating the Ordinance of '87.

This period of history, which I have run over briefly, is, I presume, as familiar to most of this assembly as any other part of the history of our country. I suppose that few of my hearers are not as familiar with that part of history as I am, and I only mention it to recall your attention to it at this time. And hence I ask how extraordinary a thing it is that a man who has occupied a position upon the floor of the Senate of the United States, who is now in his third term, and who looks to see the government of this whole country fall into his own hands, pretending to give a truthful and accurate history of the slavery question in this country, should so entirely ignore the whole of that portion of our history—the most important of all. Is it not a most extraordinary spectacle that a man should stand up and ask for any confidence in his statements, who sets out as he does with portions of history, calling upon the people to believe that it is a true and fair representation, when the leading part and controlling feature of the whole history is carefully suppressed?

But the mere leaving out is not the most remarkable feature of this most remarkable essay. His proposition is to establish that the leading men of the Revolution were for his great principle of non-intervention by the government in the question of slavery in the Territories; while history shows that they decided, in the cases actually brought before them, in exactly the contrary way, and he knows it. Not only did they so decide at that time, but they stuck to it during sixty years, through thick and thin, as long as there was one of the Revolutionary heroes upon the stage of political action. Through their whole course, from first to last, they clung to freedom. And now he asks the community to believe that the men of the Revolution were in favor of his great principle, when we have the naked history that they themselves dealt with this very subject-matter of his principle, and utterly repudiated his principle, acting upon a precisely contrary ground. It is as impudent and absurd as if a prosecuting attorney should stand up before a jury and ask them to convict A as the murderer of B, while B was walking alive before them.

I say again, if Judge Douglas asserts that the men of the Revolution acted upon principles by which, to be consistent with themselves, they ought to have adopted his popular sovereignty, then, upon a consideration of his own argument, he had a right to make you believe that they understood the principles of government, but misapplied them—that he has arisen to enlighten the world as to the just application of his principle. He has a right to try to persuade you that he understands their principles better than they did, and, therefore, he will apply them now, not as they did, but as they ought to have done. He has a right to go before the community and try to convince them of this; but he has no right to attempt to impose upon any one the belief that these men themselves approved of his great principle. There are two ways of establishing a proposition. One is by trying to demonstrate it upon reason; and the other is, to show that great men in former times have thought so and so, and thus to pass it by the weight of pure authority. Now, if Judge Douglas will demonstrate somehow that this is popular sovereignty—the right of one man to make a slave of another, without any right in that other, or any one else to object—there is no objection. But when it comes forward, seeking to carry a principle by bringing to it the authority of men who themselves utterly repudiate that principle, I ask that he shall not be permitted to do it.

I see, in the Judge's speech here, a short sentence in these words: "Our fathers, when they formed this government under which we live, understood this question just as well and even better than we do now." That is true; I stick to that. I will stand by Judge Douglas in that to the bitter end. And now, Judge Douglas, come and stand by me, and truthfully show how they acted, understanding it better than we do. All I ask of you, Judge Douglas, is to stick to the proposition that the men of the Revolution understood this subject better than we do now, *and with that better understanding they acted better than you are trying to act now.*

I wish to say something now in regard to the Dred Scott decision, as dealt with by Judge Douglas. In that "memorable debate" between Judge Douglas and myself, last year, the Judge thought fit to commence a process of catechising me, and at Freeport I answered his questions, and propounded some to him. Among others propounded to him was one that I have here now. The substance, as I remember it, is, "Can the people of a United States Territory, under the Dred Scott decision, in any lawful way, against the wish of any citizen of the United States, exclude slavery from its limits, prior to the formation of a State Constitution?" He answered that they could lawfully exclude slavery from the United States Territories, notwithstanding the Dred Scott decision. There was something about that answer that has probably been a trouble to the Judge ever since.

The Dred Scott decision expressly gives every citizen of the United States a right to carry his slaves into the United States Territories. And now there was some inconsistency in saying that the decision was right, and saying, too, that the people of the Territory could lawfully drive slavery out again. When all the trash, the words, the collateral matter, was cleared away from it—all the chaff was fanned out of it, it was a bare absurdity—*no less than that a thing may be lawfully driven away from where it has a lawful right to be.* Clear it of all the verbiage, and that is the naked truth of his proposition—that a thing may be lawfully driven from the place where it has a lawful right to stay. Well, it was because the Judge couldn't help seeing this that he has had so much trouble with it; and what I want to ask your especial attention, just now, is to remind you, if you have not noticed the fact, that the Judge does not any longer say that the people can exclude slavery. He does not say so in the copyright essay; he did not say so in the speech that he made here; and, so far as I know, since his re-election to the Senate, he has never said, as he did at Freeport, that the people of the Territories can exclude slavery. He desires that you, who wish the Territories to remain free, should believe that he stands by that position, but he does not say it himself. He escapes to some extent the absurd position I have stated by changing his language entirely. What he says now is something different in language, and we will consider whether it is not different in sense too. It is now that the Dred Scott decision, or rather the Constitution under that decision, does not carry slavery into the Territories beyond the power of the people of the Territories *to control it as other property*. He does not say the people can drive it out, but they can control it as other property. The language is different; we should consider whether the sense is different. Driving a horse out of this lot is too plain a proposition to be mistaken about; it is putting him on the other side of the fence. Or it might be a sort of exclusion of him from the lot if you were to kill him and let the worms devour him; but neither of these things is the same as "controlling him as other property." That would be to feed him, to pamper him, to ride him, to use and abuse him, to make the most money out of him "as other property"; but, please you, what do the men who are in favor of slavery want more than this? What do they really want, other than that slavery, being in the Territories, shall be controlled as other property?

If they want any thing else, I do not comprehend it. I ask your attention to this, first, for the purpose of pointing out the change of ground the Judge has made; and, in the second place, the importance of the change—that that change is not such as to give you gentlemen who want his popular sovereignty the power to exclude the institution or drive it out at all. I know the Judge sometimes squints at the argument that in controlling it as other property by unfriendly legislation they may control it to death, as you might in the case of a horse, perhaps, feed him so lightly and ride him so much that he would die. But when you come to legislative control, there is something more to be attended to. I have no doubt, myself, that if the Territories should undertake to control slave property as other property—that is, control it in such a way that it would be the most valuable as property, and make it bear its just proportion in the way of burdens as property—really deal with it as property—the Supreme Court of the United States will say, "God speed you and amen." But I undertake to give the opinion, at least, that if the Territories attempt by any direct legislation to drive the man with his slave out of the Territory, or to decide his slave is free because of his being taken there, or to tax him to such an extent that he cannot keep him there, the Supreme Court will unhesitatingly decide all such legislation unconstitutional, as long as that Supreme Court is constructed as the Dred Scott Supreme Court is. The first two things they have already decided, except there is a little quibble among the lawyers between the words *dicta* and decision. They have already decided a negro cannot be made free by territorial legislation.

What is that Dred Scott decision? Judge Douglas labors to show that it is one thing, while I think it is altogether different. It is a long opinion, but it is all embodied in this short statement. "The Constitution of the United States forbids Congress to deprive a man of his property, without due process of law; the right of property in slaves is distinctly and expressly affirmed in that Constitution; therefore if Congress shall undertake to say that a man's slave is no longer his slave, when he crosses a certain line into a Territory, that is depriving him of his property without due process of law, and is unconstitutional." There is the whole Dred Scott decision. They add that if Congress cannot do so itself, Congress cannot confer any power to do so; and hence any effort by the Territorial Legislature to do either of these things is absolutely decided against. It is a foregone conclusion by that court.

Now as to this indirect mode by "unfriendly legislation," all lawyers here will readily understand that such a proposition cannot be tolerated for a moment, because a legislature cannot indirectly do that which it cannot accomplish directly. Then I say any legislation to control this property, as property, for its benefit as property, would be hailed by this Dred Scott Supreme Court, and fully sustained; but any legislation driving slave property out, or destroying it as property, directly or indirectly, will most assuredly, by that court, be held unconstitutional.

Judge Douglas says if the Constitution carries slavery into the Territories, beyond the power of the people of the Territories to control it as other property, then it follows logically that every one who swears to support the Constitution of the United States must give that support to that property which it needs. And, if the Constitution carries slavery into the Territories, beyond the power of the people to control it as other property, then it also carries it into the States, because the Constitution is the supreme law of the land. Now, gentlemen, if it were not for my excessive modesty, I would say that I told that very thing to Judge Douglas quite a year ago. This argument is here in print, and if it were not for my modesty, as I said, I might call your attention to it. If you read it, you will find that I not only made that argument, but made it better than he has made it since.

There is, however, this difference. I say now, and said then, there is no sort of question that the Supreme Court *has* decided that it is the right of the slaveholder to take his slave and hold him in the Territory; and saying this, Judge Douglas himself admits the conclusion. He says if that is so, this consequence will follow; and because this consequence would follow, his argument is, the decision cannot, therefore, be that way—"that would spoil my popular sovereignty, and it cannot be possible that this great principle has been squelched out in this extraordinary way. It might be, it might be if it were not for extraordinary consequences of spoiling my humbug."

Another feature of the Judge's argument about the Dred Scott case is, an effort to show that that decision deals altogether in declarations of negatives; that the Constitution does not affirm anything as expounded by the Dred Scott decision, but it only declares a want of power—a total absence of power, in reference to the Territories. It seems to be his purpose to make the whole of that decision to result in a mere negative declaration of a want of power in Congress to do anything in relation to this matter in the Territories. I know the opinion of the judges states that there is a total absence of power; but that is, unfortunately, not all it states; for the judges add that the right of property in a slave is distinctly and expressly affirmed in the Constitution. It does not stop at saying that the right of property in a slave is recognized in the Constitution, is declared to exist somewhere in the Constitution, but says it is affirmed in the Constitution. Its language is equivalent to saying that it is embodied and so woven into that instrument that it cannot be detached without breaking the Constitution itself. In a word, it is a part of the Constitution.

Douglas is singularly unfortunate in his effort to make out that decision to be altogether negative, when the express language at the vital part is that this is distinctly affirmed in the Constitution. I think myself, and I repeat it here, that this decision does not merely carry slavery into the Territories, but by its logical conclusion it carries it into the States in which we live. One provision of that Constitution is, that it shall be the supreme law of the land—I do not quote the language—any Constitution or law of any State to the contrary notwithstanding. This Dred Scott decision says that the right of property in a slave is affirmed in that Constitution, which is the supreme law of the land, any State constitution notwithstanding. Then I say that to destroy a thing which is distinctly affirmed and supported by the supreme law of the land, even by a State constitution or law, is a violation of that supreme law, and there is no escape from it. In my judgment there is no avoiding that result, save that the American people shall see that constitutions are better construed than our Constitution is construed in that decision. They must take care that it is more faithfully and truly carried out than it is there expounded.

I must hasten to a conclusion. Near the beginning of my remarks, I said that this insidious Douglas popular sovereignty is the measure that now threatens the purpose of the Republican party to prevent slavery from being nationalized in the United States. I propose to ask your attention for a little while to some propositions in affirmance of that statement. Take it just as it stands, and apply it as a principle; extend and apply that principle elsewhere and consider where it will lead you. I now put this proposition, that Judge Douglas's popular sovereignty applied will reopen the African slave trade; and I will demonstrate it by any variety of ways in which you can turn the subject or look at it.

The Judge says that the peoples of the Territories have the right, by his principle, to have slaves, if they want them. Then I say that the people in Georgia have the right to buy slaves in Africa if they want them; and I deny any man on earth to show any distinction between the two things,—to show that the one is either more wicked or more unlawful; to show, on original principles, that one is better or worse than the other; or to show, by the Constitution, that one differs a whit from the other. He will tell me, doubtless, that there is no constitutional provision against people taking slaves into the new Territories, and I tell him that there is equally no constitutional provision against buying slaves in Africa. He will tell you that a people, in the exercise of popular sovereignty, ought to do as they please about that thing, and have slaves if they want them; and I tell you that the people of Georgia are as much entitled to popular sovereignty and to buy slaves in Africa, if they want them, as the people of the Territory are to have slaves if they want them. I ask any man, dealing honestly with himself, to point out a distinction.

I have recently seen a letter of Judge Douglas's in which without stating that to be the object, he doubtless endeavors to make a distinction between the two. He says he is unalterably opposed to the repeal of the laws against the African slave trade. And why? He then seeks to give a reason that would not apply to his popular sovereignty in the Territories. What is that reason? "The abolition of the African slave trade is a compromise of the Constitution!" I deny it. There is no truth in the proposition that the abolition of the African slave trade is a compromise of the Constitution. No man can put his finger on any thing in the Constitution, or on the line of history, which shows it. It is a mere barren assertion, made simply for the purpose of getting up a distinction between the revival of the African slave trade and his "great principle."

At the time the Constitution of the United States was adopted it was expected that the slave trade would be abolished. I should assert, and insist upon that, if Judge Douglas denied it. But I know that it was equally expected that slavery would be excluded from the Territories, and I can show by history, that in regard to these two things, public opinion was exactly alike, while in regard to positive action, there was more done in the Ordinance of '87 to resist the spread of slavery than was ever done to abolish the foreign slave trade. Lest I be misunderstood, I say again that at the time of the formation of the Constitution, public expectation was that the slave trade would be abolished, but no more so than the spread of slavery in the Territories should be restrained. They stand alike, except that in the Ordinance of '87 there was a mark left by public opinion, showing that it was more committed against the spread of slavery in the Territories than against the foreign slave trade.

Compromise! What word of compromise was there about it? Why, the public sense was then in favor of the abolition of the slave-trade; but there was at the time a very great commercial interest involved in it and extensive capital in that branch of trade. There were doubtless the incipient stages of improvement in the South in the way of farming, dependent on the slave trade, and they made a proposition to Congress to abolish the trade after allowing it twenty years,—a sufficient time for the capital and commerce engaged in it to be transferred to other channels. They made no provision that it should be abolished in twenty years; I do not doubt they expected it would be; but they made no bargain about it. The public sentiment left no doubt in the minds of any that it would be done away. I repeat, there is nothing in the history of those times in favor of that matter being a *compromise* of the Constitution. It was the public expectation at the time, manifested in a thousand ways, that the spread of slavery should also be restricted.

Then I say, if this principle is established, that there is no wrong in slavery, and whoever wants it has a right to have it; that it is a matter of dollars and cents, a sort of question as to how they shall deal with brutes; that between us and the negro here there is no sort of question, but that at the South the question is between the negro and the crocodile. That is all. It is a mere matter of policy; there is a perfect right, according to interest, to do just as you please—when this is done, when this doctrine prevails, the miners and sappers will have formed public opinion for the slave trade. They will be ready for Jeff. Davis and Stephens and other leaders of that company, to sound the bugle for the revival of the slave trade, for the second Dred Scott decision, for the flood of slavery to be poured over the free States, while we shall be here tied down and helpless and run over like sheep.

It is to be a part and parcel of this same idea, to say to men who want to adhere to the Democratic party, who have always belonged to that party, and are only looking about for some excuse to stick with it, but nevertheless hate slavery, that Douglas's popular sovereignty is as good a way as any to oppose slavery. They allow themselves to be persuaded easily, in accordance with their previous dispositions, into this belief, that it is about as good a way of opposing slavery as any, and we can do that without straining out old party ties or breaking up old political associations. We can do so without being called negro worshipers. We can do that without being subjected to the jibes and sneers that are so readily thrown out in place of argument where no argument can be found. So let us stick to this popular sovereignty—this insidious popular sovereignty. Now let me call your attention to one thing that has really happened, which shows this gradual and steady debauching of public opinion, this course of preparation for the revival of the slave trade, for the territorial slave code, and the new Dred Scott decision that is to carry slavery into the free states. Did you ever, five years ago, hear of anybody in the world saying that the negro had no share in the Declaration of National Independence; that it did not mean negroes at all; and when "all men" were spoken of negroes were not included?

I am satisfied that five years ago that proposition was not put upon paper by any living being anywhere. I have been unable at any time to find a man in any audience who would declare that he had ever known of anybody saying so five years ago. But last year there was not a Douglas popular sovereign in Illinois who did not say it. Is there one in Ohio but declares his firm belief that the Declaration of Independence did not mean negroes at all? I do not know how this is; I have not been here much; but I presume you are very much alike everywhere. Then I suppose that all now express the belief that the Declaration of Independence never did mean negroes. I call upon one of them to say that he said it five years ago.

If you think that now, and did not think it then, the next thing that strikes me is to remark that there has been a *change* wrought in you, and a very significant change it is, being no less than changing the negro, in your estimation, from the rank of a man to that of a brute. They are taking him down and placing him, when spoken of, among reptiles and crocodiles, as Judge Douglas himself expresses it.

Is not this change wrought in your minds a very important change? Public opinion in this country is every thing. In a nation like ours, this popular sovereignty and squatter sovereignty have already brought a change in the public mind to the extent I have stated. There is not man in this crowd who can contradict it.

Now, if you are opposed to slavery honestly, as much as anybody, I ask you to note that fact, and the like of which is to follow, to be plastered on, layer after layer, until very soon you are prepared to deal with the negro everywhere as with the brute. If public sentiment has not been debauched already to this point, a new turn of the screw in that direction is all that is wanting; and this is constantly being done by the teachers of this insidious popular sovereignty. You need but one or two turns further until your minds, now ripening under these teachings, will be ready for all these things, and you will receive and support, or submit to, the slave trade, revived with all its horrors, a slave code enforced in our Territories, and a new Dred Scott decision to bring slavery up into the very heart of the free North. This, I must say, is but carrying out those words prophetically spoken by Mr. Clay, many, many years ago—I believe more than thirty years—when he told an audience that if they would repress all tendencies to liberty and ultimate emancipation, they must go back to the era of our independence and muzzle the cannon which thundered its annual joyous return on the Fourth of July; they must blow out the moral lights around us; they must penetrate the human soul and eradicate the love of liberty; but until they did these things, and others eloquently enumerated by him, they could not repress all tendencies to ultimate emancipation.

I ask attention to the fact that in a pre-eminent degree these popular sovereigns are at this work; blowing out the moral lights around us; teaching that the negro is no longer a man but a brute; that the Declaration has nothing to do with him; that he ranks with the crocodile and the reptile; that man, with body and soul, is a matter of dollars and cents. I suggest to this portion of the Ohio Republicans, or Democrats, if there be any present, the serious consideration of this fact, that there is now going on among you a steady process of debauching public opinion on this subject. With this, my friends, I bid you adieu.

The next morning the opposing newspapers gave their readers the following reports of the meeting:

SPEECH OF MR. LINCOLN OF ILLINOIS
(*Ohio State Journal*)

We give this morning a full report of the speech of Mr. Lincoln yesterday. It was made on the eastern terrace of the State House, the same place where Douglas made his; but, Mr. Lincoln being in the hands of friends, who wished to hear instead of suppress him, the arrangement was different. Instead of being partially extinguished with a brown sheeting canopy, and surrounded with half a dozen benches on which a score or two of men standing could hide him from the audience, and then being pitted against the immense stone wall of the State House, as Douglas was, Mr. Lincoln occupied a stand placed against the State House, and was easily heard all over the terrace. Yesterday being the great day of the county fair that performance prevented so large an audience as would have otherwise attended.

It is unnecessary for us to comment on the speech, as no one who has the opportunity will omit to read it. Mr. Lincoln was enthusiastically received, and held the attention of the audience for two hours, his clear and irresistible points eliciting frequent marks of approbation. The reception of the speech exhibited a marked contrast to that of Douglas, in which, whether the audience were nearly all republicans, or whether Ohio democracy is not Douglasism, the audience absolutely declined to cheer, and every solicitation resulted in a mortifying failure. The two Illinois champions are in themselves fair illustrations of the features of democracy and republicanism; Lincoln candid, logical and clear-headed, planting himself on principles that no one can controvert and winning the entire confidence of the audience; Douglas aiming at nothing higher than a political dodge; words which talk of principle to cover up a fraud; his highest ambition to show the cunning of the trick, and the greatest admiration of his friends that he can give a cheat the semblance of a principle; "popular sovereignty" while he nor his friends dare say that this popular sovereignty can exclude slavery from the territory.

Judging by the reception of the two speeches there is but little show of any popular sovereignty of the Douglas sort in Columbus.

ABE LINCOLN IN COLUMBUS
(*Ohio Statesman*)

The Young Men's Republican Club must have been mortified at the very meagre audience in attendance at the Lincoln meeting held yesterday afternoon on the eastern terrace of the State House. The Douglas meeting on Wednesday week at the same place could well have spared a number of men equal to that which heard Lincoln on yesterday, and not missed them from the assemblage. The meeting was indeed a "beggarly account of empty boxes," and the speaker disappointed all who heard him. We should be content to have Mr. Lincoln speak on the eastern terrace every day from this time until the election. He is not an orator. He can hardly be classed as a third rate debater. The most of his time was taken up in what he supposed to be a review of Douglas' Popular Sovereignty doctrine, and the article in Harper's on that subject. He is opposed to the principle of leaving to the people of the territories the right to mould their institutions in their own way; is in favor of the intervention of Congress and the control of the people of the territories through Congressional power; and further he is of the opinion that there is an "irrepressible conflict between the states of the Union which will never end, until all are made free or all are made slave States." Mr. Lincoln is not a great man—very, very far from it; and his visit here will not pay expenses. Indeed the Republicans feel that they have burned their fingers, by bringing him here. Happily for them, however, the audience was so small that his very inferior speech will do much less damage than it would have done had the audience been large.

At the close of Mr. Lincoln's speech, the meeting adjourned to assemble at the City Hall in the evening where it was announced that Mr. Lincoln and Mr. Galloway would address the people. At the adjourned meeting the "Illinois Champion" again held forth for a short time, when Mr. Galloway was called for, but we learn he did not speak. And thus ended the day whereby the Republicans were damaged seriously. We think Mr. Lincoln will never be invited here again, and that was perhaps his opinion, as he had his daguerreotype taken in the forenoon, with a view of leaving it, we suppose, as a remembrancer for his Columbus friends. It ought to be hung up in the Young Men's Republican Club room.

Here is another description giving the observations of a young lady of sixteen, after sixty-two years had passed:[27]

It was my happy privilege, in company with my father and mother, to hear the speech of Mr. Douglas and the reply of Mr. Lincoln, both delivered to small audiences on two somber autumn afternoons. Near the northeast corner of the ten acre State House square a steam engine was boring an artesian well. It was not noisy, but the sounds were regular and insistent; and, after speaking a few minutes, Mr. Douglas, looking very weary and annoyed, stopped, saying, "I can't speak against a steam engine." As soon as word could reach the engine driver, the boring ceased and the speech went on. Appeal, not argument; entreaty to change conditions, not recognition of the great trend of events characterized his address. A perfunctory round of applause without enthusiasm punctuated its close, and silently the two hundred men who had stood on the ground throughout the harangue dispersed, seemingly not converted to the plan of voting down slavery in the territories.

Mr. Lincoln came and was apparently introduced to the same audience. There were seated on the east terrace about a score of women, when there came from the Capitol behind the group, a tall, sad-eyed, earnest, grave man. Taking up the assumptions of his rival, he showed the fallacy of the local option of dealing with the extension of slavery into the territories. He indulged in no jokes, no witticisms. The crisis was too real and too awfully pregnant with fate. The impression left on the mind by the address was the vast import of events which no trifling or jugglery or vainglorious and boastful pro-slavery or anti-slavery men could delude the Nation into excusing, viz.; the invasion of free territory by armed men and the bloody encounters which followed.

At the close of Mr. Lincoln's address, the ladies who had been seated at his right were presented to him. I did not know that I was shaking hands with the next President of the United States, the hero and martyr of the coming crisis in our history.

The next day at Dayton, while waiting for the Cincinnati train, in response to previous arrangements, Lincoln spoke; his address covered similar points to those in his speech at Cincinnati that evening. It was in relation to the influence of the Ordinance of 1787 in excluding slavery from Ohio and other states of the West and Northwest. For the historical information it contained, as well as for its repudiation of the oft-repeated declaration of Senator Douglas, the reader is referred to Lincoln's Cincinnati speech, which he will find in the next chapter.

The following from the *Weekly Dayton Journal* of September 20, describes the meeting:

> The announcement that Mr. Lincoln—"Old Abe," as he is familiarly called by the "Suckers" with whom he lives,—would speak at the Court House on Saturday afternoon, brought a large crowd of people to the appointed place, and for nearly two hours the speaker was listened to with the utmost attention. Mr. Lincoln is one of the "self-made" men—having, without the advantages of education, risen to the proud pre-eminence which he now occupies in his own State and in the United States.
>
> He is remarkable for vigor of intellect, clearness of perception, and power of argumentation, and for fairness and honesty in the presentation of facts. Every man who listened to Mr. Lincoln on Saturday was impressed with the manner as well as the matter of speech, abounding as it did in valuable historical information and in great political truths.
>
> Mr. Lincoln directed the greater part of his speech to demonstrate the falsity of the assumption contained in the question in Senator Douglas' magazine essay, by which he seeks to make the framers of this government consider slavery a desirable feature in the material out of which the Union was formed.
>
> Mr. Lincoln met this assumption by a condensed statement of the facts in the history of the government, going to show that the framers of the government found slavery existing when the constitution was formed, and got along with it as well as they could in accomplishing the Union of the States, contemplating and expecting the advent of the period when slavery in the United States should no longer exist.
>
> He referred to the limitation of the time for the continuance of the slave trade, by which the supply of slaves should be cut off—to the fact that the word slave does not occur in the constitution, for the reason given at the period of its formation, that when, in after times, slavery should cease to exist, no one should know from the language of the constitution itself, that slavery had ever existed in the United States. We cannot attempt to follow Mr. Lincoln in his statement of facts and argument in exposing the false assumption of Senator Douglas, but Mr. Lincoln showed conclusively that instead of desiring that we should have a Union made up of free and slave States, as a sort of happy admixture of political elements, the framers of our government regarded the removal of slavery as only a question of time,

and that at some day, not far distant, the people among whom it existed would get rid of it.

Mr. Lincoln referred to the assertion of Mr. Douglas that the Ordinance of 1787 had never made a free State, and that Ohio had been made free solely by the action of its own people. Mr. Lincoln spoke of the difficulty of getting rid of slavery wherever it gained a foothold. He spoke of the trouble which encompassed the formation of a free constitution in the territory where there were slaves held as property, and attributed the untrammelled action of the Convention which framed the Constitution of Ohio in 1802 to the fact that the Ordinance of 1787 had prohibited the ingress of slaves, and so had relieved the question of a free constitution of all embarrassment.

In connection with the action of the people of Ohio, Mr. Lincoln referred to what is said of the influence of climate and soil in inviting slave labor to agricultural pursuits. He contended that the soil and climate of Ohio were just as favorable to the employment of slave labor as were the soil and climate of Kentucky. And yet without the Ordinance of 1787 Kentucky was made a slave state, and with the Ordinance Ohio was made a free state.

Mr. Lincoln closed with an eloquent defense of the rights of free labor. The free white man had a right to claim that the new territories into which they and their children might go to seek a livelihood should be preserved free and clear of the incumbrance of slavery, and that no laboring white man should be placed in a position where, by the introduction of slavery into the territories, he would be compelled to toil by the side of a slave.

When Mr. Lincoln had closed, three cheers were given, and he left for Cincinnati on the 4 o'clock train.

The *Dayton Daily Empire*, the Democratic paper, in its issue of September 20, had this editorial comment:

On Saturday last, instead of tens of thousands of persons being assembled in our city, and the streets being deluged with people, as one of our morning contemporaries prophesied would be the case, upon the occasion of Mr. Lincoln's speech, a meagre crowd, numbering scarcely 200, was all that could be drummed up, and they were half Democrats, who attended from mere curiosity.

Mr. Lincoln is a very seductive reasoner, and his address although a network of fallacies and false assumptions throughout, was calculated to deceive almost any man, who would not pay very close attention to the subject, and keep continually on the guard.

Mrs. Charles W. Nickum, of Dayton, in a manuscript written by her and sent to the writer, has described as follows a very interesting event which occurred on the occasion of Lincoln's visit:

An Accidental Painting of Lincoln

One day in Dayton, Ohio, in 1859, to be more exact, on September 17, 1859, there came into Cridland's daguerreotype gallery, over Edgar's grocery store on Main Street, two gentlemen, evidently to get their photos taken, as it was almost the first of photography. The gentlemen were the late Mr. Samuel Craighead, a prominent lawyer of Dayton, and his friend a stranger.

After getting his order, Mr. Cridland thought of the lad who was doing character sketches and painting in Edmonson's studio, across the hall from him, called him to come, bring his brushes and paints, to sketch this man who was character all over, that he would keep him as long as possible, but he must work fast.

As this gentlemen was posing he noticed the lad, asked him—was he trying to make a picture of him, then in his droll way—"Keep on, you may make a good one, but never a pretty one," then as they came back to see the negatives, he posed again for the lad. With his two sittings and the photo, a little painting was made, finished, put aside, and other work begun.

In June the following year Mr. Craighead met Mr. Nickum on the street, called him to stop, wanted to know if he ever finished painting his friend's picture, he began that day at Cridland's gallery. "Yes? Where is it? I want it, that is the man nominated for President, that was Abraham Lincoln."

Then the little painting was hunted up, nicely framed, and carefully cherished ever since. First offer to buy it came from the editor of the *Philadelphia Public Ledger* in the sixties. Mr. Nickum has shown an article bewailing the fact that few good paintings were made from life of Lincoln, when he wrote to the editor, telling of his work, he asked to have it sent to him for inspection, was pleased, asked Mr. Nickum to name his price, he wanted it. Mr. Nickum had never sold a painting, and thought if others thought it was so fine, why not keep it himself. Several good offers were turned down during his lifetime.

At an examination of the Lincoln portrait, about ten years ago at the Metropolitan Art Museum in New York City, one man said he believed it recently done, mellowed by a new process, but when a revenue stamp was discovered on the back of it, put there when it was framed in the sixties, he was silent. It still had the same frame on, as when framed so many years ago. Many others have gazed on the little portrait, those too who had known Mr. Lincoln, and with tears in their eyes, said it was the best they had ever seen.

On the same day Mr. Lincoln spoke at the Court House corner, from a store box. Mr. Nickum did not know of it. Mr. Will McCrea heard him speak, and from him we got the date.

Mr. Charles W. Nickum died at Indianapolis, October 2, 1913. Mr. Whiting, Director of Cleveland Art Museum, also Mr. Burroughs, Director of Detroit Art Museum, knows of the Lincoln portrait.

Yours respectfully,
MRS. CHAS. W. NICKUM,
Dayton, Ohio.

In a letter, October 21, 1922, accompanying the above, Mrs. Nickum further says: "Mr. Nickum often remarked how kind Mr. Lincoln was, and how willing he was to pose for him, and interested, offering him words of encouragement. Once afterwards he saw President Lincoln on the reviewing stand at Washington as he passed by as one of the 131st Regiment of Ohio soldiers on their way to Baltimore, during the latter part of the Civil War—but he had changed very much in that time."

Lincoln later in the day stopped off at Hamilton, and in the brief period allowed, he spoke to a crowd expecting him. There is a scant record of this occasion in the *History of Butler County*, by Bartlow and Todhunter, from which the facts herein are drawn. When the train stopped, Lincoln appeared on the back platform with his traveling companion, Congressman John A. Gurley of Cincinnati. The crowd had caught sight of Lincoln first, and set up a great cheering, but on the appearance of Gurley, there came uproarious laughter. Lincoln was in good humor and saw the point at once. Now, Gurley was a very short man, and he whom he was chaperoning was six feet four. Standing side by side, before alighting, Lincoln, after a good laugh, said: "My friends, this is the long of it," pointing to himself, then, laying his hand on Gurley's head, "and this is the short of it." The crowd roared. He then proceeded to the improvised stand, and in the necessarily short time he could but deliver a brief address, reviewing Senator Douglas's "Popular Sovereignty" doctrine, and closing his remarks as follows:

This beautiful and far-famed Miami Valley is the garden spot of the world. My friends, your sons may desire to locate in the west; you don't want them to settle in a territory like Kansas, with the curse of slavery hanging over it. They desire the blessings of freedom, so dearly purchased by our

Revolutionary forefathers. I see that my friend Douglas is still in favor of popular sovereignty. This is a dangerous doctrine; the inhabitants of a state should apply for admission to the Union either as a free or slave state, honestly expressed at a fair election. Such were not the conditions in Kansas when she applied for admission; border ruffians from Missouri controlled their election and certified the result in favor of slavery. The American people demanded fair play, and Kansas was admitted as a free state.

CHAPTER 4

LINCOLN'S SPEECH AT CINCINNATI

The Lincoln that visited Cincinnati in September 1859 met with quite a different reception from that given the Lincoln who came there September 1855. It was four years before that he said to his hostess, "I never expect to be in Cincinnati again. I have nothing against the city, but things have so happened here as to make it undesirable for me ever to return here." In dejection he departed; in triumph he returned, for great things had happened to him in the meantime. In 1856 at the first national convention of the newly organized Republican Party, he received 110 votes for vice president against 259 for William L. Dayton. In 1858 he engaged in debate with Senator Douglas over the Kansas–Nebraska Act, and the question of slavery extension. His militant presentation of Republican principles attracted attention throughout the country, and he at once sprang into national prominence. All this while his professional reputation had grown so that he ranked with the leaders of the Illinois bar. Now we find him responding to the Macedonian cry of the Ohio Republicans to come over from Illinois to answer Douglas, thus practically continuing, at long distance, the debate of the year before.

We may digress here for a while to note an interesting phase of Cincinnati politics at this time. The reader has doubtless observed the peculiar expression of Lincoln in responding to Peter Zinn's invitation, "in relation to my appearing at Cincinnati in behalf of the Opposition is received." Note that he says "the Opposition," and not "the Republican

Party"; and these words are evidently a repetition of Zinn's language. There was a studied reason for this, and it grew out of the relations of the local Republican Party and the American Party; the former was very desirous of securing the cooperation of the latter in the local elections, and ultimately wanted to absorb it. In other words they wanted Lincoln to make a mild and rather weak partisan speech, with a view to conciliating the American Party.

The situation is well described in a letter written to Addison Peale Russell,[28] secretary of state, at Columbus, by a young man, then city solicitor of Cincinnati, who afterward rose to distinction in the nation— Rutherford B. Hayes.[29] The letter is dated September 14, two days before Lincoln spoke at Columbus, and is as follows:

> I am not a member of any executive committee and am not "one in authority" except in the humble capacity of "a sovereign." As a private, I write to make a suggestion, which I hope you will see carried to the right person. Mr. Lincoln is to speak here the last of this week (I am sorry it was not a week later, after our ticket is in the field); and all honest Americans as well as Republicans are waiting to give him a rousing reception. My suggestion is that Mr. Lincoln be informed of the facts in regard to our position here, so that he may not give a too strictly partisan cast to his address. We go by the name of "Opposition Party," and injury might be done if party names and party doctrines were used by Mr. Lincoln in a way to displease the American element of our organization. The Americans are liberal, however, and very generally sympathized with Mr. Lincoln in his contest with Douglas, although perhaps not subscribing to all his views. I understand Mr. Lincoln was an old Clay Whig, of Kentucky parentage, and with a wholesome dislike of Locofocoism. These qualities with a word of caution as to our peculiar position will enable him to make a fine impression here.
>
> If our ticket is formed without a rumpus, we are confident of carrying a majority for all. I write, supposing you will see Mr. Lincoln at Columbus. Dennison seems to be a full match, if not an overmatch, for his competitor.
> Sincerely,
> R. B. HAYES

Lincoln in his speech, however, showed no appearance of taking notice of the suggestion of not giving "a too strictly partisan cast to his address." It was strictly partisan from beginning to end. He admitted he was a "Black Republican," and declared that "slavery is wrong, morally, and politically. I desire that it should no further spread in these United

States, and I should not object if it should be gradually terminated in the whole Union." He made no reference to any local conditions. He spoke for principle to all men who agreed with the object of his party. He wanted their votes, but he did not say so; he appealed to their conscience and judgment by naked argument. His speech was singularly adroit, yet logical. Like all his speeches, it seemed to have a direct and far-reaching purpose.

Fully three-fifths of his time was directed to Kentuckians, there being many present from across the river. It was an effective discussion of Douglas's position in relation to the South, and here he planted the seeds that resulted in the dissension at Charleston the next year. Lincoln knew exactly what he was doing, but some of his auditors evidently did not, for he was interrupted with, "Speak to Ohio men and not to Kentuckians," to which he responded, "I beg permission to speak as I please." A study of this speech finds Lincoln at his best; like all his addresses, it was clear, argumentative, and logical. Its language is for a plain audience, with words almost entirely Anglo-Saxon, or its derivatives. It deserves more than a cursory reading, for it contributed more to the Republican victory of 1860 than any single speech he ever made. Not that it converted Whigs, Democrats, or Americans, but because it served to divide the Democrats of the South from the Democrats of the North on Douglas's candidacy for the presidency.

The time and place of the speech were opportune—Saturday night and the Fifth Street marketplace—now the government square. It was when the populace was at large and in the very heart of the city. Lincoln, upon his arrival at seven o'clock at the Cincinnati, Hamilton, and Dayton depot, was received by a large committee of Republicans and was immediately escorted to the Burnet House, amid cheers and the firing of cannon. At the hotel he was received by another committee, "where he shook many hands and took his tea in very great haste." From thenceforward the evening was a triumph. Amidst the blare of brass bands and the booming of cannon he was driven to the Fifth Street Market Place in an open carriage, with a mounted escort, and the German Brigade and others on foot bearing torches. Lincoln spoke from a balcony on the north side of the square.

On his arrival he found an audience of three or four thousand people, with bands playing, the square illuminated by bonfires, and sky rockets filling the air.

The following organization of the meeting was effected: president,

Benjamin Eggleston; vice presidents, Peter Zinn, Rutherford B. Hayes, Nathaniel Wright, Nicholas N. Thomas, Stephen Molliter, George Shillito, M. D. Potter, Enoch T. Carson, Miles Greenwood, M. Goepper, Richard Smith, G. W. S. Katz, Henry Price, Thomas H. Whetstone, J. L. Keck, Samuel Wiggens, A. N. Sprague, Chas. E. Fosdick, Dr. Freeman, Joseph Trounstine, Thomas Spooner, Henry Pierce, F. Hassaurek, August Willich, R. M. Corwine, C. M. Magill, J. F. Cunningham, John Steel, George N. Runyan, E. M. Johnson, C. N. Casey, Amos Moore, William Cox, George Whitcomb, Henry Mack, Dr. H. Shultz, Alfred Cutter, Leonard Swartz, C. N. Dunlap, J. S. Davis, T. H. Weasner, Frank Jobson, J. C. Butler, Moses Swasey, A. E. Swasey, Col. Hays, George Klotter, John K. Green, T. C. Day, Fred Meyer, M. B. Hogan, N. R. Looker; secretaries, John S. Gano, E. Wassenick, G. B. Wright, James Elliot, James S. Boyce, H. C. Borden, C. O. Andress, L. H. Baker, Charles Hiller, J. E. West.

The president of the meeting introduced Lincoln as "a distinguished statesman, the expounder of the Constitution, the opponent of squatter sovereignty and the friend of freedom." Thereupon "with singular clearness of enunciation and deliberation," he spoke as follows:

My Fellow Citizens of the State of Ohio:
This is the first time in my life that I have appeared before an audience in so great a city as this. I therefore—though I am no longer a young man—make this appearance under some degree of embarrassment. But, I have found that when one is embarrassed, usually the shortest way to get through with it is to quit talking or thinking about it, and go at something else.

I understand that you have had recently with you my very distinguished friend, Judge Douglas, of Illinois, and I understand, without having an opportunity (not greatly sought to be sure) of seeing a report of the speech that he made here, that he did me the honor of mentioning my humble name. I suppose that he did so for the purpose of making some objection to some sentiment at some time expressed by me. I should expect, it is true, that Judge Douglas had reminded you, or informed you, if you had never before heard it, that I had once in my life declared it as my opinion that this Government cannot "endure permanently half slave and half free; that a house divided against itself cannot stand," and, as I had expressed it, I did not expect the house to fall; that I did not expect the Union to be dissolved; but that I did expect it would cease to be divided; that it would become all one thing or the other; that either the opposition of slavery would arrest the further spread of it, and place it where the public mind would rest in the belief that it was in the course of ultimate extinction; or the friends of slavery will push it forward until it becomes alike lawful in all the States, old or new, free as well as slave. I did, fifteen months ago, express that opinion, and upon many occasions Judge Douglas has denounced it, and has greatly, intentionally or unintentionally, misrepresented my purpose in the expression of that opinion.

I presume, without having seen a report of his speech, that he did so here. I presume that he alluded also to that opinion in different language, having been expressed at a subsequent time by Governor Seward of New York, and that he took the two in a lump and denounced them; that he tried to point out that there was something couched in this opinion which led to the making of an entire uniformity of the local institutions of the various States of the Union, in utter disregard of the different States, which in their nature would seem to require a variety of institutions, and a variety of laws, conforming to the differences in the nature of the different States.

Not only so; I presume he insisted that this was a declaration of war between the free and slave States—that it was the sounding to the onset of continual war between the different States, the slave and free States.

This charge, in this form, was made by Judge Douglas on, I believe, the 9th of July, 1858, in Chicago, in my hearing. On the next evening, I made some reply to it. I informed him that many of the inferences he drew from that expression of mine were altogether foreign to any purpose entertained by me, and in so far as he should ascribe these inferences to me, as my purpose, he was entirely mistaken; and in so far as he might argue that whatever might be my purpose, actions, conforming to my views, would lead to these results, he might argue and establish if he could; but, so far as purposes were concerned, he was totally mistaken as to me.

When I made that reply to him—when I told him, on the question of declaring war between the different States of the Union, that I had not said that I did not expect any peace upon this question until slavery was exterminated; that I had only said that I expected peace when that institution was put where the public mind should rest in the belief that it was in the course of ultimate extinction; that I believed from the organization of our Government, until a very recent period of time, the institution had been placed and continued upon such a basis; that we had had comparative peace upon that question through a portion of that period of time, only because the public mind rested in that belief in regard to it, and that when we returned to that position in relation to that matter, I supposed we should again have peace as we previously had. I assured him, as I now assure you, that I neither then had, nor have, or ever had, any purpose in any way of interfering with the institution of slavery, where it exists. I believe we have no power, under the Constitution of the United States; or rather under the form of Government under which we live, to interfere with the institution of slavery, or any other of the institutions of our sister States, be they free or slave States. I declared then, and I now declare, that I have as little inclination to interfere with the institution of slavery where it now exists, through the instrumentality of the General Government, or any other instrumentality, as I believe we have no power to do so. I accidentally used this expression; I had no purpose of entering into the slave states to disturb the institution of slavery! So, upon the first occasion that Judge Douglas got an opportunity to reply to me, he passed by the whole body of what I had said upon that subject, and seized upon the particular expression of mine, that I had no purpose of entering into the slave States to disturb the institution of slavery. "Oh, no," said he, "he (Lincoln) won't enter into the slave States to disturb the institution of slavery; he is too prudent a man to do such a thing as that; he only means that he will go on to the line between the free and slave States, and shoot over at them. This is all he means to do. He means to do them all the harm he can, to disturb them all he can, in such a way as to keep his own hide in perfect safety."

Well, now, I did not think, at that time, that that was either a very dignified or very logical argument; but as it was, I had to get along with it as well as I could.

It has occurred to me here, tonight, that if I ever do shoot over the line at the people on the other side of the line into a slave State, and purpose to do so, keeping my skin safe, that I have now about the best chance I shall ever have. I should not wonder that there are some Kentuckians about this audience; we are close to Kentucky; and whether that be so or not, we are on elevated ground, and by speaking distinctly, I should not wonder if some of the Kentuckians would hear me on the other side of the river. For that reason I propose to address a portion of what I have to say to the Kentuckians.

I say, then, in the first place, to the Kentuckians, that I am what they call, as I understand it, a "Black Republican." I think slavery is wrong, morally and politically. I desire that it should be no further spread in these United States, and I should not object if it should gradually terminate in the whole Union. While I say this for myself, I say to you Kentuckians, that I understand you differ radically from me upon this proposition; that you believe slavery is a good thing; that slavery is right; that it ought to be extended and perpetuated in this Union. Now, there being this broad difference between us, I do not pretend in addressing myself to you Kentuckians, to attempt proselyting you; that would be a vain effort. I do not enter upon it. I only propose to try to show you that you ought to nominate for the next Presidency, at Charleston, my distinguished friend, Judge Douglas. In all that there is a difference between you and him, I understand he is sincerely for you, and more wisely for you, than you are for yourselves. I will try and demonstrate that proposition. Understand now, I say that I believe he is as sincerely for you, and more wisely for you, than you are for yourselves.

What do you want more than anything else to make successful your views of slavery—to advance the outspread of it, and to secure and perpetuate the nationality of it? What do you want more than anything else? What is needed absolutely? What is indispensable to you? Why! if I may be allowed to answer the question, it is to retain a hold upon the North—it is to retain support and strength from the free states. If you can get this support and strength from the free States you can succeed. If you do not get this support and strength from the free States, you are in the minority, and you are beaten at once.

If that proposition be admitted—and it is undeniable—then the next thing I say to you is, that Douglas of all the men in this nation is the only man that affords you any hold upon the free States; that no other man can give you any strength in the free States. This being so, if you doubt the other branch of the proposition, whether he is for you—whether he is really for you, as I have expressed it, I propose asking your attention for a while to a few facts.

The issue between you and me, understand, is, that I think slavery is wrong, and ought not to be outspread, and you think it is right and ought to be extended and perpetuated. (A voice, "Oh, Lord.") That is my Kentuckian I am talking to now.

I now proceed to try to show you that Douglas is as sincerely for you and more wisely for you than you are for yourselves.

In the first place we know that in a government like this, in a government of the people, where the voice of all the men of that country, substantially, enters into the execution—or administration rather—of the government—in such a government, what lies at the bottom of all of it, is public opinion. I lay down the proposition that Judge Douglas is not only the man that promises you in advance a hold upon the North, and support in the North, but that he constantly moulds public opinion to your ends; that in every possible way he can, he constantly moulds the public opinion of the North to your ends; and if there are a few things in which he seems to be against you—a few things which he says that appear to be against you, and a few that he forbears to say which you would like to have him say— you ought to remember that the saying of the one, or the forbearing to say the other, would lose his hold upon the North, and, by consequence, would lose his capacity to serve you.

Upon this subject of moulding public opinion, I call your attention to the fact—for a well established fact it is—that the Judge never says your institution of slavery is wrong; he never says it is right, to be sure, but he never says it is wrong. There is not a public man in the United States, I believe, with the exception of Senator Douglas, who has not, at some time in his life, declared his opinion whether the thing is right or wrong; but, Senator Douglas never declares it is wrong. He leaves himself at perfect liberty to do all in your favor he would be hindered from doing if he were to declare the thing to be wrong. On the contrary, he takes all the chances that he has for inveigling the sentiment of the North, opposed to slavery, into your support, by never saying it is right. This you ought to set down to his credit. You ought to give him full credit for this much, little though it be, in comparison to the whole which he does for you.

Some other things, I will ask your attention to. He said upon the floor of the United States Senate, and he has repeated it as I understand a great many times, that he does not care whether slavery is "voted up or voted down." This again shows you, or ought to show you, if you would reason upon it, that he does not believe it to be wrong, for a man may say, when he sees nothing wrong in a thing, that he does not care whether it be voted up or voted down; but no man can logically say that he cares not whether a thing goes up or goes down, which to him appears to be wrong. You therefore have a demonstration in this that to Judge Douglas's mind your favorite institution which you would have spread out, and made perpetual, is no wrong.

Another thing he tells you, in a speech made at Memphis, in Tennessee, shortly after the canvass in Illinois, last year. He there distinctly told the people, that there was a "line drawn by the Almighty across this continent, on the one side of which the soil must always be cultivated by slaves;" that he did not pretend to know exactly where that line was, but that there was such a line. I want to ask your attention to that proposition again; that there is one portion of this continent where the Almighty has designed the soil shall always be cultivated by slaves; that its being cultivated by slaves at that place is right; that it has the direct sympathy and authority of the Almighty. Whenever you can get these northern audiences to adopt the opinion that slavery is right on the other side of the Ohio; whenever you can get them, in pursuance of Douglas's views, to adopt that sentiment, they will very readily make the other argument, which is perfectly logical, that that which is right on that side of the Ohio, cannot be wrong on this, and that if you have that property on that side of the Ohio, under the seal and stamp of the Almighty, when by any means it escapes over here, it is wrong to have constitutions and laws "to devil" you about it. So Douglas is moulding the public opinion of the North, first to say that the thing is right in your State over the Ohio river, and hence to say that that which is right there is not wrong here, and that all laws and constitutions here, recognizing it as being wrong, are themselves wrong, and ought to be repealed and abrogated. He will tell you, men of Ohio, that if you choose here to have laws against slavery, it is in conformity to the idea that your climate is not suited to it, that your climate is not suited to slave labor, and therefore you have constitutions and laws against it.

Let us attend to that argument for a little while and see if it be sound. You do not raise sugar-cane (except the new-fashioned sugar-cane, and you won't raise that long), but they do raise it in Louisiana. You don't raise it in Ohio because you can't raise it profitably, because the climate don't suit it. They do raise it in Louisiana because there it is profitable. Now, Douglas will tell you that is precisely the slavery question. That they do have slaves there because they are profitable, and you don't have them here because they are not profitable. If that is so, then it leads to dealing with the one precisely as with the other. Is there then anything in the constitution or laws of Ohio against raising sugar-cane? Have you found it necessary to put any such provision in your law? Surely not. No man desires to raise sugar-cane in Ohio; but if any man did desire to do so, you would say it was a tyrannical law that forbids his doing so, and whenever you shall agree with Douglas, whenever your minds are brought to adopt his argument, as surely you will have reached the conclusion, that although slavery is not profitable in Ohio, if any man wants it, it is wrong for him not to let him have it.

In this matter Judge Douglas is preparing the public mind for you of Kentucky, to make perpetual that good thing in your estimation, about which you and I differ.

In this connection let me ask your attention to another thing. I believe it is safe to assert that five years ago, no living man had expressed the opinion that the negro had no share in the Declaration of Independence. Let me state that again; five years ago no living man had expressed the opinion that the negro had no share in the Declaration of Independence. If there is in this large audience any man who ever knew of that opinion being put upon paper as much as five years ago, I will be obliged to him now or at a subsequent time to show it.

If that be true I wish you then to note the next fact; that within the space of five years Senator Douglas, in the argument of this question, has got his entire party, so far as I know, without exception, to join in saying that the negro has no share in the Declaration of Independence. If there be now in all these United States one Douglas man that does not say this, I have been unable upon any occasion to scare him up. Now if none of you said this five years ago, and all of you say it now, that is a matter that you Kentuckians ought to note. That is a vast change in the northern public sentiment upon that question.

Of what tendency is that change? The tendency of that change is to bring the public mind to the conclusion that when men are spoken of, the negro is not meant; that when negroes are spoken of, brutes alone are contemplated. That change in public sentiment has already degraded the black man in the estimation of Douglas and his followers from the condition of a man of some sort, and assigned him to the condition of a brute. Now, you Kentuckians, ought to give Douglas credit for this. That is the largest possible stride that can be made in regard to the perpetuation of your thing of slavery.

A voice—"Speak to Ohio men, and not to Kentuckians!"

Mr. Lincoln: I beg permission to speak as I please.

In Kentucky perhaps, in many of the slave States certainly, you are trying to establish the rightfulness of slavery by reference to the Bible. You are trying to show that slavery existed in the Bible times by divine ordinance. Now, Douglas is wiser than you, for your own benefit, upon that subject. Douglas knows that whenever you establish that slavery was right by the Bible, it will occur that that slavery was the slavery of the *white* man—of men without reference to color—and he knows very well that you may entertain that idea in Kentucky as much as you please, but you will never win any northern support upon it. He makes a wiser argument for you; he makes the argument that the slavery of the *black* man, the slavery of the man who has a skin of a different color from your own, is right. He thereby brings to your support northern voters who could not for a moment be brought by your own argument of the Bible-right slavery. Will you not give him credit for that? Will you not say that in this matter he is more wisely for you than you are for yourselves?

Now, having established with his entire party this doctrine—having been entirely successful in that branch of his efforts in your behalf, he is ready for another.

At this same meeting at Memphis, he declared that, in all contests between the negro and the white man, he was for the white man, but that in all questions between the negro and the crocodile he was for the negro. He did not make that declaration accidentally at Memphis. He made it a great many times in the canvass in Illinois last year (though I don't know that it was reported in any of his speeches there), but he frequently made it. I believe he repeated it at Columbus, and I should not wonder if he repeated it here. It is, then, a deliberate way of expressing himself upon that subject. It is a matter of mature deliberation with him thus to express himself upon that point of his case. It therefore requires some deliberate attention.

The first inference seems to be that if you do not enslave the negro you are wronging the white man in some way or other; and that whoever is opposed to the negro being enslaved, is, in some way or other, against the white man. Is not that a falsehood? If there was a necessary conflict between the white man and the negro, I should be for the white man as much as Judge Douglas; but I say there is no such necessary conflict. I say that there is room enough for us all to be free, and that it not only does not wrong the white man that the negro should be free, but it positively wrongs the mass of the white man that the negro should be enslaved; that the mass of white men are really injured by the effects of slave labor in the vicinity of the fields of their own labor.

But I do not desire to dwell upon this branch of the question more than to say that this assumption of his is false, and I do hope that that fallacy will not long prevail in the minds of intelligent white men. At all events, you ought to thank Judge Douglas for it. It is for your benefit it is made.

The other branch of it is, that in a struggle between the negro and the crocodile, he is for the negro. Well, I don't know that there is any struggle between the negro and the crocodile, either. I suppose that if a crocodile (or as we old Ohio River boatmen used to call them, alligators) should come across a white man, he would kill him if he could, and so he would a negro. But what, at last, is this proposition? I believe that it is a sort of proposition in proportion, which may be stated thus: "As the negro is to the white man, so is the crocodile to the negro; and as the negro may rightfully treat the crocodile as a beast or reptile, so the white man may rightfully treat the negro as a beast or a reptile." That is really the "knip" of all that argument of his.

Now, my brother Kentuckians, who believe in this, you ought to thank Judge Douglas for having put that in a much more taking way than any of yourselves have done.

Again, Douglas's great principle, "Popular Sovereignty," as he calls it, gives you, by natural consequence, the revival of the slave trade whenever you want it. If you question this, listen awhile, consider awhile, what I shall advance in support of that proposition.

He says that it is the sacred right of the man who goes into the Territories, to have slavery if he wants it. Grant that for argument's sake. Is it not the sacred right of the man who don't go there equally to buy slaves in Africa, if he wants them? Can you point out the difference? The man who goes into the Territories of Kansas and Nebraska, or any other new Territory, with the sacred right of taking a slave there which belongs to him, would certainly have no more right to take one there than I would, who own no slave, but who would desire to buy one and take him there. You will not say—you, the friends of Judge Douglas—but that the man who does not own a slave, has an equal right to buy one and take him to the Territory, as the other does?

A voice—"I want to ask a question. Don't foreign nations interfere with the slave trade?"

Mr. Lincoln: Well! I understand it to be a principle of Democracy to whip foreign nations whenever they interfere with us.

Voice—"I only ask for information. I am a Republican myself."

Mr. Lincoln: You and I will be on the best terms in the world, but I do not wish to be diverted from the point I was trying to press.

I say that Douglas's popular sovereignty, establishing his sacred right in the people, if you please, if carried to its logical conclusion, gives equally the sacred right to the people of the States or the Territories themselves to buy slaves, wherever they can buy them cheapest; and if any man can show a distinction, I should like to hear him try it. If any man can show how the people of Kansas have a better right to slaves because they want them, than the people of Georgia have to buy them in Africa, I want him to do it. I think it cannot be done. If it is "Popular Sovereignty" for the people to have slaves because they want them, it is popular sovereignty for them to buy them in Africa, because they desire to do so.

I know that Douglas has recently made a little effort—not seeming to notice that he had a different theory—has made an effort to get rid of that. He has written a letter, addressed to somebody I believe who resides in Iowa, declaring his opposition to the repeal of the laws that prohibit the African slave trade. He bases his opposition to such repeal upon the ground that these laws are themselves one of the compromises of the Constitution of the United States. Now it would be very interesting to see Judge Douglas or any of his friends turn to the Constitution of the United States and point out that compromise, to show where there is any compromise in the constitution, or provision in the constitution, express or implied, by which the administrators of that Constitution are under any obligation to repeal the African slave trade. I know, or at least I think I know, that the framers of the constitution did expect that the African slave trade would be abolished at the end of twenty years, to which time their prohibition against its being abolished extended. I think there is abundant contemporaneous history to show that the framers of the Constitution expected it to be abolished. But while they so expected, they gave nothing for that expectation, and they put no provision in the constitution requiring it should be so abolished. The migration or importation of such persons as the States shall see fit to admit shall not be prohibited, but a certain tax might be levied upon such importation. But what was to be done after that time? The constitution is as silent about that as it is silent, personally, about myself. There is absolutely nothing in it about that subject—there is only the expectation of the framers of the constitution that the slave trade would be abolished at the end of that time, and they expected it would be abolished, owing to public sentiment, before that time, and they put that provision in, in order that it should not be abolished before that time, for reasons which I suppose they thought to be sound ones, but which I will not now try to enumerate before you.

But while they expected the slave trade would be abolished at that time, they expected that the spread of slavery into the new Territories should also be restricted. It is as easy to prove that the framers of the constitution of the United States expected that slavery should be prohibited from extending into the new Territories, as it is to prove that it was expected that the slave trade should be abolished. Both these things were expected. One was no more expected than the other, and one was no more a compromise of the constitution than the other. There was nothing said in the constitution in regard to the spread of slavery into the Territories. I grant that, but there was something very important said about it by the same generation of men in the adoption of the old Ordinance of '87, through the influence of which you here in Ohio, our neighbors in Indiana, we in Illinois, our neighbors in Michigan and Wisconsin are happy, prosperous, teeming millions of free men. That generation of men, though not to the full extent members of the convention that framed the Constitution, were to some extent members of that convention, holding seats at the same time in one body or the other, so that if there was any compromise on either of these subjects, the strong evidence is that that compromise was in favor of the restriction of slavery from the new Territories.

But Douglas says that he is unalterably opposed to the repeal of those laws; because, in his view, it is a compromise of the constitution. You Kentuckians, no doubt are somewhat offended with that! You ought not to be! You ought to be patient! You ought to know that if he said less than that, he would lose the power of "lugging" the Northern States to your support. Really, what you would push him to do would take from him his entire power to serve you. And you ought to remember how long, by precedent, Judge Douglas holds himself obliged to stick by compromises. You ought to remember that by the time you yourselves think you are ready to inaugurate measures for the revival of the African slave trade, that sufficient time will have arrived, by precedent, for Judge Douglas to break through that compromise. He says now nothing more strong than he said in 1849 when he declared in favor of the Missouri Compromise—that precisely four years and a quarter after he declared that compromise to be a sacred thing, which "no ruthless hand would ever dare to touch," he himself, brought forward the measure, ruthlessly to destroy it. By a mere calculation of time it will only be four years more until he is ready to take back his profession about the sacredness of the compromise abolishing the slave trade. Precisely as soon as you are ready to have his services in that direction, by fair calculation, you may be sure of having them.

But you remember and set down to Judge Douglas's debt, or discredit, that he, last year, said the people of the Territories can, in spite of the Dred Scott decision, exclude your slaves from these Territories; that he declared by "unfriendly legislation," the extension of your property into the new Territories may be cut off in the teeth of the decision of the Supreme Court of the United States.

He assumed that position at Freeport on the 27th of August, 1858. He said that the people of the Territories can exclude slavery, in so many words. You ought, however, to bear in mind that he has never said it since. You may hunt in every speech he has since made, and he has never used that expression once. He has never seemed to notice that he is stating his views differently from what he did then; but, by some sort of accident, he has always really stated it differently. He has always since then declared that "the constitution does not carry slavery into the Territories of the United States beyond the power of the people legally to control it, as other property." Now, there is a difference in the language used upon that former occasion and in this latter day. There may or may not be a difference in the meaning, but it is worth while considering whether there is not also a difference in meaning.

What is it to exclude? Why, it is to drive it out. It is in some way to put it out of the Territory. It is to force it across the line, or change its character, so that as property it is out of existence. But what is the controlling of it "as other property"? Is controlling it as other property the same thing as destroying it, or driving it away? I should think not. I should think the controlling of it as other property would be just about what you in Kentucky should want. I understand the controlling of property means the controlling of it for the benefit of the owner of it. While I have no doubt the Supreme Court of the United States would say "God speed" to any of the Territorial Legislatures that should thus control slave property, they would sing quite a different tune, if by the pretense of controlling it they were to undertake to pass laws which virtually excluded it, and that upon a very well known principle to all lawyers, that what a Legislature cannot directly do, it cannot do by indirection; that as the Legislature has not the power to drive slaves out, they have no power by indirection, by tax, or by imposing burdens in any way on that property, to effect the same end, and that any attempt to do so would be held by the Dred Scott court unconstitutional.

Douglas is not willing to stand by his first proposition that they can exclude it, because we have seen that that proposition amounts to nothing more or less than the naked absurdity, that you may lawfully drive out that which has a lawful right to remain. He admitted at first that the slave might be lawfully taken into the Territories under the Constitution of the United States, and yet asserted that he might be lawfully driven out. That being the proposition, it is the absurdity I have stated, he is not willing to stand in the face of that direct, naked and imprudent absurdity; he has, therefore, modified his language into that of being *"controlled as other property."*

The Kentuckians don't like this in Douglas! I will tell you where it will go. He now swears by the court. He was once a leading man in Illinois to break down a court, because it had made a decision he did not like. But he now not only swears by the court, the courts having got to working for you, but he denounces all men that do not swear by the courts, as unpatriotic, as bad citizens. When one of these acts of unfriendly legislation shall impose such heavy burdens as to, in effect, destroy property in slaves in a Territory and show plainly enough that there can be no mistake in the purpose of the Legislature to make them so burdensome, this same Supreme Court will decide that law to be unconstitutional, and he will be ready to say for your benefit, "I swear by the court; I give it up"; and while that is going on he has been getting all his men to swear by the courts, and to give it up with him. In this again he serves you faithfully, and as I say, more wisely than you serve yourselves.

Again: I have alluded in the beginning of these remarks to the fact, that Judge Douglas has made great complaint of my having expressed the opinion that this Government "cannot endure permanently half slave and half free." He has complained of Seward for using different language, and declaring that there is an "irrepressible conflict" between the principles of free and slave labor. (A voice—"He says it is not original with Seward. That it is original with Lincoln.") I will attend to that immediately, sir. Since that time, Hickman of Pennsylvania expressed the same sentiment. He has never denounced Mr. Hickman: why? There is a little chance, notwithstanding that opinion in the mouth of Hickman, that he may yet be a Douglas man. That is the difference! It is not unpatriotic to hold that opinion if a man is a Douglas man.

But neither I, nor Seward, nor Hickman, is entitled to the enviable or unenviable distinction of having first expressed that idea. That same idea was expressed by the Richmond *Enquirer* in Virginia, in 1856; quite two years before it was expressed by the first of us. And while Douglas was pluming himself, that in his conflict with my humble self, last year, he had "squelched out" that fatal heresy, as he delighted to call it, and had suggested that if he only had had a chance to be in New York and meet Seward he would have "squelched" it there also, it never occurred to him to breathe a word against Pryor. I don't think that you can discover that Douglas ever talked of going to Virginia to "squelch" out that idea there. No. More than that. That same Roger A. Pryor was brought to Washington City and made the editor of the *par excellence* Douglas paper, after making use of that expression, which, in us, is so unpatriotic and heretical. From all this, my Kentucky friends may see that this opinion is heretical in his view only when it is expressed by men suspected of a desire that the country shall all become free, and not when expressed by those fairly known to entertain the desire that the whole country shall become slave. When expressed by that class of men, it is nowise offensive to him. In this again, my friends of Kentucky, you have Judge Douglas with you.

There is another reason why you southern people ought to nominate Douglas at your convention in Charleston. That reason is the wonderful capacity of the man; the power he has of doing what would seem to me impossible. Let us call your attention to one of these apparently impossible things.

Douglas had three or four very distinguished men of the most extreme anti-slavery views of any men in the Republican party, expressing their desire for his re-election to the Senate last year. That would, of itself, have seemed to be a little wonderful, but that wonder is heightened when we see that Wise of Virginia, a man exactly opposed to them, a man who believes in the Divine right of slavery, was also expressing his desire that Douglas should be re-elected; that another man that may be said to be kindred to Wise, Mr. Breckinridge, the Vice President, and of your own State, was also agreeing with the anti-slavery men in the North, that Douglas ought to be re-elected. Still, to heighten the wonder, a Senator from Kentucky, whom I have always loved with an affection as tender and endearing as I have ever loved any man; who was opposed to the anti-slavery men for reasons which seemed sufficient to him, and equally opposed to Wise and Breckinridge, was writing letters into Illinois to secure the re-election of Douglas. Now that all these conflicting elements should be brought, while at daggers' points, with one another, to support him, is a feat that is worthy for you to note and consider. It is quite probable that each of these classes of men thought, by the re-election of Douglas, their peculiar views would gain something; it is probable that the anti-slavery men thought their views would gain something; that Wise and Breckinridge thought so too, as regards their opinions; that Mr. Crittenden thought that his views would gain something, although he was opposed to both these other men. It is probable that each and all of them thought that they were using Douglas, and it is yet an unsolved problem whether he was not using them all. If he was, then it is for you to consider whether that power to perform wonders is one for you lightly to throw away.

There is one other thing that I will say to you in this relation. It is but my opinion, I give it to you without a fee. It is my opinion that it is for you to take him or be defeated; and that if you do take him you may be beaten. You will surely be beaten if you do not take him. We, the Republicans and others forming the opposition of the country, intend to "stand by our guns," to be patient and firm, and in the long run to beat you whether you take him or not. We know that before we fairly beat you, we have to beat you both together. We know that you are "all of a feather," and that we have to beat you altogether, and we expect to do it. We don't intend to be very impatient about it. We mean to be as deliberate and calm about it as it is possible to be, but as firm and resolved as it is possible for men to be. When we do as we say, beat you, you perhaps want to know what we will do with you.

I will tell you, so far as I am authorized to speak for the opposition, what we mean to do with you. We mean to treat you, as near as we possibly can, as Washington, Jefferson and Madison treated you. We mean to leave you alone, and in no way to interfere with your institution; to abide by all and every compromise of the constitution, and, in a word, coming back to the original proposition, to treat you, so far as degenerated man (if we have degenerated) may, according to the examples of those noble fathers—Washington, Jefferson and Madison. We mean to remember that you are as good as we; that there is no difference between us other than the difference of circumstances. We mean to recognize and bear in mind always that you have as good hearts in your bosoms as other people, or as we claim to have, and treat you accordingly. We mean to marry your girls when we have a chance—the white ones I mean, and I have the honor to inform you that I once did have a chance in that way.

I have told you what we mean to do. I want to know, now, when that thing takes place, what do you mean to do. I often hear it intimated that you mean to divide the Union whenever a Republican or anything like it, is elected President of the United States. (A voice—"That is so.") "That is so," one of them says; I wonder if he is a Kentuckian? (A voice—"He is a Douglas man.") Well, then, I want to know what you are going to do with your half of it? Are you going to split the Ohio down through, and push your half off a piece? Or are you going to keep it right alongside of us outrageous fellows? Or are you going to build up a wall some way between your country and ours, by which that moveable property of yours can't come over here any more to the danger of your losing it? Do you think you can better yourselves on that subject, by leaving us here under no obligation whatever to return those specimens of your movable property that come hither? You have divided the Union because we would not do right with you, as you think, upon that subject; when we cease to be under obligations to do anything for you, how much better off do you think you will be? Will you make war upon us and kill us all? Why, gentlemen, I think you are as gallant and as brave men as live; that you can fight as bravely in a good cause, man for man, as any other people living; that you have shown yourselves capable of this upon various occasions; but man for man, you are not better than we are, and there are not so many of you as there are of us. You will never make much of a hand at whipping us. If we were fewer in numbers than you, I think that you could whip us; if we were equal it would likely be a drawn battle, but being inferior in numbers, you will make nothing by attempting to master us.

But perhaps I have addressed myself as long, or longer, to the Kentuckians than I ought to have done, inasmuch as I have said that whatever course you take we intend in the end to beat you. I propose to address a few remarks to our friends, by way of discussing with them the best means of keeping that promise, that I have in good faith made.

It may appear a little episodical for me to mention the topic of which I shall speak now. It is a favorable proposition of Douglas's that the interference of the General Government, through the Ordinance of '87, or through any other act of the General Government, never has made or ever can make a Free State; that the Ordinance of '87 did not make free states of Ohio, Indiana or Illinois. That these states are free upon his "great principle" of popular sovereignty, because the people of those several states have chosen to make them so. At Columbus, and probably here, he undertook to compliment the people that they themselves have made the State of Ohio free, and that the Ordinance of '87 was not entitled in any degree to divide the honor with them. I have no doubt that the people of the State of Ohio did make her free according to their own will and judgment, but let the facts be remembered.

In 1802, I believe, it was you who made your first constitution, with the clause prohibiting slavery, and you did it I suppose very nearly unanimously; but you should bear in mind that you—speaking of you as one people—that you did so unembarrassed by the actual presence of the institution amongst you; that you made it a free state, not with the embarrassment upon you of already having among you many slaves, which if they had been here, and you had sought to make a free state, you would not know what to do with. If they had been among you, embarrassing difficulties, most probably, would have induced you to tolerate a slave constitution instead of a free one, as indeed these very difficulties have constrained every people on this continent who have adopted slavery.

Pray what was it that made you free? What kept you free? Did you not find your country free when you came to decide that Ohio should be a free state? It is important to inquire by what reason you found it so? Let us take an illustration between the states of Ohio and Kentucky. Kentucky is separated by this River Ohio, not a mile wide. A portion of Kentucky, by reason of the course of the Ohio, is further north than this portion of Ohio, in which we now stand. Kentucky is entirely covered with slavery—Ohio is entirely free from it. What made that difference? Was it climate? No! A portion of Kentucky was further north than this portion of Ohio. Was it soil? No! There is nothing in the soil of the one more favorable to slave labor than the other. It was not climate or soil that caused one side of the line to be entirely covered with slavery and the other side free of it. What was it? Study over it. Tell us, if you can, in all the range of conjecture, if there be anything you can conceive of that made that difference, other than that there was no law of any sort keeping it out of Kentucky while the Ordinance of '87 kept it out of Ohio. If there is any other reason than this, I confess that it is wholly beyond my power to conceive it. This, then I offer to combat the idea that that ordinance has never made any state free.

I don't stop at this illustration. I come to the State of Indiana; and what I have said as between Kentucky and Ohio, I repeat as between Indiana and Kentucky; it is equally applicable. One additional argument is applicable also to Indiana. In her Territorial condition she more than once petitioned Congress to abrogate the ordinance entirely, or at least so far as to suspend its operation for a time, in order that they should exercise the "Popular Sovereignty" of having slaves if they wanted them. The men then controlling the general government, imitating the men of the Revolution, refused Indiana that privilege. And so we have the evidence that Indiana supposed she could have slaves, if it were not for that ordinance; that she besought Congress to put the barrier out of the way; that Congress refused to do so, and it all ended at last in Indiana being a free state. Tell me not then that the Ordinance of '87 had nothing to do with making Indiana a free state, when we find men chafing against and only restrained by that barrier.

Come down again to our State of Illinois. The great Northwest Territory, including Ohio, Indiana, Illinois, Michigan, and Wisconsin, was acquired first, I believe, by the British Government, in part at least, from the French. Before the establishment of our independence, it becomes a part of Virginia; enabling Virginia afterward to transfer it to the General Government. There were French settlements in what is now Illinois, and at the same time there were French settlements in what is now Missouri—in the tract of country that was not purchased till about 1803. In these French settlements negro slavery had existed for many years—perhaps more than a hundred, if not as much as two hundred years—at Kaskaskia, in Illinois, and at St. Genevieve, or Cape Girardeau, perhaps, in Missouri. The number of slaves was not very great, but there was about the same number in each place. They were there when we acquired the Territory. There was no effort made to break up the relation of master and slave, and even the Ordinance of 1787 was not so enforced as to destroy that slavery in Illinois; nor did the ordinance apply to Missouri at all.

What I want to ask your attention to, at this point, is that Illinois and Missouri came into the Union about the same time, Illinois in the latter part of 1818, and Missouri, after a struggle, I believe some time in 1820. They had been filling up with American people about the same period of time; their progress enabling them to come into the Union about the same. At the end of that ten years, in which they had been so preparing (for it was about that period of time), the number of slaves in Illinois had actually decreased; while in Missouri, beginning with very few, at the end of that ten years, there were about ten thousand. This being so, and it being remembered that Missouri and Illinois are, to a certain extent, in the same parallel of latitude—that the northern half of Missouri and the southern half of Illinois are in the same parallel of latitude—so that climate would have the same effect upon one as upon the other, and that in the soil there is no material difference so far as bears upon the question of slavery being settled upon one or the other—there being none of those natural causes to produce a difference in filling them, and yet there being a broad difference in their filling up, we are led again to inquire what was the cause of that difference.

It is most natural to say that in Missouri there was no law to keep that country from filling up with slaves, while in Illinois there was the Ordinance of '87. The ordinance being there, slavery decreased during that ten years—the ordinance not being in the other, it increased from a few to ten thousand. Can anybody doubt the reason of the difference?

I think all these facts most abundantly prove that my friend Judge Douglas's proposition, that the Ordinance of '87, or the national restriction of slavery, never had a tendency to make a Free State, is a fallacy—a proposition without the shadow or substance of truth about it.

Douglas sometimes says that all the states (and it is part of this same proposition I have been discussing) that have become free, have become so upon his "great principle"; that the State of Illinois itself came into the Union as a slave State, and that the people, upon the "great principle" of popular sovereignty, have since made it a free state. Allow me but a little while to state to you what facts there are to justify him in saying the Illinois came into the Union as a slave state.

I have mentioned to you that there were a few old French slaves there. They numbered, I think, one or two hundred. Besides that, there had been a Territorial law for indenturing black persons. Under that law, in violation of the Ordinance of '87, but without any enforcement of the ordinance to overthrow the system, there had been a small number of slaves introduced as indentured persons. Owing to this the clause for the prohibition of slavery was slightly modified. Instead of running like yours, that neither slavery nor involuntary servitude, except for crime, of which the party shall have been duly convicted, should exist in the state, they said that neither slavery nor involuntary servitude should thereafter be introduced, and that the children of indentured servants should be born free; and nothing was said about the few old French slaves. Out of this fact, that the clause for prohibiting slavery was modified because of the actual presence of it, Douglas asserts again and again that Illinois came into the Union as a slave state. How far the facts sustain the conclusion that he draws, it is for intelligent and impartial men to decide. I leave it with you with these remarks, worthy of being remembered, that that little thing, those few indentured servants being there, was of itself sufficient to modify a Constitution made by a people ardently desiring to have a free Constitution; showing the power of the actual presence of the institution of slavery to prevent any people, however anxious to make a Free State, from making it perfectly so.

I have been detaining you longer perhaps than I ought to.

I am in some doubt whether to introduce another topic upon which I could talk awhile. (Cries of "Go on," and "Give us it.") It is this then; Douglas's popular sovereignty, as a principle, is simply this: If one man chooses to make a slave of another man, neither that man nor anybody else has a right to object. Apply it to Government, as he seeks to apply it, and it is this: If, in a new Territory, into which a few people are beginning to enter for the purpose of making their homes, they choose to either exclude slavery from their limits, or to establish it there, however one or the other may affect the persons to be enslaved, or the infinitely greater number of persons who are afterward to inhabit that Territory, or the other members of the family of communities, of which they are but an incipient member, or the general head of the family of States as parent of all—however their action may affect one or the other of these, there is no power or right to interfere. That is Douglas's popular sovereignty applied. Now I think that there is a real popular sovereignty in the world. I think a definition of popular sovereignty, in the abstract, would be about this—that each man shall do precisely as he pleases with himself, and with all those things which exclusively concern him. Applied in government, this principle would be, that a general government shall do all those things which pertain to it, and all the local governments shall do precisely as they please in respect to those matters which exclusively concern them.

Douglas looks upon slavery as so insignificant that the people must decide that question for themselves, and yet they are not fit to decide who shall be their Governor, Judge or Secretary, or who shall be any of their officers. These are vast national matters, in his estimation, but the little matter in his estimation is that of planting slavery there. That is purely of local interest, which nobody should be allowed to say a word about.

Labor is the great source from which nearly all, if not all, human comforts and necessities are drawn. There is a difference in opinion about the elements of labor in society. Some men assume that there is a necessary connection between capital and labor, and that connection draws within it the whole of the labor of the community. They assume that nobody works unless capital excites them to work. They begin next to consider what is the best way. They say there are but two ways; one is to hire men and to allure them to labor by their consent; the other is to buy the men and drive them to it, and that is slavery. Having assumed that, they proceed to discuss the question of whether the laborers themselves are better off in the condition of slaves or of hired laborers, and they usually decide that they are better off in the condition of slaves.

In the first place, I say that the whole thing is a mistake. That there is a certain relation between capital and labor, I admit. That it does exist, and rightfully exists, I think is true. That men who are industrious, and sober, and honest in the pursuit of their own interests should after a while accumulate capital, and after that should be allowed to enjoy it in peace, and also if they should choose, when they have accumulated it, to use it to save themselves from actual labor and hire other people to labor for them, is right. In doing so they do not wrong the man they employ, for they find men who have not of their own land to work upon, or shops to work in, and who are benefitted by working for others, hired laborers, receiving their capital for it. Thus a few men that own capital, hire a few others, and these establish the relation of capital and labor rightfully, a relation of which I make no complaint. But I insist that that relation after all does not embrace more than one-eighth of the labor in the country.

(The speaker proceeded to argue that the hired laborer, with his ability to become an employer, must have every precedence over him who labors under the inducement of force. He continued:)

I have taken upon myself in the name of some of you to say that we expect upon these principles to ultimately beat them. In order to do so, I think we want and must have a national policy in regard to the institution of slavery, that acknowledges and deals with that institution as being wrong. Whoever desires the prevention of the spread of slavery and the nationalization of that institution, yields all, when he yields to any policy that either recognizes slavery as being right, or as being an indifferent thing. Nothing will make you successful but setting up a policy which shall treat the thing as being wrong. When I say this, I do not mean to say that this general government is charged with the duty of redressing or preventing all the wrongs in the world; but I do think it is charged with preventing and redressing all wrongs which are wrongs to itself. This Government is expressly charged with the duty of providing for the general welfare. We believe that the spreading out and perpetuity of the institution of slavery impairs the general welfare. We believe—nay, we know, that that is the only thing that has ever threatened the perpetuity of the Union itself. The only thing which has ever menaced the destruction of the government under which we live, is this very thing. To repress this thing, we think, is providing for the general welfare. Our friends in Kentucky differ from us. We need not make our argument for them, but we who think it is wrong in all its relations, or in some of them at least, must decide as to our own actions, and our own course, upon our own judgment.

I say that we must not interfere with the institution of slavery in the States where it exists, because the Constitution forbids it, and the general welfare does not require us to do so. We must not withhold an efficient Fugitive Slave law because the constitution requires us, as I understand it, not to withhold such a law. But we must prevent the outspreading of the institution, because neither the Constitution nor general welfare requires us to extend it. We must prevent the revival of the African slave trade, and the enacting by Congress of a Territorial slave code. We must prevent each of these things being done by either Congress or the courts. The people of these United States are the rightful masters of both congresses and courts, not to overthrow the Constitution, but to overthrow the men who pervert the Constitution.

To do these things we must employ instrumentalities. We must hold conventions; we must adopt platforms, if we conform to ordinary custom; we must nominate candidates, and we must carry elections. In all these things, I think we ought to keep in view our real purpose, and in none do any thing that stands adverse to our purpose. If we shall adopt a platform that fails to recognize or express our purpose, or elect a man that declares himself inimical to our purpose, we not only take nothing by our success, but we tacitly admit that we act upon no other principle than a desire to have "the loaves and fishes," by which, in the end, our apparent success is really an injury to us.

I know that this is very desirable with me, as with everybody else, that all the elements of the opposition shall unite in the next Presidential election and in all future time. I am anxious that that should be, but there are things seriously to be considered in relation to that matter. If the terms can be arranged, I am in favor of the union. But suppose we shall take up some man and put him upon one end or the other of the ticket, who declares himself against us in regard to the prevention of the spread of slavery—who turns up his nose and says he is tired of hearing anything more about it, who is more against us than against the enemy, what will be the issue? Why, he will get no slave states after all—he has tried that already until being beat is the rule for him. If we nominate him upon that ground, he will not carry a slave state, and not only so, but that portion of our men who are highstrung upon the principle we really fight for, will not go for him, and he won't get a single electoral vote anywhere, except, perhaps, in the State of Maryland. There is no use in saying to us that we are stubborn and obstinate, because we won't do some such thing as this. We cannot do it. We cannot get our men to vote it. I speak by the card, that we cannot give the State of Illinois in such case by fifty thousand. We would be flatter down than the "Negro Democracy" themselves have the heart to wish to see us.

After saying this much, let me say a little on the other side. There are plenty of men in the slave States that are altogether good enough for me to be either President or Vice President, provided they will profess their sympathy with our purpose, and will place themselves on the ground that our men, upon principle, can vote for them. There are scores of them, good men in their character for intelligence and talent and integrity. If such a one will lace himself upon the right ground, I am for his occupying one place upon the next Republican or Opposition ticket. I will heartily go for him. But, unless he does so place himself, I think it a matter of perfect nonsense to attempt to bring about a union upon any other basis; that if a union be made, the elements will scatter so that there can be no success for such a ticket, nor anything like success. The good old maxims of the Bible are applicable, and truly applicable, to human affairs, and in this, as in other things, we may say here that he who is not for us is against us; he who gathereth not with us scattereth. I should be glad to have some of the many good, and able, and noble men of the South to place themselves where we can confer upon them the high honor of an election upon one or the other end of our ticket. It would do my soul good to do that thing. It would enable us to teach them that, inasmuch as we select one of their own number to carry out our principles, we are free from the charge that we mean more than we say.

But, my friends, I have detained you much longer than I expected to do. I believe I may do myself the compliment to say that you have stayed and heard me with great patience, for which I return you my most sincere thanks.

The speech was received by the Cincinnati press with varied feelings. The Republican organ—the *Gazette*—published it in full, thus doing the greatest service to its cause, and by reason of this, was compelled to limit its news features. The *Commercial* was more detailed in its description of the meeting. The *Enquirer* reported the whole affair fully and fairly, but its comments on the speech itself were very denunciatory and severely critical. Its attitude was frankly the Douglas view. It realized the weight of Lincoln's argument, and sought to break its force, because he was dealing a death-blow to Douglas's ambition for the presidency by making it impossible for him to receive the united support of the Democracy. The following are excerpts from these papers:

(*Daily Gazette*)
The Honorable Abraham Lincoln, of Illinois, arrived in this city, Saturday evening, from Dayton, at which place, we understand, he made a speech prior to the leaving of the cars. Upon reaching the depot he was met by a large concourse of persons, who had assembled to greet the champion of Freedom in the "Sucker State." The reception must have reminded him of his tour through his own state when, as here, the guns thundered welcome, music greeted, and people cheered at each place of stopping.

Conducted by the committee to the Burnet House, he there received some few persons, who desired to show him by personal visit that respect which his honesty and talent has procured for him at home and wherever his name is known. About eight o'clock he was conveyed to the Fifth street marketplace, where from the balcony of Mr. Kinsey's house he delivered himself of a speech occupying two hours and a half.

(*Commercial*)
We give in another place an abstract of the remarks of Hon. Abraham Lincoln, of Illinois, in the Fifth street market-place, Saturday night. He made a very able and long speech, and commanded the attention of a very large body of citizens for more than two hours. He was clear headed and plain spoken, and made his points with decided effect. We have not room for a verbatim report, and presume that the great majority of our readers would prefer an impartial and intelligible abstract, giving the substance of the thing in such form that it may be found without a protracted effort of speech reading. The principle effort of Mr. Lincoln's speech was an argument addressed to Kentuckians, assuring them that Douglas was on their side of the slavery question, that they had reason to trust him, and that he was the man they should select at Charleston as their standard bearer in the presidential contest of 1860. He contended that Douglas was as sincerely in favor of the Southern policy as the South itself, and more wisely working for the extension of slavery than the Southerners themselves—and that he did all that he could do for the slavery interests, compatible with the retention of political power in the North. Mr. Douglas's friends in the South might find it worth while to give Mr. Lincoln's speech the widest possible circulation, it would not, however, be palatable to the Douglas democracy of the North. . . .

One of the prominent political topics of the town, for a few days, even where our local politics assumes importance, as now, will be the strong and peculiar speech of the able and singular Hon. Abe. Lincoln, of Illinois in Fifth street market space, Saturday night. It was understood and avowed that Mr. Lincoln was to speak "in opposition to the view recently expressed in Ohio by the Hon. S. A. Douglas." The republicans proposed that, as the democrats had made an immense lion of Mr. Douglas, they would cause Mr. Lincoln to play the lion on a scale equally extensive. But Mr. Douglas had a great advantage. He has become the most noted politician in the country. For some years he has been the central figure of American politics. There are thousands of persons who have an abiding faith that he is to be some day the president of the United States, and, animated by a lively sense of favors to come, they take every occasion to show their devotion to this person. Mr. Lincoln is not conspicuous as a presidential candidate.

(*Daily Enquirer*)
A "verbatim report" of the speech of Mr. Lincoln was given by our enterprising neighbor of the *Gazette*, in their yesterday's impression. Mr. Lincoln—so

we are informed by the editor of that journal—"is deficient in clap-trap, *but excels in logic and honesty*; and herein"—our contemporary continues—"he differs from Judge Douglas." We thank him for his endorsement.

We have glanced over the speech of Mr. Lincoln in the *Gazette*. We do not say that we have read it: it is not worth reading. It contains nothing that is calculated to make any man wiser, or more learned; to make him a better citizen or a better man; to give him any insight into the character of the Government, or into his duty as a part of the governing power. It is in a single expressive word, *trash*—trash from beginning to end; trash without one solitary oasis to relieve the dreary waste that begins with its nearest and ends with its furthest boundary. Among public addresses from the stump, the speech of Mr. Lincoln belongs to the lowest order. It is not the speech of a statesman; it is not the speech of a politician; it is not even the speech of a fair partisan. It is the speech of a pettifogging demagogue, devoted to an uncandid and one-sided discussion of the real or presumed party and doctrinal status of a third person. It is not a business of the display of either logic or honesty, and, therefore—we beg pardon of our contemporary, for disagreeing with him—there is no appearance of these qualities....

The speech of Mr. Lincoln was well received. His audience was in excellent humor with itself and with its orator. His remarks were interrupted—as appears by the report—by frequent laughter and applause. One of Mr. Lincoln's strongest points is his propensity to misstate the positions and exaggerate the remarks of his antagonist, in the indulgence of which we observe he was so happy as to bring down the crowd on several occasions. When he told his hearers that Douglas' popular sovereignty, as a principle, is simply this: "If one man chooses to make a slave of another man, neither that other man nor anybody else has a right to object," he was answered with "cheers and laughter." It was undoubtedly received as an excellent joke. As a truth it would not have been at all laughable; we must, therefore, take the applause as a tribute to the author's wit at the expense of his credit for veracity. His speech was full of jokes of a similar character—well calculated to reduce to less than nothing the reputation of their utterer as a man of truth and candor. Indeed, it appears that the crowd was not long in finding out its man; for the rambling dialogue between the orator and his hearers into which the speech degenerated indicated well enough the respect in which he had come to be holden, who was not too proud to stand up and utter palpable lies for their amusement....

Hon. Mr. Lincoln is a tall, dark-visaged, angular, awkward, positive-looking individual with character written in his face and energy expressed in his every movement. He has the appearance of what is called in the Northeast a Western man—one who, without education or early advantages, has risen by his own exertions from an humble origin. Indeed, in this respect he resembles Douglas, to whom, however, in largeness of thought, profundity of penetration, and excellence of judgment, he is greatly inferior.

At the same time Moncure D. Conway, a distinguished Unitarian clergyman and author of his time, was in Cincinnati, and he has left us his impressions of Lincoln and his speech:[30]

One warm evening in 1859, passing through the market-place in Cincinnati, I found there a crowd listening to a political speech in the open air. The speaker stood on the balcony of a small brick house, some lamps assisting the moonlight. Something about the speaker, and some words that reached me, led me to press nearer. I asked the speaker's name, and learned that it was Abraham Lincoln. Browning's description of the German professor, "Three parts sublime to one grotesque," was applicable to this man. The face had a battered and bronzed look, without being hard. His nose was prominent, and buttressed a strong and high forehead. His eyes were high-vaulted, and had an expression of sadness; his mouth and chin were too close together, the cheeks hollow. On the whole, Lincoln's appearance was not attractive until one heard his voice, which possessed variety of expression, earnestness, and shrewdness in every tone. The charm of his manner was that he had no manner; he was simple, direct, humorous. He pleasantly repeated a mannerism of his opponent,—"This is what Douglas calls his *gur-reat per-rinciple."* But the next words I remember were these: *"Slavery is wrong."*

The young man, Rutherford B. Hayes, before referred to, who was present at the meeting as a vice president, has also given us a first hand impression in his diary kept at the time:[31]

Mr. Lincoln has an ungainly figure, but one loses sight of that, or rather the first impression disappears in the absorbed attention which the matter of his speech commands. He is an orator of an unusual kind, so calm, so undemonstrative, but nevertheless an orator of great merit. It is easy to contrast him after the manner of Plutarch, but his like has not been heard in these parts. His manner is more like Crittenden's, and his truth and candor are like what we admire in the Kentuckian, but his speech has greater logical force, greater warmth of feeling.

Lincoln returned home recognized as having greatly advanced the interests of his party in Ohio, and as having increased the chances of

Dennison's election. His speeches were widely circulated throughout the state, and he made many friends that were useful to him in the future. His farewell, unlike that of four years before, was full of cheer.

CHAPTER 5

OHIO'S PART IN LINCOLN'S NOMINATION

The Lincoln–Douglas debate in 1858 resulted in decided advantages for the Republican Party; its state ticket was elected by a substantial majority—125,430 votes to the Democratic poll of 121,609; and as a further result the opposition to slavery extension had reached such a degree of understanding and approval as the people of the North never before attained. It was a personal, but very close triumph for Douglas; his majority in the joint session was but eight. This was the exact number of Democrats serving over in the Senate from the last legislature. But for Lincoln it was a defeat that was felt keenly, more keenly, perhaps, because the margin was so small, and because he expected success. It begot one of his temperamental moods of depression. In the following days of his melancholia, when encircled by deepening shadows, he felt that even his friends neglected and ignored him. This mood, however, passed away, and he said he felt "like the boy that stubbed his toe—'it hurt too bad to laugh, and he was too big to cry.'"

As many a candidate, before and since, he was not only beaten, but "broke"; and in addition there was the inevitable aftermath of every campaign—party debts. This was called to his attention by N. B. Judd, his close friend and the chairman of the Republican State Committee. He had no money, and he wrote Judd, "I have been on expense so long without earning anything, that I am absolutely without money now even for household expenses." "Still," he says, "if you can put in two hundred and fifty dollars for me towards discharging the debt of the Committee,

I will allow it when you and I settle the private matter between us."

This was two weeks after the election. There was no thought in Lincoln's mind, nor in that of any of his immediate friends, of the presidency; indeed, some of them were of the opinion that his political career was ended. Many of them charged his defeat to his famous speech opening the campaign at Springfield, in which he declared that "this government cannot endure, permanently, half slave and half free." Leonard Swett, his closest friend, was of this opinion. After the election Mr. Swett said: "The first ten lines of that speech defeated him. The sentiment of the 'house divided against itself' seemed wholly inappropriate. It was a speech made at the commencement of a campaign, and apparently made for the campaign. Viewing it in this light alone nothing could have been more unfortunate or more inappropriate. It was saying the wrong thing first."

After a while the gloom wore away, and as word came from the country, his friends began to discover that Lincoln was the real victor in the recent struggle. He had become a national character and had presented the principle of the new party before the North as it had never been presented before. He had furnished the issue for 1860. His friends in Illinois at first, however, had no thought of him beyond the vice presidency. His supporters in the legislature in the spring of 1859 discussed this subject. Lincoln answered, to one of the members who said that while they would not be able to make him president, they might make him vice president, that he did not consider himself material for president, and that the minor office was not big enough for one who had been a candidate for United States senator. It was not until the spring of 1860 that he actually consented to be a candidate for president, and that he formally held conferences with his friends on that subject.

Long before this, however, there came from Ohio the first declaration of organized Republicans favoring him as a candidate for president. The Illinois election involving his defeat for United States senator was on November 2, 1858; three days afterward a meeting was held in Mansfield, Ohio, nominating him for president, as will be seen by the following published in the *Sandusky Commercial-Register,* November 9, 1858:

LINCOLN FOR PRESIDENT

We are indebted to a friend at Mansfield for the following dispatch:

MANSFIELD, Nov. 5th, 1858.

Editor Sandusky Register: An enthusiastic meeting is in progress here tonight in favor of Lincoln for the next Republican candidate for President.

REPORTER.

This news was repeated in Lincoln's home paper at Springfield, the *Illinois State Journal,* of November 19, as follows:

LINCOLN FOR PRESIDENT

The *Sandusky* (Ohio) *Register* announces the nomination of Hon. Abraham Lincoln for the next President, by an enthusiastic meeting at Mansfield in that State.

This journal of his own town, although differing with Lincoln in politics, seems to have been ready to reprint the favorable expressions of his Ohio friends, for we find on the 19th this item:

(From the *New York Herald.*)

ANOTHER PRESIDENTIAL TEAM.—The following ticket has just been brought out at Cincinnati: For President, Abraham Lincoln, of Illinois; for Vice President, John P. Kennedy, of Maryland—with a platform embracing protection to American industry, the improvement of western rivers and harbors, and opposition to the extension of slavery by free emigration into the territories.

This early Ohio movement toward Lincoln was based on admiration for him, growing out of his courageous opposition to Douglas. The spectacular debate had something to do with it, but more than all was his steady, temperate, and irrefutable arguments against the extension of slavery. Unlike Seward, Wade, and Sumner, he was practical, unemotional and constitutional. It was apparent that Lincoln's arguments were the only ones upon which could be built an antislavery party; abolitionism as advocated was revolutionary, and instinctively rejected by the mass of the Northern people. This, too, notwithstanding that the immorality of slavery was generally admitted. So great an impression did the Lincoln–Douglas debates, including the former's speeches at Columbus and Cincinnati make, that a general demand for them prevailed. In Illinois they had been printed as campaign documents by different committees, but in Ohio another view obtained. When both sides had been read and studied, it was discovered that no better propaganda for the support of the new party could be made than to publish all the arguments, for and against slavery extension, and let the North judge. Far-seeing leaders saw that in Lincoln's speeches was the unanswerable appeal of the new crusade, and they believed that the wider their circulation the stronger became their cause.

Therefore, early in December, 1859, George M. Parsons, chairman, and the members of the Republican committee wrote to Lincoln requesting copies of all the speeches in the debates as well as his Ohio speeches in the recent campaign. They regarded them, they said, "as luminous and triumphant expositions of the doctrines of the Republican party, successfully vindicated from the aspersions of its foes, and calculated to make a document of great practical service to the Republican party in the approaching Presidential contest." They also enclosed a supplementary letter signed by governor-elect Dennison, the state officers, and the Republican members of the State Board of Equalization representing the several senatorial districts of the state, then assembled at Columbus.

This expression from the Republican Party of Ohio was very significant, for at this very time Governor Chase and his friends were doing all possible with a view to presenting him [Chase] as the state's presidential candidate at the national convention of the coming year. It will also be observed that the governor did not join his colleagues in signing the letter, which, with its reply, follows:[32]

COLUMBUS, OHIO, Dec. 7, 1859.

HON. ABRAHAM LINCOLN:
DEAR SIR:—As members of the Republican party of Ohio, from different portions of the State, met together for the first time since the election, we thank you in the name of the party for the prompt and efficient aid rendered us in the late campaign, by your speeches at Columbus and Cincinnati. The pro-slavery Democracy, driven to despair by repeated defeats, entered the late contest openly ignoring a defense of the present Administration, and raising the specious flag of popular sovereignty, called the Little Giant himself into the field to tickle the public ear with rehearsals of his "Harper's Magazine" article.

The experience acquired in seven pitched battles with him as an antagonist, enabled you to make such a searching and thoroughly practical expose of the fallacies of his position, in your Ohio speeches, which were scattered by thousands by our Central Committee among the people, that Douglasism, with its inconsistent theory, that "a thing (slavery) may lawfully be driven away, from where it has a right to be," by the action or non-action of a Territorial Legislature, in spite of the decision of the Supreme Court of the United States in the Dred Scott case, was no where among the voters when the polls were closed. Proclaimed victor by a majority of the popular vote of your own State, in the famous debates which have attracted the universal attention of the party as containing the doctrines of the Republican creed, thoroughly discussed and completely vindicated from the misrepresentations of its foes: we would request that you cause to be collected for publication in permanent form, authentic copies of those debates, together with your two Ohio speeches, as a document that will be of essential service to the cause in the approaching Presidential campaign. The results of the late elections indicate a glorious triumph then, if Republican principles are properly discussed and rightly diffused among the people. The signs of the times bespeak, that there is a West, no longer to be used as a mere voting appendage to carry out the schemes of other interests, but a political power united to assert her own dignity in the confederacy and carry out to their legitimate consummation the immortal principles of the Ordinance of 1787, under which she was organized, by standing by its champions and indignantly spurning the whole tribe of trading Dough faces, who flout at the sacred birthright of their own States.

Respectfully yours,

S. WILLIAMSON, Cuyahoga,
ERASTUS SPENCER, Geauga,
A. C. RAMAGE, Belmont,
N. W. CARROLL, Preble,
S. T. CUNARD, Morrow,
W. S. RUSSELL, Sandusky,
P. N. O'BANNON, Licking,
GEO. CLIFTON, Lorain,
S. W. MCCULLOUGH, Logan,
SAM'L C. JOHNSON, Lawrence,
WM. DENNISON, JR.
F. M. WRIGHT,
A. P. RUSSELL,
A. P. STONE
W. B. THRALL

A. L. NORTHRUP, Darke,
O. D. BIGELOW, Hancock,
JAMES H. LADD, Jefferson,
JACOB EGBERT, Warren,
B. NESBITT, Greene,
SETH WOODFORD, Washington,
DANIEL HAYNES, Mahoning,
JOHN HOY, Summit,
WM. MCDONALD, Champaign,
AMOS CARR, Carroll,
JOHN WADDLE,
JOHN L. MARTIN,
C. P. WOLCOTT,
ANSON SMITH,

SPRINGFIELD, ILLINOIS, December 19.

Messrs. GEO. M. PARSONS AND OTHERS,
  Central Executive Committee, etc.
GENTLEMEN:—Your letter of the 7th instant, accompanied by a similar one from the governor-elect, the Republican State officers, and the Republican members of the State Board of Equalization of Ohio, both requesting of me, for publication in permanent form, copies of the political debates between Senator Douglas and myself last year, has been received. With my grateful acknowledgments to both you and them for the very flattering terms in which the request is communicated, I transmit you the copies. The copies I send you are as reported and printed by the respective friends of Senator Douglas and myself, at the time—that is, his by his friends, and mine by mine. It would be an unwarrantable liberty for us to change a word or a letter in his, and the changes I have made in mine, you perceive, are verbal only, and very few in number. I wish the reprint to be precisely as the copies I send, without any comment whatever.
  Yours very truly,
  A. LINCOLN.

The result of this was the publication of a volume containing not only the debates and Ohio speeches, but others of Lincoln and Douglas in the Illinois campaign of 1858, delivered at Springfield, Chicago, and Bloomington. Lincoln's famous "house-divided-against-itself" speech at Springfield opened the volume. Nearly fifty thousand copies were printed and sold throughout the country by the publishers, Follett, Foster & Co., of Columbus, Ohio.[33]

The initiation of this work by the Ohio Republicans, for its promotion was purely political, did much to advance the cause. It also added in a pronounced way to Lincoln's standing, especially in the East. An eminent historian has written this:[34]

> Since "nothing succeeds like success," it was for the most part supposed in the East that as Douglas had won the prize, he had overpowered his antagonist in debate. This remained the prevalent opinion until, in 1860, the debates were published in book form. Since then the matured judgment is that in the dialectic content, Lincoln got the better of Douglas.

The circulation of this book had a powerful influence in the East. It gave Lincoln a new standing among its editors and wise men. Heretofore, when from Illinois and Ohio there came suggestions of him for the presidency, they were regarded as a joke.[35] It was not long, however, before a different estimate was placed upon the western lawyer. His speeches indicated a powerful personality. Their simple but irrefutable logic, their serious spirit in behalf of a great cause, and their genuine statesmanship commanded from those who read them the greatest respect. There came a curiosity to see this man, and then invitations to speak in the East, culminating in his Cooper Institute speech in New York. Before a critical audience presided over by William Cullen Bryant, in an address remarkable for its keen historical analysis of the slavery question and for its wise counsels to the Republican Party, he made it apparent to his eastern critics that William H. Seward had a serious rival for the presidency.[36] From New York he went up to New England, speaking in Vermont, Rhode Island, and Connecticut. When Lincoln returned home, his candidacy was no longer regarded as a joke. This eastern trip was the most potent factor up to this time in making Lincoln a presidential candidate of consequence.

That this situation developed was due almost wholly to the actions of his admirers in Ohio.

Since the debates, many Ohioans had openly expressed their preference for him for president. They were free in writing to offer him their services. Lincoln in return wrote as freely, and at times did not hesitate to give his opinions on Ohio politics. Witness his letter to Governor Chase on the Fugitive Slave Law, and the following to Hon. Samuel Galloway on the defeat of Judge Swan. It is to be regretted that but very few of these letters are extant, but such as are throw an interesting light on the politics of those days as well as contribute to the history of the times. One of the most valuable, as well as characteristic, is the one last referred to, in which he comments critically on Ohio political affairs, and also refers to the presidency:[37]

SPRINGFIELD, ILL., July 28, 1859.

HON. SAMUEL GALLOWAY.

MY DEAR SIR:—Your very complimentary, not to say flattering, letter of the 23rd inst. is received. Dr. Reynolds had induced me to expect you here; and I was disappointed not a little by your failure to come. And yet I fear you have formed an estimate of me which can scarcely be sustained on a personal acquaintance.

Two things done by the Ohio Republican convention—the repudiation of Judge Swan, and the "plank" for a repeal of the Fugitive Slave law—I very much regretted. These two things are of a piece; and they are viewed by many good men, sincerely opposed to slavery, as a struggle against, and in disregard of, the Constitution itself. And it is the very thing that will greatly endanger our cause, if it be not kept out of our national convention. There is another thing our friends are doing which gives me some uneasiness. It is their leaning toward "popular sovereignty." There are three substantial objections to this: First, no party can command respect which sustains this year what it opposed last. Secondly, Douglas (who is the most dangerous enemy of liberty, because the most insidious one) would have little support in the North, and by consequence, no capital to trade on in the South, if it were not for his friends thus magnifying him and his humbug. But lastly, and chiefly, Douglas's popular sovereignty, accepted by the public mind as a just principle, nationalizes slavery, and revives the African slave trade inevitably. Taking slaves into new Territories, and buying slaves in Africa, are identical things, identical rights or identical wrongs, and the argument which establishes one will establish the other. Try a thousand years for a sound reason why Congress shall not hinder the people of Kansas from having slaves, and, when you have found it, it will be an equally good one why Congress should not hinder the people of Georgia from importing slaves from Africa.

As to Governor Chase, I have a kind side for him. He was one of the few distinguished men of the Nation who gave us, in Illinois, their sympathy last year. I never saw him, but suppose him to be able and right-minded; but still he may not be the most suitable as a candidate for the Presidency.

I must say I do not think myself fit for the Presidency. As you propose a correspondence with me, I shall look for your letters anxiously.

I have not met Dr. Reynolds, since receiving your letter; but when I shall, I will present your respects as requested.

Yours very truly,
A. LINCOLN.

With the approach of the national convention we find evidences of Lincoln's industry among his Ohio friends. The "Mr. Parrott of the legislature," referred to in the following letter was Edwin A. Parrott of Dayton, the member from Montgomery County:

CHICAGO, March 24, 1860.

HON. SAMUEL GALLOWAY.
MY DEAR SIR: I am here attending a trial in court. Before leaving home I received your kind letter of the 15th. Of course I am gratified to know I have friends in Ohio who are disposed to give me the highest evidence of their friendship and confidence. Mr. Parrott, of the legislature, had written me to

the same effect. If I have any chance, it consists mainly in the fact that the whole opposition would vote for me, if nominated. (I don't mean to include the pro-slavery opposition of the South, of course.) My name is new in the field, and I suppose I am not the first choice of a very great many. Our policy, then, is to give no offense to others—leave them in a mood to come to us if they shall be compelled to give up their first love. This, too, is dealing justly with all, and leaving us in a mood to support heartily whoever shall be nominated. I believe I have once before told you that I especially wish to do no ungenerous thing toward Governor Chase, because he gave us his sympathy in 1858 when scarcely any other distinguished man did. Whatever you may do for me, consistently with these suggestions, will be appreciated and gratefully remembered. Please write me again.

Yours very truly,
A. LINCOLN.

The Lincoln sentiment seems to have developed in Cincinnati contemporaneously with that in Mansfield, as will be remembered by the report of the *New York Herald*, which registered a movement for a ticket composed of Lincoln and Kennedy. At the same time there was a pronounced opinion favoring Judge John McLean of the United States Supreme Court, and a resident nearby Cincinnati, which was the home of Governor Chase. Richard M. Corwine, a prominent lawyer of Cincinnati (at one time a partner of Rutherford B. Hayes) and a delegate afterward to the Chicago convention, where he voted to the end for Judge McLean, was in correspondence with Lincoln, doubtless for the purpose of feeling out the chances for his friend. He evidently wrote cautiously; Lincoln replied in the same spirit. To Corwine's first letter he answered:

SPRINGFIELD, April 6th, 1860.
HON. R. M. CORWINE.
MY DEAR SIR:—Reaching home yesterday after an absence of more than two weeks, I found your letter of the 24th of March. Remembering that when a not very great man begins to be mentioned for a very great position, his head is very likely to be a little turned, I concluded I am not the fittest person to answer the questions you ask. Making due allowance for this, I think Mr. Seward is the very best candidate we could have for the North of Illinois, and the very worst for the South of it. The estimate of Governor Chase here is neither better nor worse than that of Seward, except that he is a newer man. They are regarded as being almost the same,

seniority giving Seward the inside track. Mr. Bates, I think, would be the best man for the South of our State, and the worst for the North of it. If Judge McLean was fifteen, or even ten years younger, I think he would be stronger than either, in our state, taken as a whole; but his great age, and the recollection of the deaths of Harrison and Taylor have, so far, prevented his being spoken much of here.

I really believe we can carry the state for either of them, or for any one who may be nominated; but doubtless it would be easier to do it with some than with others.

I feel myself disqualified to speak of myself in this matter. I feel that this letter will be of little value to you; but I can make it no better, under the circumstances. Let it be strictly confidential, not that there is anything really objectionable in it, but because it might be misconstrued.

Yours very truly,
A. LINCOLN.

Again, two weeks before the national convention he wrote:

SPRINGFIELD, May 2nd, 1860.

HON. R. M. CORWINE,
DEAR SIR:—
Private.
Yours of the 30th ult. is just received. After what you have said, it is perhaps proper I should post you, so far as I am able, as to the "lay of the land."

First, I think the Illinois delegation will be unanimous for me at the start; and no other delegation will. A few individuals in the other delegations would like to go for me at the start, but may be restrained by their colleagues. It is represented to me by men who ought to know, that the whole of Indiana might not be difficult to get. You know how it is in Ohio. I am certainly not the first choice there; and yet I have not heard that anyone makes any positive objection to me. It is just so everywhere as far as I can perceive. Everywhere, except here in Illinois and possibly in Indiana, one or another is preferred to me, but there is no positive objection. This is the ground as it now appears. I believe you personally know C. M. Allen of Vincennes, Indiana. He is a delegate and has notified me that the entire Indiana delegation will be in Chicago the same day you name, Saturday, the 12th. My friends, Jesse K. Dubois, our auditor, and Judge David Davis, will probably be there ready to confer with friends from other States. Let me hear from you again when anything occurs.

Yours very truly,
A. LINCOLN.

It is worth noting that Galloway and Corwine had both written Lincoln after the Republicans of Ohio had declared in convention that their choice for the presidency was Governor Chase. There is no doubt but that scores of prominent Republicans throughout the state were doing the same thing, almost to the date of the national convention. Very little of this correspondence has been preserved, or has come to light, to the loss of a wide and interesting knowledge of the politics of that period.

Now for a review of the state situation. On March 1, 1860, the Republicans held a state convention to select delegates-at-large to the second Republican National Convention to be held at Chicago, May 16. The state convention assembled in the Odeon, next to the Neil House in Columbus. The following were elected delegates-at-large: David Kellogg Cartter, of Cuyahoga County; Conrad Brodbeck, of Montgomery; Thomas Spooner, of Hamilton; and Valentine B. Horton, of Meigs. The convention also adopted the following resolution:

> *Resolved,* That while the Republicans of Ohio will give their united support to the nominee of the Chicago Convention, they would indicate as their first choice and recommend to said Convention the name of Salmon P. Chase, of Ohio.

In the light of the presidential state endorsements of today, this seems to lack enthusiasm, but it met the requirements of the times, which confined such expressions to brevity of language. The resolution, however, was not passed unanimously. The vote, being taken by counties, showed that sixty-five were unanimous for the resolution; seventeen were divided; four were unanimous against it; and two not voting. The remainder of the Ohio delegation was selected by congressional district conventions. Under this sifting and testing system the party secured able and distinguished representatives. By its results delegations were formed of men prominent in business in their community, or men who, by political careers had already gone through a process of selection, or men of mature age and judgment, who in the past enjoyed party honors and confidences. The haphazard process of electing delegates by the primary system, where selections are arrived at by active minorities welded together by outside organizations regardless of party loyalty, was then unknown.

The Ohio delegation to Chicago was as follows:[38]

AT LARGE

David K. Cartter, Cleveland,
Valentine B. Horton, Pomeroy,
Thomas Spooner, Redding,
Conrad Brodbeck, Dayton.

DISTRICTS

1. Benjamin Eggleston, Cincinnati,
   Fred Hassaurek, Cincinnati,
2. R. M. Corwine, Cincinnati,
   Joseph H. Barrett, Cincinnati,
3. William Beckett, Hamilton,
   P. P. Lowe, Dayton,
4. G. D. Burgess, Troy,
   John E. Cummings, Sidney,
5. David Taylor, Defiance,
   E. Graham, Perrysburg,
6. John M. Barrere, New Market,
   Reeder W. Clarke,
7. Thomas Corwin, Lebanon,
   A. Hivling, Xenia,
8. W. H. West, Bellefontaine,
   Levi Geiger, Urbana,
9. Earl Bill, Tiffin,
   D. W. Swigart, Bucyrus,
10. J. V. Robinson, Jr., Portsmouth,
    Milton L. Clark, Chillicothe,
11. N. H. Van Voorhees, Athens,
    A. C. Sands, Zaleski,
12. Willard Warner, Newark,
    Jonathan Renick, Circleville,
13. John J. Gurley, Mt. Gilead,
    P. N. Schuyler, Norwalk,
14. James Monroe, Oberlin,
    G. U. Harn, Wooster,

15. Columbus Delano, Mt. Vernon,
    R. K. Enos, Millersburg,
16. Daniel Applegate, Zanesville,
    Caleb A. Williams, Chesterfield,
17. C. J. Allbright, Cambridge,
    Wm. Wallace, Martin's Ferry,
18. H. Y. Beebe, Ravenna,
    Isaac Steese, Massillon,
19. Robert F. Paine, Cleveland,
    R. Hitchcock, Painesville,
20. Joshua R. Giddings, Jefferson,
    Milton Sutliffe, Warren,
21. Samuel Stokely, Steubenville,
    D. Arter, Carrollton.

Although the Republicans of Ohio, through their state convention, had designated Governor Chase as their presidential preference, this declaration was considered binding only upon the delegates-at-large. The district delegates regarded themselves as representing local sentiment. Governor Chase soon discovered, as has many a candidate since, that state convention instructions are "more honored in the breach than in the observance." Shortly a divergence of choice developed, and there was talk of Justice John McLean and Senator "Ben" Wade as candidates. The Chase delegates were especially embittered against the Wade movement and declared they would vote for Lincoln or Seward first. This settled that diversion. It was openly charged by Chase's friends that this conspiracy, as they called it, in behalf of Wade was promoted by delegates D. K. Cartter, Joshua R. Giddings, C. P. Wolcott, William Dennison, Jr., Thomas Corwin, and Columbus Delano, with a view of creating a senatorial vacancy for which each of the gentlemen named would be a candidate.[39] So this reduced Ohio's candidates to two—Chase and McLean.

Salmon P. Chase was a worthy candidate of a great state. He was an antislavery partisan from his youth. He followed his convictions to the extreme. Leaving the Democratic Party on account of its proslavery position, he first joined the Liberty, then the Republican Party. He opposed the operation of the Fugitive Slave Law, and when a young man entering the practice of law, he defended the fugitive slave in the courts at Cincinnati, when by so doing he invited social ostracism and professional failure. He maintained throughout his political career that Congress could not constitutionally impose on state officials the enforcement of the Fugitive Slave Law. He was elected United States Senator from Ohio by a combination of Democrats and Free Soilers in 1849. He left the Democratic Party upon the election of Franklin Pierce in 1852, and from that time was prominent in antislavery affairs. He was one of the founders of the Republican Party and was its candidate for governor of Ohio in 1855 and 1857, and both times elected. He was a man of conscience and courage, of impressive personal bearing, narrow in his views, of non-reliable temperament and impracticable judgment, which his subsequent life proved.

John McLean was one of the really able men of the country. He commenced his political career early. In 1812 he entered Congress, and from that time to his death was in public life. He served on the Supreme Bench of Ohio, was appointed commissioner of the Land Office, was Postmaster General under President Monroe, was appointed associate justice of the Supreme Court by President Jackson, and was in this position at the time of the Chicago convention. Thus he had a continuous record of forty-eight years of conspicuous and pure official life and was in his seventy-sixth year. Lincoln in his letter to R. M. Corwine had called attention to Judge McLean's age and the possibility of a repetition of the cases of Presidents Harrison and Taylor.

Just what Lincoln feared happened: Judge McLean died April 4, 1861, just thirty days after inauguration day; if he had been president, Harrison's case would have been paralleled.

On the third day of the convention, May 18, came the nomination of the candidates. It will be observed that the style of nominating speeches is in sharp contrast to that of the present day. Those presenting the candidates we are interested in are here given in full:[40]

> MR. JUDD of Illinois: "I desire on behalf of the delegation from Illinois, to put in nomination, as a candidate for President, of the United States, Abraham Lincoln of Illinois." (Immense applause, long continued.)
>
> MR. CARTTER of Ohio: "Ohio presents to the consideration of this Convention as a candidate for President, the name of Salmon P. Chase of Ohio." (Applause.)
>
> MR. CORWIN of Ohio: "I rise, Mr. President, at the request of many gentlemen, part of them members of this Convention, and many of them of the most respectable gentlemen known to the history of this country and its politics, to present the name of John McLean." (Applause.)

MR. DELANO of Ohio: "I rise on behalf of a portion of the delegation from Ohio, to put in nomination the man who can split rails and maul Democrats." (Great applause.)

Thus Ohio alone, of all the states, joined with Illinois in presenting Lincoln's name to the convention. This was no surprise, as for more than a year there had been developing a trend to this end. From the night of the meeting of Lincoln's friends at Mansfield, his strength had been growing. So this speech of Mr. Delano was not the result of spontaneous enthusiasm, neither was it the fruit of intrigue. Its effect was tremendous; well it might be, for here was Ohio with one of the great men of the nation as her candidate, presenting the name of Lincoln.

Murat Halstead, the famous editor, who as a young man was present as correspondent of the *Cincinnati Commercial*, thus described the scene:[41]

> As Mr. Delano of Ohio, on behalf "of a portion of the delegation of that State," seconded (?) the nomination of Lincoln, the uproar was beyond description. Imagine all the hogs ever slaughtered in Cincinnati giving their death squeals together, a score of big steam whistles going (steam at 160 lbs. per inch), and you conceive something of the same nature. I thought the Seward yell could not be surpassed; but the Lincoln boys were clearly ahead, and feeling their victory, as there was a lull in the storm, took deep breaths all round, and gave a concentrated shriek that was positively awful, and accompanied it with stamping that made every plank and pillar in the building quiver.

On the call of the roll of the states, Ohio's vote for president on the first ballot was as follows:[42]

FOR SALMON P. CHASE

Allbright, Applegate, Barrett, Beckett, Beebe, Bill, Brodbeck, Cartter, Clarke, R. W., Eggleston, Ennis, Giddings, Graham, Gurley, Harn, Hassaurek, Hitchcock, Horton, Lowe, Paine, Sands, Schuyler, Steese, Spooner, Stokely, Sutliffe, Swigart, Taylor, Townshend,[43] Van Voorhees, Wallace, Warner, West, and Williams—34.

FOR ABRAHAM LINCOLN

Burgess, Clark, M. L., Cummings, Delano, Geiger, Hivling, Renick, and Robinson—8.

FOR JOHN MCLEAN

Arter, Barrere, Corwin, and Corwine—4.

The second ballot developed the following vote:

FOR SALMON P. CHASE

Allbright, Applegate, Beebe, Bill, Brodbeck, Cartter, Eggleston, Ennis, Graham, Hassaurek, Hitchcock, Horton, Lowe, Paine, Sands, Schuyler, Steese, Spooner, Stokely, Sutliffe, Swigart, Taylor, Townshend, Van Voorhees, Wallace, Warner, West, and Williams—29.

FOR ABRAHAM LINCOLN

Arter, Barrere, Beckett, Burgess, Clarke, R. W., Clark, M. L., Cummings, Delano, Geiger, Gurley, Harn, Hivling, Renick, and Robinson—14.

FOR JOHN MCLEAN

Barrett, Corwin, and Corwine—3.

The third ballot was as follows:

FOR ABRAHAM LINCOLN

Allbright, Applegate, Arter, Barrere, Barrett, Beckett, Burgess, Clarke, R. W., Clark, M. L., Cummings, Delano, Eggleston, Ennis, Geiger, Gurley, Harn, Hivling, Lowe, Renick, Robinson, Sands, Schuyler, Stokely, Swigart, Van Voorhees, Wallace, Warner, West, and Williams—29.

For Salmon P. Chase

Beebe, Bill, Brodbeck, Cartter, Giddings, Graham, Hassaurek, Hitchcock, Horton, Paine, Steese, Spooner, Sutliffe, Taylor, and Townshend—15.

For John McLean

Corwin and Corwine—2.

During the session of a national convention, where nominations are hotly contested, there is no period of such intense interest as that of the roll call of the states for the selection of a candidate for president. It is one of silence and suspense. And yet, notwithstanding all the attendant anxiety, there are hundreds among the delegates and spectators who keep accurate records of the poll as the states respond. So, on that day at Chicago, it was known throughout the convention before the third ballot was announced that Lincoln had received 231½ votes, thus lacking only 1½ votes necessary for the nomination. Then it was that a well-schooled Ohio politician snatched Opportunity in its flight and made him the nominee.

Among the things happening at this time, an incident related by Joseph Medill of the *Chicago Tribune*, in an interview published in the *Saturday Evening Post* (Philadelphia) August 5, 1899, adds to the history of the convention. Mr. Medill said:

> After the second ballot, I whispered to Cartter, of Ohio: "If you can throw the Ohio delegation for Lincoln, Chase can have anything he wants." "H—how d–d'ye know?" stuttered Cartter. "I know, and you know I wouldn't promise if I didn't know."

David K. Cartter, the Ohio chairman, was a hard and loyal worker for Governor Chase, as well as a farsighted man who knew a situation when he saw it. Therefore, he was able at what he deemed the right time to give to Lincoln four additional votes. This was effected by the change from Governor Chase of H. Y. Beebe, of Ravenna, David K. Cartter, of Cleveland, Fred Hassaurek, of Cincinnati, and from Judge McLean of Thomas Corwin, of Lebanon. Thereupon, before the result of the third ballot could be announced, Cartter got the floor amidst great expectation and excitement, and said:[44]

> I arise, Mr. Chairman, to announce the change of four votes from Mr. Chase to Abraham Lincoln.

Then came a scene that can be witnessed in no place in the world except in an American national convention. Ten thousand Lincoln worshippers, in and out of the convention, that were serious, sober, and anxious during the roll call, now changed into a cheering, howling, dancing, stamping mob. It seemed as if they abandoned their thinking faculties and substituted a wild disposition that was a cross between the recklessness of childhood and the irresponsibility of a mild lunacy. By night all Chicago seemed bereft; the streets were filled with shouting, singing, marching men with torch lights, and these processions of light wended their way through the streets like serpents of fire. Their sole cry was of the new leader from the West—"Lincoln," "Lincoln."

Murat Halstead, the "eye-witness," wrote the following vivid description of the dramatic scenes attending the nomination:[45]

> While this ballot was taken amid excitement that tested the nerves, the fatal defection from Seward in New England still further appeared—four votes going over from Seward to Lincoln in Massachusetts. The latter received four additional votes from Pennsylvania and fifteen additional votes from Ohio. It was whispered about—"Lincoln's the coming man—will be nominated this ballot." When the roll of States and Territories had been called, I had ceased to give any attention to any votes but those for Lincoln, and had his vote added up as it was given. The number of votes necessary to a choice were two hundred and thirty-three, and I saw under my pencil as the Lincoln column was completed, the figures 231½—one vote and a half to give him the nomination. In a moment the fact was whispered about. A hundred pencils had told the same story. The news went over the house wonderfully, and there was a pause. There are always men anxious to distinguish themselves on such occasions. There is nothing that politicians like better than a crisis. I looked up to see who would be the man to give the decisive vote. The man for the crisis in the Cincinnati Convention—all will remember—was Col. Preston of Kentucky. He broke the Douglas line and precipitated the nomination of Buchanan, and was rewarded with a foreign mission. In about ten ticks of a watch, Cartter of Ohio was up. I had imagined Ohio would be slippery enough for the crisis. And sure enough! Every eye was on Cartter, and every body who

understood the matter at all, knew what he was about to do. He is a large man with rather striking features, a shock of bristling black hair, large and shining eyes, and is terribly marked with the smallpox. He has also an impediment in his speech, which amounts to a stutter; and his selection as chairman of the Ohio delegation was, considering its condition, altogether appropriate. He had been quite noisy during the sessions of the Convention, but had never commanded, when mounting his chair, such attention as now. He said, "I rise (eh), Mr. Chairman (eh), to announce the change of four votes of Ohio from Mr. Chase to Mr. Lincoln." The deed was done. There was a moment's silence. The nerves of thousands, which through the hours of suspense had been subjected to terrible tension, relaxed, and as deep breaths of relief were taken, there was a noise in the wigwam like the rush of a great wind, in the van of the storm—and in another breath, the storm was there. There were thousands cheering with the energy of insanity.

To Governor Chase, Lincoln's nomination was a severe blow, one from which he never recovered. Naturally a poor loser, his dissatisfaction was nursed and fomented by his brilliant, ambitious, and intriguing daughter. His biographer records him as complaining of the Ohio delegation, that its lack of unity "gave an opportunity to the partisans of the other candidates to foment divisions." His letter of congratulations to Lincoln was in exceeding bad taste, being mostly devoted to praising Seward's friends for adhering to him, and condemning his (Chase's) for deserting him. It was an exhibition of disappointment and soreness characteristic of this otherwise great man:[46]

> MY DEAR SIR: I congratulate you, most heartily, on your nomination; and shall support you, in 1860, as cordially and earnestly as I did in 1858.
>
> The excellent platform adopted, and the selection of that true and able man, Hannibal Hamlin, as your associate on the ticket, completes my satisfaction with the results of the convention. They will prove, I am confident, as auspicious to the country as they are honorable to the nominees.
>
> Mr. Seward has much reason to be gratified by the large and cordial support which he received, and especially by the generous, unanimous, and constant adhesion, without regard to personal preferences, of the entire delegation from his own great State. Doubtless, the similar adhesion of the Illinois delegation affords a higher gratification to you than the nomination itself. The only regret I feel connected with the convention is excited by the failure of the delegation from Ohio to evince the same generous spirit. In this regret I am quite sure you must participate; for I err

greatly in my estimate of your magnanimity if you do not condemn, as I do, the conduct of delegates from whatever State, who disregard, while acting as such, the clearly expressed preference of their own State convention.
Yours cordially,
S. P. CHASE.

HON. ABRAHAM LINCOLN.

The Republicans of Ohio responded to Lincoln's candidacy with genuine satisfaction—far more enthusiastically than they would have done to that of Chase or Seward. These men were recognized as great statesmen, friends of liberty, and founders of the party; but they failed to reach the hearts of the people—especially those of the West. Again they had records that were too radical for a great many Republicans. Their very dignity and scholarship handicapped them, and their long career in politics had developed powerful enemies. But above all, they failed to appeal to the rank and file. Therefore, they met the same fate as did Webster and Clay before them, and Blaine, Thurman, and Sherman since. Lincoln, on the other hand, satisfied the conservative Republicans and appealed to the masses of his party. His life, struggles, and accomplishments under adversity touched their hearts. In Ohio there were thousands of voters of Lincoln's age, whose early youth was passed in similar surroundings. They were born in log cabins, split rails, and lived lives of labor and hardship. These environments were those of the pioneers; and in 1860, Ohio was yet an agricultural state, still fresh with the memories of early days.

Lincoln grew stronger as the campaign progressed; it was apparent that public sentiment in Ohio strongly favored him. According to the *Ohio State Journal*, at the time, the position of the newspapers of the state was a striking evidence of that fact. The support of the press was divided among the four presidential tickets thus: Lincoln and Hamlin, 126; Douglas and Johnson, 80; Breckinridge and Lane, 8; Bell and Everett, 2. Of the German newspapers, eight were for Lincoln and fourteen for Douglas. Ten daily papers supported Lincoln, six Douglas, one Breckinridge, and one Bell.

During the campaign it was Lincoln's policy to avoid public expressions, either oral or written. He permitted no authorized statements. He was consequently much annoyed when Samuel Galloway advised him that the Columbus publishing house, which printed the "Lincoln–Douglas Debates," was about to issue an "authorized biography of

Lincoln." This doubtless was inspired by the phenomenal success of the former work. Lincoln was quick to repudiate this, as the following letter shows:

SPRINGFIELD, ILL., June 19, 1860.

HON. SAM'L GALLOWAY.
MY DEAR SIR:—Your very kind letter of the 15th is received. Messrs. Follett, Foster, & Co.'s Life of me is *not* by my authority; and I have scarcely been so much astounded by anything, as by their public announcement that it is authorized by me. They have fallen into some strange misunderstanding. I certainly knew they contemplated publishing a biography, and I certainly did not object to their doing so, *upon their own responsibility.* I even took pains to facilitate them. But, at the same time, I made myself tiresome, if not hoarse, with repeating to Mr. Howard, their only agent seen by me, my protest that I *authorized nothing*—would be *responsible for nothing.* How they could so misunderstand me, passes comprehension. As a matter *wholly my own,* I would authorize no biography, without *time* and *opertunity* [sic] to carefully examine and consider every word of it; and, in this case, in the nature of things, I can have no such time and opertunity [sic]. But, in my present position, when, by the lessons of the past, and the united voice of all discreet friends, I can neither write nor speak a word for the public, how dare I to send forth, by my authority, a volume of hundreds of pages, for adversaries to make points upon without end? Were I to do so, the convention would have a right to re-assemble and substitute another name for mine.

For these reasons, I would not look at the proof sheets—I am determined to maintain the position of truly saying I never saw the proof sheets, or any part of their work, before its publication.

Now, do not mistake me—I feel great kindness for Messrs. F., F., & Co.—do not think they have intentionally done wrong. There may be nothing wrong in their proposed book—I sincerely hope there will not. I barely suggest that you, or any of the friends there, on the party account, look it over, and exclude what you may think would embarrass the party— bearing in mind, at all times, that I *authorize nothing*—will *be responsible* for *nothing.*

Your friend, as ever,
A. LINCOLN.

The author of the biography was William Dean Howells, from Ashtabula County, and then one of the editorial writers on the *Ohio State Journal.* He was but twenty-three years of age, and his work did not augur the rich literary accomplishments of his after years. He kept in mind Lincoln's injunction, and in the preface said: "It is hardly necessary to add, that no one but the writer is responsible for his matter of treating events and men."

After a most exciting campaign, the Lincoln electors carried fifty-nine of the eighty-eight counties of Ohio and were elected by a plurality of 44,388 and a majority of 20,655.

So ends Ohio's record in helping to make Lincoln president; and it justifies saying that next to his own Illinois, no state was more instrumental in contributing to the events that framed his destiny and led to his immortal fame.

CHAPTER 6

LINCOLN IN OHIO ON HIS WAY TO INAUGURATION

It was a bright day in February, 1861, that Lincoln made the greatest entrance of his life into Ohio—his journey to Washington to be inaugurated president of the United States. His first visit, in 1849, was one made in obscurity; his second, in 1855, one that ended in humiliation; his third, in 1859, was one of party glorification; this, the last, was one of great dignity, enthusiastic acclamation accompanied with all its triumphal accessories. Yet beneath it all there was a feeling in the popular mind of seriousness and anxiety, for the country was in a perilous state. Already, so far as the South could go, the Union was dissolved.

Lincoln started on his way to Washington from his home in Springfield, Illinois, on February 11, 1861. He was met at Indianapolis the next day by Mayor R. M. Bishop of Cincinnati and a large reception committee from that city which filled two cars of the special train of four passenger cars and a baggage car. It is worthy of note that on this committee was a future president and his wife—Mr. and Mrs. Rutherford B. Hayes. The party reached Cincinnati in the afternoon.[47] Thousands of citizens for hours crowded about the Indianapolis and Cincinnati depot, anxiously and patiently awaiting the arrival of the president-elect. Soon the city police and the military organizations arrived, and the booming of cannon announced the approach of the train. When Lincoln stepped from his car, followed by his suite and the committee, the crowd became wild in enthusiasm and welcomed the future president with prolonged cheering. Through a cleared way, with Mayor Bishop, he walked to his carriage. His towering form, clad in black with a gray shawl across his shoulders and crowned with a tall silk hat, was like Saul's, "head and shoulders above his fellows." Stepping into his carriage he remained standing, hat in hand, bowing to the right and to the left in response to the greeting cheers of thousands of people. His carriage was drawn by six white horses, and the procession which escorted him through the city to the Burnet House was composed of, and moved in the following order:[48]

> Miles Greenwood, Grand Marshal, and Aids, mounted.
> Major-General Lytle and Staff, mounted.
> Brigadier-General Bates and Staff.
> Steuben Artillery, Captain Ammis.
> First Cincinnati Battalion, in command of Major Kennett,
>   composed of the following companies:
> Lafayette, Guards, Captain Miller.
> German Yagers, Captain Sommer.
> Rover Guards, Lieutenant Hubbell, commanding.
> Cincinnati Zouaves, Lieutenant Anderson, commanding.
> First Company Second Cincinnati Battalion, Captain Pendry.
> Continental Battalion, in command of Colonel Jones, as follows:
> Company A, Captain Jackson.
> Company B, Captain Whitcom.
> Independent Guthrie Greys Battalion—two companies, in
>   command of Major Bosley.
> Detachment of Washington Dragoons, acting as special guard
>   to the carriage, Captain Pfau.
> Abraham Lincoln, President elect, in carriage, drawn by six
>   white horses.
> Second Detachment of Washington Dragoons, Captain Pfau.
> Carriages with the suite of President elect.
> Citizens on horseback.
> Citizens in carriages.

The line of march was from the depot to Sixth Street, up Sixth to Mound, out Mound to Eighth, on Eighth to Elm Street, up Elm to Fifteenth, out Fifteenth to Vine Street, down Vine to the Burnet House. The route was profusely decorated in a very artistic way, the patriotic idea dominating throughout. The Stars and Stripes were everywhere. The most impressive and patriotic decorations in the city were those of the Gibson house. They were the most striking and attractive of the day, and well worthy of description. A great transparency sixty feet long and twenty feet wide was spread across the hotel; on one end of which was a portrait of Lincoln and on the other one of Hamlin, and in the center one of Washington with the coat of arms of the United States. Over the remaining surface were the mottoes: "The people will sustain the people's choice." "Honor to a President, not to a partisan." "A union of hearts, a union of hands." "A union that nothing can sever." "A Union of States, a union of lands." "The American Union, forever." "The Union must and shall be preserved." "Protection to the Rights of all Sections." "Maintenance of the Letter and Spirit of the Constitution and Preservation of the Union at all hazards." "The time has come when Demagogues must go under." "The security of a Republic is in the maintenance of the Laws." Beneath all this, on a pink groundwork, were the names of the thirty-four states, each encircled with evergreens. Under those which seceded were the words: "Out on paper." The whole was exceedingly patriotic and apropos. The transparency, with the entire hotel front, was brilliantly illuminated in the evening.

As the procession passed the orphan asylum, all the children were assembled, and as Lincoln's carriage passed, they sang "Hail Columbia"; further on, groups of little girls sang "The Star Spangled Banner," and one of them presented him with flowers, upon receiving which, he kissed the little child. The whole march was filled with touching, patriotic, and beautiful incidents. The day was fine and the whole city was abroad. From the crowded streets, from every window and every roof came cheers and demonstrations of waving flags and handkerchiefs. It was five o'clock when the Burnet House was reached. Here in the presence of an immense crowd of people Mayor Bishop delivered to him an address of welcome as follows:[49]

> *Honored Sir:* In the name of the people of all classes of my fellow-citizens, I extend to you a cordial welcome, and in their behalf I have the honor of offering you the hospitalities of Cincinnati. Our city needs no eulogy from me. Her well known character for enterprise, liberality and hospitality, is not more distinguished than is her undying devotion to the Union of these States, and a warm, filial and affectionate regard for that glorious ensign which has

"Braved the battle and the breeze,"

upon land and sea so many years. The people under the solemn and dignified forms of the Constitution have chosen you as President of the United States, and as such I greet you. And you will believe me, when I say, that it is the earnest and united desire of our citizens that your administration of the General Government may be marked by wisdom, patriotism and justice, to all sections of the country, from the Atlantic to the Pacific oceans, from the northern boundary of Maine to the Gulf of Mexico; so that when you retire from office your fellow-citizens may greet you everywhere with the cheering words, "Well done, thou good and faithful servant."

But, sir, I see in this great and anxious concourse not only the citizens of Ohio, but also many from our sister state, Kentucky,—the land of Clay, the former home of your parents and mine, and the place of your birth. These, too, greet you, for they, like us, are, and ever will be, loyal to the Constitution and the Union. I again welcome you to our noble city, and trust that your short stay with us may be an agreeable one, and that your journey to our Federal Capital may be pleasant and safe.

To this Lincoln replied as follows:

Mr. Mayor, Ladies and Gentlemen: Twenty-four hours ago, at the Capital of Indiana, I said to myself, I have never seen so many people assembled together in winter weather. I am no longer able to say that. But it is what might reasonably have been expected—that this great city of Cincinnati would thus acquit herself on such an occasion. My friends, I am entirely overwhelmed by the magnificence of the reception which has been given, I will not say to me, but to the President elect of the United States of America. Most heartily do I thank you one and all for it. I am reminded by the address of your worthy Mayor, that this reception is given, not by one political party, and even if I had not been so reminded by His Honor, I could not have failed to know the fact by the extent of the multitude I see before me now. I could not look upon this vast assemblage without being made aware that all parties were united in this reception. This is as it should be. It is as it should have been if Senator Douglas had been elected; as it should have been if Mr. Breckinridge had been elected; as it should ever be when any citizen of the United States is constitutionally elected President of the United States. Allow me to say that I think what has occurred here today could not have occurred in any other country on the face of the globe, without the influence of the free institutions which we have unceasingly enjoyed for three-quarters of a century. There is no country where the people can turn out and enjoy this day precisely as they please, save under the benign influence of the free institutions of our land. I hope that, although we have some threatening national difficulties now, while these free institutions shall continue to be in the enjoyment of millions of free people of the United States, we will see repeated every four years what we now witness. In a few short years I and every other individual man who is now living will pass away. I hope that our national difficulties will also pass away, and I hope we shall see in the streets of Cincinnati—good old Cincinnati—for centuries to come, once every four years, the people give such a reception as this to the constitutionally elected President of the whole United States. I hope you shall all join in that reception, and that you shall also welcome your brethren across the river to participate in it. We will welcome them in every State in the Union, no matter where they are from. From away South, we shall extend to them a cordial good will, when our present differences shall have been forgotten and blown to the winds forever.

I have spoken but once before this in Cincinnati. That was a year previous to the late presidential election. On that occasion, in a playful manner but with sincere words, I addressed much of what I said to the Kentuckians. I gave my opinion that we as Republicans would ultimately beat them as Democrats, but that they could postpone that result longer by nominating Senator Douglas for the presidency than they could in any other way. They did not in the true sense of the word nominate Douglas, and the result has come certainly as soon as I expected. I also told them how I expected they would be treated after they should have been beaten; and I now wish to call or recall their attention to what I said upon that subject. I then said: "When we do, as we say, beat you, you perhaps will want to know what we will do with you. We mean to treat you as near as we possibly can as Washington, Jefferson and Madison treated you. We mean to leave you alone and in no way interfere with your institutions, to abide by all and every compromise of the Constitution; and, in a word, coming back to the original proposition to treat you as far as degenerate men, if we have degenerated, may according to the examples of those noble fathers, Washington, Jefferson and Madison. We mean to remember that you are as good as we—that there is no difference between us—other than the difference of circumstances. We mean to recognize and bear in mind always that you have as good hearts in your bosoms as other people, or as good as we claim to have and treat you accordingly."

Fellow-citizens of Kentucky, friends, brethren: May I call you such? In my new position I see no occasion and feel no inclination to retract a word of this. If it shall not be made good be assured that the fault shall not be mine.

Concerning this speech and another that Lincoln made in the evening,

William Henry Smith,[50] who was at the time an editorial writer on the *Cincinnati Daily Gazette*, and present on this occasion, reveals some history, from personal knowledge, not recorded by any other writer. The usual report of Lincoln's response to Mayor Bishop is as given above; but Mr. Smith says that the following sentiments, in an additional paragraph, "omitted by Mr. Raymond and all other biographers," were also expressed, and were included in the *Gazette's* report of the speech the next morning:

> And now, fellow-citizens of Ohio, have you who agree in political sentiment with him who now addresses you ever entertained other sentiments towards our brethren of Kentucky than those I have expressed to you? (Loud and repeated cries of "No!" "No!") If not, then why shall we not, as heretofore, be recognized and acknowledged as brethren again, living in peace and harmony, one with another? (Cries of "We will!") I take your response as the most reliable evidence, trusting to the good sense of the American people, on all sides of all rivers in America, under the Providence of God, who has never deserted us, that we shall again be brethren, forgetting all parties—ignoring all parties.

According to Mr. Smith,[51] the effect of the expression of this conservative opinion was to alarm some of the Republicans, who feared that the new president was going to betray his party and the principles upon which he was elected. It was therefore determined by these alarmists to secure from Lincoln a positive declaration as to his policy. On this subject he had evidently made up his mind to let his inaugural be his sole instrument in expressing his future course of conduct. He knew well how easily speeches can be misconstrued. He said at Indianapolis: "Solomon says, 'There is a time to keep silence'; and when men wrangle by the mouth, with no certainty that they mean the same thing while using the same words, it perhaps were as well if they would keep silence." Nevertheless, there were some who thought they could force an expression. How this was done and how it was successfully repelled, is told by Mr. Smith: "In the evening," he says, "I called, with other citizens, at Mr. Lincoln's rooms at the Burnet House[52] to pay my respects. Mr. Lincoln had put off the melancholy mood that appeared to control him during the day, and was entertaining those present with genial, even lively, conversation. The pleasant entertainment was interrupted by the announcement that a delegation of German workingmen were about to serenade Mr. Lincoln. Proceeding to the balcony, there were seen the faces of nearly two thousand of the substantial German citizens who had voted for Mr. Lincoln because they believed him to be a stout champion of free labor and free homesteads."

The object of the serenade was disclosed when Frederick Oberkleine stepped forward and in almost aggressive tones spoke as follows:[53]

> We, the German free workingmen of Cincinnati, avail ourselves of this opportunity to assure you, our chosen Chief Magistrate, of our sincere and heartfelt regard. You earned our votes as the champion of Free Labor and Free Homesteads. Our vanquished opponents have, in recent times, made frequent use of the terms "Workingmen" and "Workingmen's Meetings," in order to create an impression that the mass of workingmen were in favor of compromises between the interests of free labor and slave labor, by which the victory just won would be turned into a defeat. This is a despicable device of dishonest men. We spurn such compromises. We firmly adhere to the principles which directed our votes in your favor. We trust that you, the self-reliant because self-made man, will uphold the Constitution and the laws against secret treachery and avowed treason. If to this end you should be in need of men, the German free workingmen, with others, will rise as one man at your call, ready to risk their lives in the effort to maintain the victory already won by freedom over slavery.

"This," says Mr. Smith, "was bringing the rugged issue boldly to the front, and challenging the President-elect to meet the issue or risk the loss of the support of an important section of his own party. Oberkleine spoke with great effect, but the remarks were hardly his own. Some abler man had put into his mouth these significant words." Lincoln saw at once the purpose of the speaker, and without hesitation, yet with a deliberation that was intended to impress his hearers that he thoroughly understood their aim, spoke as follows:

> *Mr. Chairman:*—I thank you, and those you represent, for the compliment paid me by the tender of this address. In so far as there is an allusion to our present national difficulty, and the suggestion of the views of the gentlemen who present this address, I beg you will excuse me from entering particularly upon it. I deem it due to myself and the whole country, in the present extraordinary condition of the country and of public opinion, that I should wait and see the last development of public opinion before I give my views or express myself at the time of my inauguration. I hope at that time to be false to nothing you have been taught to expect of me.

I agree with you, Mr. Chairman, and with the address of your constituents, in the declaration that workingmen are the basis of all governments. That remark is due to them more than to any other class, for the reason that there are more of them than of any other class. And as your address is presented to me, not only on behalf of workingmen, but especially of Germans, I may say a word as to classes. I hold that the value of life is to improve one's condition. Whatever is calculated to advance the condition of the honest, struggling laboring man, so far as my judgment will enable me to judge of a correct thing, I am for that thing.

An allusion has been made to the Homestead Law. I think it worthy of consideration, and that the wild lands of the country should be distributed so that every man should have the means and opportunity of benefiting his condition. (Cheers.) I have said that I do not desire to enter into details, nor will I.

In regard to Germans and foreigners, I esteem foreigners no better than other people—nor any worse. (Laughter and cheers.) They are all of the great family of men, and if there is one shackle upon any of them it would be far better to lift the load from them than to pile additional loads upon them. (Cheers.) And inasmuch as the continent of America is comparatively a new country, and the other countries of the world are old countries, there is more room here, comparatively speaking, than there is elsewhere; and if they can better their condition by leaving their old homes, there is nothing in my heart to forbid them coming, and I bid them all Godspeed. (Cheers.) Again, gentlemen, thanking you for your address, I bid you good night.

This interesting and sensational incident was not generally noted at the time of its occurrence, and to Mr. Smith we are indebted for its being recorded. Says he, regarding this: "If anyone had expected to trap Mr. Lincoln into imprudent utterances, or the indulgence of the rhetoric of a demagogue, this admirable reply showed how completely they were disappointed. The preservation of this speech is due to my accidental presence. The visitation of the Germans was not on the programme, and none of the representatives of the press charged with the duty of reporting the events of the day were present. Observing this, I took shorthand notes on the envelope of an old letter loaned for the occasion, and afterwards wrote them out. The words of Mr. Lincoln, exactly as spoken, are given above."

Rutherford B. Hayes, in a letter to his uncle, gives his summary of this occasion, "all of which he saw, and part of which he was":[54]

The reception given to the President-elect here was most impressive. He rode in an open carriage, standing erect with head uncovered, and bowing his acknowledgements to greetings showered upon him. There was a lack of comfort in the arrangements, but the simplicity, the homely character of all was in keeping with the nobility of this typical American. A six-in-hand with gorgeous trappings, accompanied by outriders and a courtly train, could have added nothing to him; would have detracted from him, would have been wholly out of place. The times are unsuited to show. The people did not wish to be entertained with display; they did wish to see the man in whose hands is the destiny of our country.

You will read the speeches in the papers, and search in vain for anything to find fault with. Mr. Lincoln was wary at all times, wisely so I think, and yet I hear no complaint. Our German Turners, who are radical on the slavery question and who are ready to make an issue of war, planned to draw from him some expression in sympathy with their own views. They serenaded him and talked at him, but they were baffled. In private conversation he was discreet but frank. He believes in a policy of kindness, of delay to give time for passions to cool, but not in a compromise to extend the power and the deadly influence of the slave system. This gave me great satisfaction. The impression he made was good. He undoubtedly is shrewd, able, and possesses strength in reserve. This will be tested soon.

In the evening the young men of Cincinnati gave a brilliant banquet at the Burnet House in honor of Robert, eldest son of the president-elect. According to press accounts it was a lively affair.[55] "Edibles and drinkables in profusion were discussed, particular attention being paid to Longworth's sparkling Catawba. Indeed, the volley of corks that flew for a time reminded one very forcibly of the attacking of Fort Sumter, the seizure of Fort Pickens, or other hostile operations." About fifty young men were present, and Fred Hassaurek was toastmaster. To a committee that invited the president-elect to be present, he excused himself on account of fatigue.

The next morning Lincoln and his suite left on a special train over the Little Miami Railway for Columbus. At various places on the way he was greeted with cheering crowds. A newspaper correspondent who accompanied him reported that the journey was very agreeable, and that the president-elect, although a good deal fatigued and slightly indisposed, engaged almost constantly in conversation.[56] The newspaper man observed that he was "a very delightful talker, and his style as a story teller and relator of anecdotes has not been exaggerated." He avoided discussing the political questions of the day. The nearest he would come to it was to illustrate with quaint humor and simplicity the demands of the South upon the North by a little home story. He said it reminded him of a dispute that once occurred between his two younger boys, Tom and Bill, a pair of mischievous rogues of eight and ten years. One of them had a toy that the other wanted and demanded in terms emphatic and boisterous. At length he was told to let his brother have it in order to quiet him. "No, sir," was the sturdy response, "I must have it to quiet myself." Lincoln was of the opinion that the quiet of the South at the expense of the North did not amount to much.

The state government by a joint resolution passed January 31, invited the president-elect to visit the capital on his way to Washington; to this Lincoln responded in a letter to the governor:

SPRINGFIELD, ILLINOIS, February 7, 1861.

SIR: Your letter of the 31st ultimo, on behalf of the legislature of Ohio, to visit Columbus on my way to Washington, has been received.

With profound gratitude for the mark of respect and honor thus cordially tendered me by you, I accept the invitation.

Please arrange no ceremonies which will waste time.

Your obedient servant,

A. LINCOLN.

HIS EXCELLENCY, WILLIAM DENNISON.

The arrangements for the reception were placed in the hands of a committee composed of members of the Senate, the House of Representatives and the city council of Columbus. The joint committee was composed as follows: For the Senate, James Monroe, of Lorain; F. P. Cuppy, of Montgomery; and G. W. Holmes, of Hamilton. For the House, S. E. Brown, of Miami; J. Scott, of Warren; W. G. Flagg, of Hamilton; John Welsh, of Athens; G. W. Andrews, of Auglaize; and E. Parrott, of Montgomery. On the part of the city council, A. B. Buttles, Joseph H. Riley, and S. E. Ogden. They announced the program on February 13 to be as follows:[57]

"The President-elect and suite accompanied by the committees appointed on the part of the General Assembly and the Executive, will reach Columbus about 2 o'clock P.M. today, and will proceed at once to the State Capitol in carriages, under escort of the 1st Battalion, 2d Regiment, Lieut. Col. Mills, commanding. The Governor will receive the President-elect at the Executive Rooms; thence, accompanied by the committee of Escort, they will proceed to the Hall of Representatives, when the Governor will present the President-elect to the General Assembly, through Lieutenant Governor Kirk, its presiding officer; after which the President-elect will proceed to the rotunda of the Capitol, where he will receive the citizens until 5 o'clock P. M. From 8½ o'clock to 10 P. M. there will be a levee at the House of Representatives for ladies and their escorts. This levee, and all ceremonies, will close at 10 o'clock precisely. The President-elect will be the guest of the Governor during his stay in the city, and with his suite, accompanied by the Governor's aids and the proper committees, will leave for Pittsburg by special train at 8 o'clock A. M. on Thursday. The execution of this programme will be entrusted to Brig. Gen. Lucian Buttles, who is appointed Marshal of the day. Proper salutes will be fired on the arrival and departure of the President-elect."

Thousands of people were at the depot when the special train arrived. When Lincoln appeared on the platform of the rear end, he was greeted with tumultuous applause. The march on High Street to the Statehouse was between crowds enthusiastic with welcoming demonstrations. On the western portico and steps of the Statehouse was a multitude of densely packed people. Through this crowd, escorted by his reception committee, the president-elect with difficulty reached his way to the Capitol. Accompanied by Governor Dennison, he was escorted to the House of Representatives where both houses were assembled.

As the towering form of Lincoln appeared in the chamber, the legislators arose in a body to pay their respects. Governor Dennison presented him to the presiding officer, Lieutenant Governor Robert C. Kirk, who addressed him as follows:[58]

SIR: On this day, and probably this very hour, the Congress of the United States will declare the verdict of the people, making you their President. It is my pleasurable duty, in behalf of the people of Ohio, speaking through this General Assembly, to welcome you to their Capital. Never in the history of this Government has such fearful responsibility rested upon the Chief Executive of the nation as will now devolve upon you. Never since the memorable time our patriotic fathers gave existence to the American Republic, have the people looked with such intensity of feeling to the inauguration and future policy of a President, as they do to yours. I need not assure you that the people of Ohio have full confidence in your ability and patriotism, and will respond to you in their loyalty to the Union and the Constitution. It would seem, sir, that the great problem of self-government is to be solved under your administration. All nations are deeply interested in its solution, and they wait with breathless anxiety to know whether this form of government which has been the admiration of the world is to be a failure or not. It is the earnest and united prayer of our people, that the same kind Providence which protected us in our colonial struggles and has attended us thus far in our prosperity and greatness, will so imbue your mind with wisdom, that you may dispel the dark clouds that hang over our political horizon, and thereby secure the return of harmony and fraternal feeling to our now distracted and unhappy country. God grant their prayer may be fully realized! Again I bid you a cordial welcome to our Capital.

The president-elect then spoke as follows:

Mr. President and Mr. Speaker, and Gentlemen of the General Assembly of Ohio: It is true, as has been said by the President of the Senate, that very great responsibility rests upon me in the position to which the votes of the American people have called me. I am duly sensible of that weighty responsibility. I can but know what you all know, that, without a name—perhaps without a reason why I should have a name—there has fallen upon me a task such as did not rest even upon the Father of his Country. And so feeling, I can only turn and look for those supports without which it will be impossible for me to perform that great task. I turn, then, and look to the American people, and to that God who has never forsaken the American people.

Allusion has been made to the interest felt in relation to the policy of the new administration. In reference to this, I have received from some sources some degree of credit for having kept silence; from others, some degree of deprecation. I still think I was right. In the varying and repeatedly shifting scenes that never could enable us to judge by the past, it has seemed fitting that before speaking upon the difficulties of the country I should have seen the whole ground to be sure—after all, being at liberty to modify and change the course of policy as future events may make a change necessary. I have not maintained silence from want of any real anxiety; for there is nothing going wrong. It is a consoling circumstance that when we look out, there is nothing that really hurts anybody. We entertain different views upon political questions, but nobody is suffering anything. This is the most consoling circumstance, and from it we may conclude that all we want is time, patience and a reliance on God who has never forsaken this people.

Fellow Citizens, what I have said, I have said altogether extemporaneously, and will now come to a close.

An eyewitness has given us a good description of Lincoln on this occasion:[59]

> The impression which the appearance of the President-elect created was most agreeable. His great height was conspicuous even in that crowd of goodly men, and lifted him fully in view as he walked up the aisle. When he took the Speaker's stand, a better opportunity was afforded to look at the man upon whom more hopes hang than upon any other living. At first the kindness and amiability of his face strikes you; but as he speaks, the greatness and determination of his nature are apparent. Something in his manner, even more than in his words, told how deeply he was affected by the enthusiasm of the people; and when he appealed to them for encouragement and support, every heart responded with mute assurance of both. There was the simplicity of greatness in his unassuming and confiding manner, that won its way to instant admiration. He looked somewhat worn with travel and the fatigues of popularity, but warmed to the cordiality of his reception.

In the meantime the great concourse of people massed before the west front of the Capitol, and, increasing every moment, were waiting for an address from the president-elect. He soon appeared on the steps and spoke as follows:

> *Ladies and Gentlemen:* I appear before you only to address you very briefly. I shall do little else than to thank you for this very kind reception; to greet you and bid you farewell. I should not find strength, if I were otherwise inclined, to repeat speeches of very great length, upon every occasion similar to this—although few so large—which will occur on my way to the Federal Capital. The General Assembly of the great State of Ohio has just done me the honor to receive me, and to hear a few broken remarks from myself. Judging from what I see, I infer that the reception was one without party distinction, and one of entire kindness—not that had nothing in it beyond the feeling of the citizenship of the United States of America. Knowing, as I do, that any crowd, drawn together as this has been, is made up of the citizens near about, and that in this county of Franklin there is great difference of political sentiment, and those agreeing with me having a little the shortest row; from this and the circumstances I have mentioned, I infer that you do me the honor to meet me here without distinction of party. I think this is as it should be. Many of you who were not favorable to the election of myself to the Presidency, were favorable to the election of the distinguished Senator from the State in which I reside. If Senator Douglas had been elected to the Presidency in the late contest, I

think my friends would have joined heartily in meeting him on his passage through your Capital, as you have me today. If any of the other candidates had been elected, I think it would have been altogether becoming and proper for all to have joined in showing honor quite as well to the office and the country as to the man. The people are themselves honored by such a concentration. I am doubly thankful that you have appeared here to give me this greeting. It is not much to me, for I shall very soon pass away from you; but we have a large country and a large future before us, and the manifestations of good will towards the Government, and affection for the Union, which you may exhibit, are of immense value to you and your posterity forever. In this point of view it is that I thank you most heartily for the exhibition you have given me; and with this, allow me to bid you an affectionate farewell.

Lincoln then returned to the rotunda where it was understood he would shake hands with all who desired to meet him. It was an unfortunate arrangement, for the entire crowd in mob order followed him. The scene which followed is vividly pictured by William T. Coggeshall,[60] state librarian, who was present:[61]

Mr. Lincoln took his position in the rotunda near the stairway leading to the Library, and the people admitted at the south door, passed through and out at the north door. Almost immediately the vast rotunda was crowded with eager, turbulent, pushing, crowding, jostling sovereigns, frantic to wrench the hand of the President-elect. An attempt was made to preserve a lane through which the hand-shakers might pass to Mr. Lincoln, and furious and heroic were the struggles to keep this avenue open. With a sublime devotion, which demands the highest praise, a few spartans held back the crowd, which heaved and surged to and fro. For a while the President greeted the people with his right hand only, but as the officers gave way before the irresistible crowd, he shook hands right and left, with astonishing rapidity. The physical exertion must have been tremendous. People plunged at his arms with frantic enthusiasm, and all the infinite variety of shakes, from the wild and irrepressible pump-handle movement to the dead grip, was executed upon the devoted sinister and dexter of the President. Some glanced into his face as they grasped his hand; others invoked the blessings of heaven upon him; others affectionately gave him their last gasping assurance of devotion; others, bewildered and furious, with hats crushed over their eyes, seized his hand in a convulsive grasp, and passed on as if they had not the remotest idea who, what, or where they were, nor what anything was at all about. But at last the performance become intolerable to the President, who retired to the staircase in exhaustion, and contented himself with looking at the crowd as it swept before him. It was a very good natured crowd, nothing occurred to mar the harmony of the occasion, and the utmost enthusiasm prevailed.

After this strenuous reception Lincoln retired to the governor's residence for a rest. But his labors were not over. In the evening he received, at the residence of Governor Dennison, the state officers, the members of the legislature and the city council; later he held another reception at the Statehouse in the executive chamber, where again he met the general public.

The next morning, February 14, he continued his journey, leaving at eight o'clock. The weather had changed, but in the pouring rain he was greeted by large crowds at Newark, Dresden, Coshocton, Newcomerstown, and Uhrichsville.

At Steubenville he received formal greetings from the city authorities, and in response, said:

> *My Fellow Citizens:* I fear that great confidence in my abilities is unfounded. The place I am about to assume is encompassed by vast difficulties. As I am, nothing shall be wanting on my part; unless sustained by the American people and God, I cannot hope to be successful. I believe the devotion to the Constitution is equally great on both sides of the river; it is only the different understandings of it. The only dispute is, what are their rights? If the majority should not rule, who should be the judge? When such a judge is found we must all be bound by his decision. That judge is the majority of the American people; if not, then the minority must control. Would that be right, just or generous? Assuredly not. He reiterated that the majority should rule. If he adopted a wrong policy, the opportunity to condemn it would occur in four years; then I can be turned out, and a better man, with better views, be put in my place.

At Pittsburgh he was given a reception, from which he started to Cleveland. According to the *Cleveland Herald* of February 15, it was one continued ovation from Ohioans.

At Wellsville there was a stop for a few moments to change engines. A large crowd had assembled, and Lincoln went out on the platform. He excused himself from making a speech, having made a few remarks there on the previous day. At this moment a man stepped forward and offered a couple of apples to the president-elect. A little boy in the crowd yelled out, "Say, Mr. Linkin, that man is running for postmaster!" The donor of the apples collapsed amid screams of laughter.

At Alliance there was a stop of twenty minutes for an elegant dinner furnished by the Cleveland and Pittsburgh Railroad Company. Here the crowd was so large that it was only by the strenuous efforts of the Canton Zouaves, who were on duty in full uniform, that a passage could be cleared. After dinner a temporary stand was placed in front of the station, and from it Lincoln addressed a few short remarks expressive of his gladness to see such an outpouring of the people.

At Ravenna the largest crowd that had been seen after leaving Allegany City was assembled. The approach of the train was greeted with double-loaded cannon, which boomed its welcome far and wide. Here it was found necessary to stop for a few minutes, and, in response to loud calls, Lincoln made a short speech, expressing his gratitude for the noble efforts of Ohio in the right cause, and his pleasure at hearing that men of all parties in this state had joined in the defense of the Union. Cheers and blessings were showered on him as the cars moved away. As the train moved, the cannon gave a parting salute.

But the largest crowd was at Hudson. At that point not less than five thousand people were assembled. Eight cars came up from the Akron branch, crowded inside and out, and accompanied by a band of music. Cheer on cheer rent the air as Lincoln appeared and bowed to the crowd.

At four o'clock cannon announced the approach to Cleveland. Here elaborate preparations had been made for the reception of the president-elect. The committee of arrangements consisted of the mayor, G. B. Senter, the president of the city council, I. U. Masters, and the following members thereof: C. L. Russell, W. H. Haywood, and O. M. Oviatt. Cooperating with this committee was one from the citizen body of which S. J. Andrews was chairman and Merrill Barlow secretary. The city was profusely decorated; the federal and city buildings, the hotels, business houses, and newspaper offices leading in variety and brilliancy. The city was filled with thousands of people from the Western Reserve, and the immense and surging crowds on the streets called for the greatest exertions of the city police force. This was especially so at the Euclid Street Station of the Cleveland and Pittsburgh Railroad. At four o'clock in the afternoon of February 15, Lincoln entered Cleveland, saluted by the booming of artillery and the unbounded enthusiasm of the people. He was escorted to a carriage drawn by four white horses. His escort consisted of the following:[62]

Cleveland Regiment Light Artillery, Colonel James Barnett,
    commanding; consisting of the following companies:
Company A, Captain Simmons;
Company B, Captain Mack;
Company D, Captain Rice;
Company E, Captain Hechman.
Cleveland Light Dragoons, Captain Holtnorth.
Cleveland Greys, Captain Paddock.
City council, in carriages.
The president-elect in an open barouche.
The president's suite in carriages.
Citizen's committee in carriages.
Firemen—Phoenix No. 4 and Firemen's Board.
Citizens in carriages, manufacturing establishments, and various
    representations of the business interests of the city.

The Weddell House where the reception was held, at half past four o'clock, was illuminated with colored lanterns. Mr. Masters, the president of the city council, on behalf of the authorities, spoke as follows:

Honored Sir:—The pleasant duty devolves upon me to extend to you, in behalf of the citizens of Cleveland, through their municipal representatives, a cordial welcome to this city and community. In extending this welcome, I am but speaking the voice of our men of business; our mechanics, whose representatives are around me; of farmers, who have largely gathered here; of men of all trades, avocations, professions and parties, who merge all distinction in that name common to them all, of highest distinction to them all, and best beloved by them all—American citizens. They bid me welcome you as the official representative of their country, chosen in accordance with the Constitution which they venerate with love. They bid me express to you their unconditional loyalty to the Constitution and country, which their fathers transmitted to them, and which they fervently hope may, by the blessing of God, be transmitted unimpaired to their children and their children's children. Again I bid you a hearty welcome.

Sherlock J. Andrews, chairman of the citizen's committee, then delivered the following address:

Mr. Lincoln—Sir: I have the honor, on behalf of the citizens of Cleveland, to repeat the welcome you have already received through the official organ of that city, and to express the great satisfaction that we all derive from this personal interview. We come today, sir, forgetful of party distinctions, and as citizens of a common country, to tender you the homage of our sincere respect, both for your personal character and for the high station to which you have been called by the popular will; and, though unexampled difficulties and embarrassments stand upon the threshold of your administration, we still cherish the hope that, by the blessing of Divine Providence, you may be enabled so to execute the great trust confided to you as to allay excitement, correct misapprehension, restore harmony, and reinstate this glorious Union of ours in the affections and confidence of the whole people. It is true, indeed, that in the late peaceful contest for the Chief Magistracy, we have acted under various political organizations, and have differed as to men and measures. Yet, sir, in every enlightened effort to support the prerogatives and honor of the General Government, in every determination to uphold the supremacy of law, in every measure wisely designed to maintain unimpaired the constitutional rights of all the States or of any of the States, and every concession consistent with truth and justice, that looks to the promotion of peace and concord, there is not a man in the vast multitude here assembled to do you honor, who will not give you his cordial and earnest support. Such, I am persuaded, sir, are the views of those I represent, and to whom, for any further expression of their sentiments, I shall now refer you.

Fellow citizens, I have the honor of introducing to you the Honorable Abraham Lincoln, the President elect of the United States.

To this the president-elect responded:[63]

Mr. Chairman and Fellow Citizens: We have been marching in procession for about two miles through snow, rain, and deep mud. The large number that have turned out under these circumstances testify that you are in earnest about something or other. But do I think so meanly of you as to suppose that earnestness is about me personally? I should be doing you an injustice to suppose it was. You have assembled to testify your respect to the Union, the Constitution and the laws. And here let me say that it is with you, the people, to advance the great cause of the Union and the Constitution, and not with any one man. It rests with you alone. This fact is strongly impressed on me at present. In a community like this, whose appearance testifies to their intelligence, I am convinced that the cause of Liberty and the Union can never be in danger.

Frequent allusion is made to the excitement at present existing in our national politics. It is well that I should also allude to it here. I think there is no occasion for any excitement. The crisis, as it is called, is altogether an artificial crisis. In all parts of the nation there are differences of opinion on politics. There are differences of opinion even here. You did not all vote for the person who now addresses you. What is happening now will not hurt those who are farther away. Have they not all the rights now they ever had? Do they not have their fugitive slaves returned as ever? Have they not the same Constitution that they have lived under for the last seventy odd years? Have they not a position as citizens of this common country, and have we any power to change that position? [Cries of "No!] What, then, is the matter with them? Why all this excitement? Why of all these complaints? As I said before, this crisis is all artificial. It has no foundation in facts. It is not argued up, as the saying is, and therefore cannot be argued down. Let is alone, and it will go down of itself. [Laughter.]

Mr. Lincoln said they must be content with but very few words from him, as he was much fatigued, and had spoken so frequently that he was already hoarse. He thanked them then for the cordial and magnificent reception they had given him—not the less did he thank them for the votes they gave him last fall, and quite as much he thanked them for the efficient aid they had given the cause which he represented—a cause which he would say was a good one. He had one more word to say: He was given to understand that this reception was tendered not only by his own party supporters, but by men of all parties. This is as it should be. If Judge Douglas had been elected, and had been here on his way to Washington, as I am tonight, the Republicans should have joined his supporters in welcoming him, just as his friends have joined with mine tonight. If all don't join now to save the good old ship of Union in this voyage, nobody will have a chance to pilot her on another.

The Weddell House was the scene of a crushing and unorganized evening reception, which Lincoln simply reviewed, and afterward abandoned from fatigue. Later, with Mrs. Lincoln, he received a few friends in another part of the hotel. An early departure was made the next morning without demonstration, although a large crowd was on hand to bid a cheering good-bye. Lincoln waved a farewell, and the train sped eastward; the party was accompanied to the state line by Colonels George S. Mygatt and George O'Hara of Governor Dennison's staff.

He was greeted enthusiastically at Willoughby. At Painesville he mounted a platform that had been arranged for the occasion and spoke briefly. At Madison he acknowledged the greetings of a large crowd by bowing from the platform of his car.

At Geneva the approach of the special was announced by the booming of the cannon. As the train pulled into the station there was great cheering. One of the banners displayed bore the inscription, "The

Lord is God; let all the people praise Him." As Lincoln appeared on the platform, a man stepped forward and read from a paper as follows:

> Abraham Lincoln, the People's representative and President: Aided by Divine Providence may he so guide the Ship of State (now floating among the reefs and breakers of Disunion) that she may be brought back to her original mooring: The Constitution as it is; the Union as it was; and Liberty uncompromised.

The reading was followed by loud cheers. Lincoln responded in a few words expressive of his thorough devotion to the principles enunciated in the speaker's remarks. This was followed by prolonged applause.

Lincoln spoke briefly at Ashtabula, assuring the people that the warm manifestations of approval that he met there and everywhere on his journey strengthened him for the duties awaiting him.

The stop at Conneaut was so brief that he had time only to bow in recognition of the ovation tendered.

In Lincoln's journey through Ohio there was nothing lacking in the demonstrations of loyalty and enthusiasm by its people, regardless of party. But on the other hand there was a plain feeling of disappointment among the Republicans and Union Democrats over his speeches. This, we have seen, was publicly exhibited at Cincinnati, while at Columbus[64] and Cleveland the criticism was widespread but private. This attitude was not one of unfriendliness, but of grave concern and regret over Lincoln's apparent inability to realize the seriousness of the national situation. His optimism as to the future, his constant reiteration that everything would come out all right, and, as he said at Columbus, "It is a good thing there is not more than anxiety, for there is nothing going wrong," and, "When we look out, there is nothing that really hurts anybody"; all this threw many of the leading Republicans, not only in Ohio, but throughout the country, into a condition of alarm which they dared not express. It looked to them as if the policy of the triumphant party was to be one of *laissez faire*. They could not understand how the future president could say "all's well" while the very foundations of the Union were rocking and its rafters were cracking over their heads. In rapid succession, commencing December 20, 1860, South Carolina, Mississippi, Florida, Alabama, Louisiana, and Texas had passed ordinances of secession. They had formed the "Confederate States of America" February 8, and on the next day Jefferson

Davis and Alexander H. Stephens were elected president and vice president, respectively, of the new "nation," as they loved to call it. While Lincoln was making his speeches, this "government" was functioning *de facto*; it was seizing for its own use scores of millions of dollars' worth of national property, consisting of forts, arsenals, custom-houses, post offices, and monies.

In this fateful period, senators and representatives of the remaining southern states were openly conspiring under the very roof of their nation's Capitol for the further dissolution of the Union by speeches, telegrams, and letters urging their states to join the Southern Confederacy. It was under these conditions that thousands of thoughtful Republicans and Democrats asked themselves, "What does Lincoln mean by his persistent ignoring of conditions?" "Why does he sedulously refrain from taking the nation into his confidence?" "Why all these generalities in time of danger?"

As much as the North knew Lincoln at this time, it had thus far little opportunity to assess the greatness of his statesmanship or the depth of his shrewdness. The people generally did not know that he, far more than they, was informed of the situation and its danger, as well as the daily reproaches heaped upon him by reason of his speeches. He felt his responsibility and carried his burdens alone, and, while he advised with close friends, he knew they could neither share nor divide them with him. Knowing this, we can better understand his pathetic farewell to his neighbors, when he said that a duty was upon him, "Greater than that which has devolved upon any other man since the days of Washington." This dangerous duty was laid upon him early, for during the critical period between his election and inauguration his responsibility was as great and weighty as that in the darkest days of the war. He saw clearly that in order to save the Union and prevent the extension of slavery, there were certain vital and essential measures to be consummated. The first in order, paramount and absolutely necessary, was that he should be inaugurated president.

Jefferson Davis and his associates, backed by the slaveholders of the South, were bold in their designs and actions. They were resolved to go out of the Union. They firmly believed that the North in the "long run" would not oppose. There were evidences of this disposition cropping out. Horace Greeley in the *New York Tribune* as early as November 9, 1860 (three days after the election and forty days before South Carolina seceded), declared in favor of letting the southern states go in peace.[65]

Seward, who was known to be the coming secretary of state, made a statement to the effect that everything would be settled in sixty days. The Republicans in the second session of the Thirty-sixth Congress in December 1860 went to the fullest length to conciliate, even guaranteeing the perpetual existence of slavery in the southern states. This was to be done by a constitutional amendment, which they recommended the states to adopt. Strange to say, it was adopted by Ohio;[66] only one other accepted it, Maryland. This, and other manifestations of conciliation on the part of the Republicans, was construed by the southern leaders as obsequiousness or cowardice—they cared little which—and they were satisfied that they could bluff their scheme to consummation. All they wanted was "to be let alone." Add to all this the horrible possibility of assassination (a plot for which was discovered and thwarted), and we can see how much wiser it was for Lincoln to refrain from aggressive and prophetic speeches. Therefore, he proceeded "on the even tenor of his way" to Washington, noncommittal as to what his policy would be as to the new "government" of the South.

The man best posted on the southern situation was William H. Seward. He was in the senate in the last session of Congress wherein Jefferson Davis served—1860–61. He was sure that Davis expected a peaceful dissolution of the Union. Seward knew as long as Davis felt that way, there would be no obstruction to Lincoln's inauguration. On the contrary, Seward was equally certain that if Lincoln foreshadowed his policy, as expressed in his inaugural address, that war would be commenced earlier, and the southern contingent in Congress would have forced some method to prevent the canvass of the electoral vote. Seward, about that time, made a speech at the Astor House in New York. It was very conciliatory and persuasive. He said, in the same vein Lincoln said it in Ohio, that there is "going to be no trouble," and "it would be over in sixty days." Afterward he was severely criticized for this speech by a leading New York Democrat. His explanation was given later, at a dinner at the Willard Hotel, Washington, as follows:[67]

> Oakey Hall says I am the most august liar in the United States; that I said in the winter before the war, in a speech at the Astor House, that the trouble would all be over and everything settled in sixty days. I would have Mr. Oakey Hall to know that when I made that speech the electoral vote was not counted, and I knew it never would be if Jeff Davis believed there would be war. We both knew that he was to be President of the Southern Confederacy, and that I was to be Secretary of State under Mr. Lincoln. I

wanted the vote counted and Lincoln inaugurated. I had to deceive Davis, and I did it. That's why I said it would all be settled in sixty days.

It will be apparent now that Lincoln's negative speeches had the same object as Seward's affirmative declaration, viz.: the holding of the southern leaders in *status quo*. If this had not been done, and had Lincoln followed the popular demands, the open hostilities against the Union would have been commenced in Buchanan's administration instead of in his own.

The second condition that worried Lincoln greatly, and which was another factor in restraining his public expressions, was a growing tendency toward conciliation and the surrender of the principles of the Chicago platform upon which the Republicans were placed in power. If there was any reason for the existence of the Republican Party, it was based on the two cardinal declarations of its platform: 1) "that the Federal Constitution, the rights of the States, and the Union of the States must and shall be preserved," and 2) "we deny the authority of Congress, of a territorial legislature, or of any individual, to give legal existence to slavery in any territory of the United States."

Lincoln saw that if these principles were to be surrendered, the party might as well be abandoned. So far as the question of the Union was concerned, there was no difference in the stand of the Republicans and the Democrats of the North. Douglas was as firm on that subject as Lincoln, yet in a certain element of the Republican Party there was a growing sentiment of peaceable dissolution of the Union in order to have peace. We shall afterward see the motives which produced this feeling. Lincoln, however, was adamant on this: With him "the Union must and shall be preserved." Although he made no reference in his February speeches in Ohio as to what he would do in regard to the seceding states, he long before had made up his mind as to his program. The very next day after South Carolina seceded, December 21, he wrote to his confidential friend, E. B. Washburne, congressman from Illinois, and chairman of the Republican National Committee, as follows:

CONFIDENTIAL
SPRINGFIELD, Dec. 21, 1860.

HON. E. B. WASHBURNE.
MY DEAR SIR:—Last night I received your letter, giving an account of your interview with General Scott, and for which I thank you. Please present my respects to the General and tell him confidentially I shall be obliged to him

to be as well prepared as he can to either *hold,* or retake, the forts, as the case may require, at and after the inauguration.

Yours, as ever,
A. LINCOLN.

On the compromise over slavery extension, which was then being debated in Congress, and had assumed the shape of legislation, December 13, he wrote as follows:

HON. E. B. WASHBURNE.
MY DEAR SIR:—Your long letter received. Prevent as far as possible any of our friends from demoralizing themselves and our cause by entertaining propositions for compromise of any sort on slavery extension. There is no possible compromise upon it, but which puts us under again, and all our work to do over again. Whether it be a Missouri line or Eli Thayer's Popular Sovereignty, it is all the same.—Let either be done, and immediately filibustering and extending slavery recommences. On that point hold firm as a chain of steel.

Yours, as ever,
A. LINCOLN.

If the general citizenship had knowledge of what Lincoln's mental attitude was while he was making speeches, they would have been satisfied, but its publicity would have been disastrous. From his vantage ground at Springfield he was in full touch with the situation, which called for the exercise of the greatest wisdom as well as caution. Under the threats of secession he saw the influence of Greeley's appeal spreading throughout the North. It found a willing lodgment in two classes of his own party: the commercial element and the pre-abolition Republicans. The former feared war, as destructive to trade and credits; they had the spirit of the silversmiths of Ephesus against Paul, "this our craft is in danger to be set at nought." The motive of the latter was hatred of slavery, which was stronger in their minds than love for the Union. One of the declarations of an old abolitionist was that the Constitution was a "covenant with death and an agreement with hell." Many Republicans had not fully forgotten their abolition feeling and were willing to see the slave states go in order that *their* Union might be all free.

While Lincoln was delivering his speeches in Ohio—without "punch" as his critics complained—he was wise enough not to be provocative, for he was upon territory in which his party had been inoculated with the germ of "peaceful separation." A week after his election the *Ohio State Journal* of Columbus commenced a series of remarkable editorials,[68] arguing to that end. In its issue of November 13, 1860, more than a column was devoted to the proposition that there was no power under the Constitution to forcibly maintain the Union. A paragraph will show its reasoning:

> The object of the American Union is to provide for the common defence, general welfare, etc. It is so stated in the preamble to the Constitution. The general government is but the representative of the states. It is not a genuine federal center of power. Now if any state or states wish to renounce the benefits of this general protection, how can they be compelled to continue the recipient of such advantages? The Cotton States are not rebelling against the federal authority nor nullifying any particular general law. They simply request to be relieved from the Union compact. To coerce them to remain in the Union, by the forces of the United States government is to entirely change the nature of Federal authority. It will be to make the Federal government not a representative of the states, their instrument in providing for the common defence, &c., but a superior, centralized power having an existence independent of the states. We regret being compelled to take this view of the matter, but it seems inevitable.

In the issue of November 17, the editor naively proposes the expulsion of South Carolina from the Union for the reason that she has never been anything but a source of vexation, trouble, and expense. The way to do this is thus set forth:

> Let the thing be regularly and deliberately done. Petitions circulated among the people for the expulsion of South Carolina would receive innumerable signatures; and on the meeting of Congress, we might "batter the gates of" the Capital "with storms of prayer" for that purpose. The body which has the power to admit a state into the Union has the power to expel a State, and we hope that our members may be instructed to act promptly in this matter.

On November 28, in a long discussion, there is a disposition to modify the former expression on the question of peaceable secession, as the following extract shows:

> We have been thus explicit upon this point because a former article which appeared in the *Journal* of the 13th inst., has been misapprehended in

several important particulars. The writer did not intend to assert that secession was a right to be exercised by any State at will; but that it was the right of any State to take the initiative step towards secession, by applying for release from the Federal compact of Union embodied in the Constitution. In that article it was assumed that a peremptory refusal to recognize the right to make such application, especially if accompanied by an attempt at coercion into an unwilling continuance in the Union, the particular case referred to, would bring about a war of sections, which would amount to virtual dissolution. As to whether such application would be favorably received by the people of the other states, is a question for them to consider, whenever it shall be presented in due form. But all will admit that a peaceable solution of the question should first be sought; and that a resort to coercion should be postponed until all other alterations are exhausted.

As late as March 27, 1861, after Lincoln's inauguration, there is a long editorial on the failure of the Union under the Constitution:

The Africanized people of the South have precipitated a work which we believe advancing civilization and the teachings of Christianity would have, ere long, demanded at the hands of the free people of the North. The complicity with the barbarism of slavery which the latter have had forced upon them by the Union has become more burthensome every year, and must have been thrown off voluntarily before the lapse of many years. The Union has done nothing in reality for freedom. Its legislation has all been in favor of slavery, when required to decide differences between these antipodes.—Then why should free men deplore the loss of the Union? Separate peaceful existences of the sections are preferable to a Union which is dissatisfactory to one and which retards the progress of the other.

The creators of the Union sowed the seeds of its inevitable death at the creation. They thought to beget a healthy body by an unnatural cross between right and wrong. They thought to produce a harmonious, symmetrical whole by blending two conflicting systems of industry—two civilizations. How could they expect to be successful when all history is against them? All nations that recognize the right of one man to oppress another sooner or later crumble into dissolution, and in that extinction we are bound to recognize the decree of justice. And why should the American people alone hope to enjoy immunity from this universal doom?

In southern Ohio the leading exponent of pacifism was the *Cincinnati Daily Commercial*. Representing a community closely connected with Southern trade, naturally its commercial interests looked with fearful apprehension upon all interruption of business relations. War meant a loss of millions of dollars, not only in present and future profits, but in credits already due. There was a distinct, but silent and small, element with this view. On February 1, 1861, the *Commercial*, which might be said to represent this minority, in more positive terms than heretofore, expressed itself on the situation. On the day before it had advocated calling a national convention to release the dissatisfied states. This day, February 1, it declared:

> If it be possible for the disaffected states to separate themselves from the Union peaceably, we are in favor of given them full permission and all needful assistance to go.

After arguing at length against war and condemning the southern states for their treasonable intentions and acts, the editorial proceeds:

> But if one state cannot withdraw from the Union, a convention of the people of all the states can take the general welfare into consideration and yield the disaffected States the independence that they seem to covet. It is vain to talk of coercing the people of the states from the Potomac to the Rio Grande, and the Ohio to the Gulf. The General Assemblies of New York and Ohio by almost unanimous votes tendered the general government money and men to enforce the laws. Virginia and Kentucky instead of responding to this movement by the passage of similar resolutions, defiantly took the side of rebellious South Carolina and of the mobs that robbed the Federal Government of its property in states that had not intended to withdraw from the Union. This we fear is decisive. We must, therefore, permit the establishment of a Cotton Empire; and if the border slave states prefer the dominion of the peculiar politicians who possess authority under King Cotton to the old-fashioned American Republic, they must be permitted to go their way, and in peace, if peace if possible. If mad man will make war it must be met, but we must make peace if we can.

Among the Republicans of the Western Reserve were thousands of old abolitionists who heard of the secession of the South with little regret. This grew out of their antecedent history. They went into the Republican Party on the theory that it afforded the only practical agency for the ultimate destruction of slavery. In doing this they did not leave behind their abhorrence of the system and the determination to destroy it. It was a bitter dose to accept the Republican doctrine of non-interference with slavery as it was and to accept the Fugitive Slave Law.

But they did it. They had a hope that by "boring from within" they could finally accomplish their end. They were right, for in the subsequent march of events, they were the most potential factor in destroying slavery, even though it was done as a military necessity. These people never ceased to look upon the South as the sinful member of the Union, and they were now ready even to follow the scriptural injunction, "if thy right hand offend thee, cut if off, and cast it from thee."

Representing this element, Joshua R. Giddings being the leader, was the *Ashtabula Sentinel* edited by W. C. Howells, the father of William Dean Howells. The father was a political Covenanter and was dominated in politics solely by his moral convictions. Nothing meant much to him that did not have right and justice for a foundation. Hence he was not disposed to look with disfavor upon secession. On February 6, 1861, he wrote to his paper from Columbus that the dissolution of the Union seemed inevitable and that the public was preparing for it. A week later, in referring to the attitude of the Cincinnati papers on this question, he wrote to the *Sentinel* as follows:[69]

> It is really surprising now to see how generally the public and private expression of the people of the border is in favor of peaceable separation. Its entire practicability is demonstrated to a large portion of the thinkers of the country, while the idea of coercing or fighting them to make them stay in, is looked upon as ridiculous.

This survey of newspaper sentiment in Ohio shows the atmosphere through which Lincoln moved on his way to Washington, and that it continued even after his inauguration. Here and there lightning flashes of rebellion in his own party against its basic doctrines, and again, continuing rumbles of discontent. But to all these he said not a word in any of his utterances.

On his way to Washington he made nineteen speeches in as many leading cities. These were distributed as follows: Illinois, one; Indiana, one; Ohio, six; New York, five; New Jersey, two; and Pennsylvania, four.

It has been said,[70] "the journey can only be looked upon as a sad failure, and his speeches except his touching farewell to his old neighbors at Springfield, and his noble address in Independence Hall at Philadelphia, had better not have been delivered." This opinion can well be challenged and ought to be. The speeches were well planned, and what was said was only what should have been said. It was his first critical situation, and it was managed so as to successfully attain the result desired. Few men could have safely run such a gauntlet. Amidst the excitement of that day, men did not see with the precision that he did. This wisdom would have been useless without the force of will to carry it out.

So that we are compelled to measure him as Seward did after his "dream of domination" failed: "Executive skill and vigor are rare qualities. The President is the best of us."

CHAPTER 7

LINCOLN'S RELATIONS WITH OHIO DURING THE WAR; THE CASE OF VALLANDIGHAM; THE DEFECTION OF SALMON P. CHASE

In the war for the Union, Ohio assumed foremost rank among the greater states of the North in furnishing men and money to suppress the revolution of the South. Up to December 31, 1864, nearly 365,000 of her citizens had enlisted in the federal armies; its political divisions, including the state itself, paid out for war purposes over $65,000,000. In the field, Ohio led the states in furnishing the military commanders. By birth or residence she was credited with Generals Grant, Sherman, and Sheridan; Major Generals Buell, Cox, Crook, Custer, Garfield, Gilmore, Hazen, Leggett, McClellan, McCook, McDowell, Mitchel, Rosecrans, Stanley, Steedman, Swayne, and Weitzel. To these may be added 150 brigadier generals.

On the civil side of the war, Ohio was equally conspicuous and dominant. The two most powerful members of Lincoln's cabinet were Ohioans. Salmon P. Chase, twice governor and twice senator from Ohio, was a secretary of the treasury whose success in trying times ranks him with Alexander Hamilton; Edwin M. Stanton, the great war minister, was Lincoln's right hand whose executive force more than once organized victory out of defeat. If we turn to Congress for Ohio's place and influence, we find in the Senate John Sherman as chairman of the Finance Committee carrying into legislation the policies of

Secretary Chase; and Benjamin F. Wade as chairman of the Committee on the Conduct of the War. In the House, General Robert C. Schenck was at the head of the Committee on Military Affairs. Into the hands of these men were committed the financial and military legislation of the nation.

Nevertheless, with this record of patriotic contribution to the Union cause, Ohio was the source of much disloyal activity, the result and purpose of which was to embarrass and oppose Lincoln and the prosecution of the war. It was to Ohio, more than any other state, that he gave his personal attention at one time, for its movements were destroying the morale of the Union army and handicapping the power of government. In order that we may get an intelligent view of the condition and times referred to, it will be necessary to go back to the period just before the war.

It will be remembered that Governor Dennison was elected in 1859 after a strictly partisan campaign, in which Lincoln actively and effectively took part. The next year was filled with great events—Lincoln's nomination, his election, and the secession of the southern states; after these came his inauguration and the firing on Fort Sumter. This latter event, so tragic and so foolish, melted away all party lines; and the North, at first dazed, arose with the anger of a giant to prevent the dissolving of the Union.

The general assembly of Ohio was in session when the storm broke. Within twenty-four hours after Lincoln's call for troops, every vestige of party lines vanished; Democrats vied with Republicans in rallying to the support of the Union. One million dollars was voted unanimously by both houses to be expended in furnishing arms to Ohio troops and for other military purposes.[71] Specifically $500,000 was appropriated to carry into effect the requisitions of the president; $450,000 for equipping the militia of the state; and $50,000 for the governor to use as he might find necessary. Later $1,500,000 was appropriated for use in case of invasion of the state. This was followed by a law providing for raising by taxation a fund for the relief of families of volunteers, which relief was to be continued for a year after the death of such volunteers in the service. Other legislation made necessary by the exigencies of the times was also passed. This was Ohio's answer to the southern Confederacy, and it was given without regard to party.

While this patriotic legislation was being considered, there came to Columbus for the purpose of urging the Democrats of the legislature to oppose it, Clement L. Vallandigham,[72] the Democratic congressman from the Dayton district. He met with no success in his endeavor to dissuade his party associates to oppose these measures.

Vallandigham was one of the outstanding characters of the war period. His brief but meteoric career forms one of the dramatic episodes of that time. The sinister influence which he cast over Ohio and the nation, resulting finally in Lincoln's interference, was dangerous to the morale of both people and army. There were times when Vallandigham was worth a division to the Confederate cause. With this in view, a more than general reference to his personality will better enable us to assess his place in history and also understand a character that gave Lincoln more concern and trouble than any man outside the southern Confederacy.

We have already seen that preceding the war the Republican Party held its element of pacifism which, however, disappeared with the firing upon Fort Sumter. A similar element existed in the Democratic Party, but on the other hand it continued throughout the war, having gained and held control of that organization. Of this Vallandigham was the talented and aggressive leader, possessing magnetic powers of oratory, which in their climax gave speech to words of eloquent disloyalty. He was of mixed Huguenot and Scotch–Irish stock, and his heritage was conscience, courage, and combativeness. His mind was narrow and single-tracked. He would rather see the Union destroyed than to deviate a hair's breadth from the Constitution, which it was made to preserve. He had no sense of adjustment; his egoism was overdeveloped. He was not a Democrat of the Jefferson or Jackson type. He belonged to that class of men that Macaulay characterized as "architects of ruin."

When he came to Columbus to influence his fellow Democrats against supporting war legislation, he came with a reputation for prosouthern sentiments. He had already, November 20, 1860, in a speech in Cooper Institute, New York, declared that:[73]

> If any one or more of the states of this Union should at any time secede, for the reasons of the suffering and justice of which, before God and the tribunal of history, they alone may judge, much as I deplore it, I never would, as a Representative in the Congress of the United States, vote one dollar of money whereby one drop of American blood should be shed in a Civil War.

In the House of Representatives on February 20, 1861, he gave further evidence of his position by advocating a constitutional amendment introduced by him providing for the division of the Union into four sections, to be known as, the North, the West, the Pacific, and the South.[74] One of its provisions was that:

> No State shall secede without the consent of the Legislature of the States of the section to which the State proposing to secede belongs. The President shall have power to adjust with seceding States all questions arising by reason of their secession; but the terms of adjustment shall be submitted to the Congress for their approval before the same shall be valid.

In this speech, which was bold in expression, Vallandigham claimed that his aim was to save the Union, but his plan had in it essentially the opposite purpose.

Now if these expressions of Vallandigham were the sum of his offending, he might be absolved from his sin of disloyalty. In his Cooper Institute speech, his declared attitude was practically that of Horace Greeley, but expressed in a flamboyant and exaggerated style. His proposed constitutional amendment to divide the Union into four sections was but another form of plan that the *Tribune* and other Republican papers were willing to acquiesce in as the price for peace. They, as well as some prominent Republicans, were willing to have a North and a South. If division was to come, there was not any difference in principle in a "peaceful separation" into four sections. As we view it today, all these propositions were absurd and impracticable. It was far better for the country to fight it out to a finish. Let separation be accomplished, and a dozen fragments of a once glorious Union would have been the result.

These vagaries as to plans for peace were so common in both parties at this time, that Vallandigham was only one of many "running round in circles," devising some way to avoid war. But when he kept up this antagonism to the government after its flag was fired upon, he crossed the Rubicon of his life. This is the reason that when he came to his fellow Democrats in the general assembly, he found himself without standing.

Thwarted at Columbus, he sought by personal appeal to his party associates to check the rising Union sentiment among them. To more than twenty prominent Democrats of Ohio, he sent a private circular letter calling a conference at Chillicothe, May 15, 1861, "to concert measures to arouse the people to a sense of danger which was so imminent from the bold conspiracy to usurp all power in the hands of the Executive," as well as "to rescue the Republic from all impending military despotism." To this call there were but four answers; three were favorable to its purposes, and one adverse to the conference. There was no meeting.[75]

This failure served to intensify his feelings, and he started, more strenuously than before, to create a public sentiment against the war for the Union, which he led with power and malevolence. He cleft his party in twain; those favoring the war, joining with the Republicans, formed the Union Party, and his followers retaining the organization of the old Democratic Party were known as the "Peace Democracy." This alignment in Ohio, the Union and Peace Democracy, was the partisan division during and after the war—from 1861 to 1867. It is not the purpose to dwell upon the relations of these parties during this period, although it might be made very interesting reading.[76] The object herein being to deal with the career of a single man, reference to the parties will be only as associated with him.

In the extra session of Congress called by Lincoln for July 4, 1861, Vallandigham made what might be called his first official declaration against the war. On July 10, he delivered a speech in the House of Representatives, which for bold antagonism dazed the Union sentiment of the country. His attitude received little sympathy from his party colleagues. This speech, under the title "After Some Time Be Past," was widely circulated, not only in this country, but in England and on the continent.[77]

In the fall of 1862 he was defeated for reelection to congress by the Union general, Robert C. Schenck of Dayton; and as expected, he returned to Washington to complete his term, more hostile than ever. He manifested this in a remarkable speech in the House on "The Great Civil War in America," January 14, 1863.[78] It was a pessimistic philippic against the continuance of the war and a bitter indictment of Lincoln and his administration. Its practical effect was to encourage the southern armies and to give hope to the Davis government. Said he, "You can never subdue the seceded states. Two years of fearful experience have taught you that"; then he asks, "Why carry on this war? If you persist, it can only end in final separation between the North and the South. And in that case, believe me, as you did not my former warning, the whole Northwest will go with the South." He then proceeded to plead for peace, either by domestic agreement or foreign intervention. He held that slavery must be recognized in any event. "In my deliberate judgment," said he, "African slavery, as an institution, will come out of this conflict fifty-fold stronger than when it was begun."

This speech had three effects: by it Vallandigham burned his bridges behind him and became an open antagonist of the government. With all his talk of Union and peace he was directly aiding and encouraging the enemy. Again, it spread the peace sentiment throughout the country; and lastly, it served to obstruct enlistments as well as to discourage the army in the field. By the friends of the Union everywhere, it was regarded as "words of brilliant and polished treason." When the Thirty-seventh Congress adjourned, Vallandigham made speeches of the same tenor in New York and Philadelphia. He reached Dayton on March 13, receiving an enthusiastic welcome from his followers. He addressed meetings in Ohio in March and April. The greatest demonstration of his tour was to be at Mt. Vernon, May 1, where he was to be welcomed by the Peace Democracy of central Ohio.

At this time the states of Ohio, Indiana, Kentucky, and Illinois formed a military district designated as the "Department of Ohio," under the command of General Ambrose E. Burnside. Within this territory there had developed the most violent feeling against the government and the war. It had no parallel throughout the country. Here the seditious teachings of Vallandigham bore fruit in the form of resistance to the draft; in the organization of secret treasonable societies, of one of which, the "Sons of Liberty," he became supreme commander; in open and armed resistance to the government and a general disposition to sympathize with and aid the enemy. In a word, there existed in this district a well-organized conspiracy to obstruct the military authorities of the United States.[79]

To meet this situation, General Burnside issued "General Orders No. 38" in which was the following:

> The habit of declaring sympathies for the enemy will not be allowed in this Department. Persons committing such offences will be at once arrested, with a view to being tried as above stated, or sent beyond our lines into the lines of their friends. It must be distinctly understood that treason, expressed or implied, will not be tolerated in this Department. All officers and soldiers are strictly charged with the execution of this order.

In accordance with arrangements, Vallandigham addressed a meeting of great magnitude and enthusiasm at Mt. Vernon. It lasted throughout the day, and the Peace Democracy of the surrounding counties was there in force. They gloried in the name of "Butternut" and "Copperhead," for there were butternut boughs in profusion for ornaments, and on the breasts of thousands were pins made of the liberty heads cut from copper cents. The orator was at his best, and his adoring audience readily surrendered to his magnetic eloquence. After his opening, he proceeded to denounce "Lincoln and his minions"; he said, "This was a wicked, cruel, and unnecessary war"; "a war not waged for the preservation of the Union"; "a war for the purpose of crushing out liberty and erecting a despotism." He denounced General Burnside's order as, "a base usurpation of arbitrary authority," and added "that the sooner the people inform the minions of usurped power they will not submit to such restrictions upon their liberties, the better." He declared "that he was at all times, and upon all occasions, resolved to do what he could to defeat the attempts now being made to build up a monarchy upon the ruins of our free government." He declared that "he was a free man and did not ask David Tod, Abraham Lincoln, or Ambrose E. Burnside for his rights to speak as he had done and was doing"; "his authority for so doing was higher than General Orders No. 38—it was General Orders No. 1—the Constitution"; that, "General Orders No. 38 was a base usurpation of arbitrary power"; "he had the most supreme contempt for such power, he despised it, spat upon it, trampled it under this feet"; on the draft, he said, "an attempt would shortly be made to enforce the conscription act; they should remember that this was not a war for the preservation of the Union—it was a wicked Abolition war, and that if those in authority were allowed to accomplish their purpose, the people would be deprived of their liberties, and a monarchy established." During his speech someone hurrahed for "Jeff Davis"; this Vallandigham promptly denounced.[80]

The meeting was on Friday; Vallandigham was arrested on the following Monday by order of General Burnside. He was tried by a military commission, and on May 16 was found guilty of "publicly expressing, in violation of General Orders No. 38 from Headquarters of the Department of Ohio, sympathy for those in arms against the Government of the United States, and declaring disloyal sentiments and opinions, with the object and purpose of weakening the power of the Government in its efforts to suppress an unlawful rebellion." He was sentenced to confinement in Fort Warren, in Boston Harbor, during the continuance of the war. This sentence was changed by Lincoln, who directed General Burnside to send Vallandigham "under secure guard to the headquarters of General Rosecrans" and "by him to be delivered into the Confederate lines," and that in case he returned, the original sentence should be enforced. While being tried before the military commission, application for a writ of *habeas corpus* was made in the United States Circuit Court, Judge H. H. Leavitt, presiding. Upon a full hearing the writ was refused.

The banishment of Vallandigham made him immediately the idol and martyr of the Peace Democracy. At their New York state convention, May 16, resolutions of protest against his arrest, trial, and sentence were passed, and these, with a long letter were sent to Lincoln.[81] He answered at length. His reasoning was unanswerable. For instance, this:

> I understand the meeting, whose resolutions I am considering, to be in favor of suppressing the rebellion by military force—by armies. Long experience has shown that armies cannot be maintained unless desertions shall be punished by the severe penalty of death. The case requires, and the law and the Constitution sanction, this punishment. Must I shoot a simple-minded soldier-boy who deserts, while I must not touch a hair of a wily agitator who induces him to desert? This is none the less injurious when effected by getting a father, or brother, or friend, into a public meeting, and there working upon his feelings till he is persuaded to write the soldier-boy that he is fighting in a bad cause, for a wicked Administration of a contemptible government, too weak to arrest and punish him if he shall desert. I think that in such a case to silence the agitator and save the boy is not only constitutional, but withal, a great mercy. [82]

The Ohio Peace Democracy met in state convention to nominate a governor on June 11, at Columbus, amidst great excitement. The exile of their leader, who was now within the lines of the southern Confederacy, had stirred them into a state of hysterical devotion to him. The unfriendly press estimated the attendance at 25,000; inflamed by the passionate appeals of extravagant orators, all feelings of reason and conservation had been banished. There were a few thoughtful Democrats who saw the folly of it all. They urged General McClellan, who was still a resident of Ohio, to be a candidate; he refused. They called on Rufus P. Ranney; he refused. Finally, Hugh J. Jewett, a Union man and

War Democrat, consented. On a trial ballot they gave him thirteen votes and Vallandigham 411, and at once nominated the latter unanimously. As to the platform, the delegates cried "Vallandigham is platform enough." The leaders, however, presented resolutions dealing entirely with the alleged prosecution and persecution of their nominee. There was no reference to the terrible trial through which the country was passing; no words of condemnation for those who were seeking to dissolve the Union; and no praise even for the tens of thousands of Ohio Democrats who were in the field fighting for the flag. On all the events that would appeal to patriotism, the platform was as silent as the grave.[83] The resolutions concluded by calling upon the president "respectfully but most earnestly to restore Clement L. Vallandigham to his home in Ohio." A committee of one from each congressional district was selected by the presiding officer of the convention to present an application for such purpose to the president.

Lincoln from the beginning viewed the peace movement in the North with grave concern. He knew it was dangerous, and he called it "the fire in the rear." He realized the power of Vallandigham over his party, and in commuting his sentence from imprisonment to exile among his friends, whom he constantly eulogized as unconquerable, Lincoln displayed his usual shrewdness as well as humor. He did not propose to martyrize the head of the peace party by making Fort Warren a shrine for all the disloyal and dissatisfied elements of the North. At the same time he would have preferred not to have this situation on his hands, and on this his cabinet agreed with him. He did not hesitate to say as much to General Burnside.[84]

The committee provided by the convention was composed of prominent Peace Democrats, including every Democratic congressman except Samuel S. ("Sunset") Cox. Why he was not on the committee is not known, but he never was in sympathy with Vallandigham's extreme views. They met at Washington on June 26 and prepared an elaborate address to the president urging the revocation of his order against their leader and nominee. The address, Lincoln's reply, and the committee's rejoinder are important historical documents and throw a flood of light on the Ohio situation of that period. The committee's address is as follows:

WASHINGTON CITY, June 26, 1863.

To His Excellency, the President of the United States:
The undersigned having been appointed a committee, under the authority of the resolutions of the State convention held at the city of Columbus, Ohio, on the 11th instant, to communicate with you on the subject of the arrest and banishment of Clement L. Vallandigham, most respectfully submit the following as the resolutions of that convention, bearing upon the subject of this communication, and ask of your Excellency their earnest consideration. And they deem it proper to state that the convention was one in which all parts of the State were represented, and one of the most respectable as to numbers and character, one of the most earnest and sincere in support of the Constitution and the Union ever held in that State.

Resolved, 1. That the will of the people is the foundation of all free government; that to give effect to this will, free thought, free speech, and a free press are indispensable. Without free discussion there is no certainty of sound judgment; without sound judgment there can be no wise government.

Resolved, 2. That there is an inherent and constitutional right of the people to discuss all measures of their Government, and to approve or disapprove, as to their best judgment seems right. They have a like right to propose and advocate that policy which, in their judgment, is best, and to argue and vote against whatever policy seems to them to violate the Constitution, to impair their liberties, or to be detrimental to their welfare.

Resolved, 3. That these, and all other rights guaranteed to them by their Constitution, are their rights in time of war as well as times of peace, and of far more value and necessity in war than peace; for in the time of peace liberty, security, and property are seldom endangered; in war they are ever in peril.

Resolved, 4. That we now say to all whom it may concern, not by way of threat, but calmly and firmly, that we will not surrender these rights, nor submit to their forcible violation. We will obey the laws ourselves, and all others must obey them.

Resolved, 11. That Ohio will adhere to the Constitution and the Union as the best, and it may be the last, hope of popular freedom, and for all wrongs which may have been committed, or evils which may exist, will seek redress under the Constitution, and within the Union, by the peaceful and powerful agency of the suffrages of the people.

Resolved, 14. That we will earnestly support every constitutional measure tending to preserve the Union of the States. No men have a greater interest in its preservation than we have, none desire more; there are none who will make greater sacrifices or endure more than we will to accomplish that end. We are, as we have ever been, the devoted friends of the Constitution and the Union, and we have no sympathy with the enemies of either.

Resolved, 15. That the arrest, imprisonment, pretended trial, and actual banishment of Clement L. Vallandigham, a citizen of the State of Ohio, not belonging to the land or naval forces of the United States, nor to the militia in actual service, by alleged military authority, for no other pretended crimes than that of uttering words of legitimate criticism upon the conduct of the Administration in power, and of appealing to the ballot-box for a change of policy—(said arrest and military trial taking place where the courts of law are open and unobstructed, and for no act done within the sphere of active military operations in carrying on the war)—we regard as a palpable violation of the following provisions of the Constitution of the United States:

1. "Congress shall make no law...abridging the freedom of speech or of the press, or the rights of the people peaceably to assemble, and to petition the Government for a redress of grievances."

2. "The right of the people to be secure in their persons, houses, papers and effects, against unreasonable searches and seizures, shall not be violated; and no warrant shall issue but upon probable cause, supported by oath or affirmation, and particularly describing the place to be searched, and the person or things to be seized."

3. "No person shall be held to answer for a capital or otherwise infamous crime, unless on a presentment or indictment of a grand jury, except in cases arising in the land or naval forces, or in the militia when in actual service in time of war or public danger."

4. "In all criminal prosecutions the accused shall enjoy the right to a speedy and public trial by an impartial jury of the State and district wherein the crime shall have been committed; which district shall have been previously ascertained by law."

5. And we furthermore denounce said arrest, trial and banishment, as a direct insult offered to the sovereignty of the people of Ohio, by whose organic law it is declared that no person shall be transported out of the State for any offense committed within the same.

Resolved, 16. That C. L. Vallandigham was, at the time of his arrest, a prominent candidate for nomination by the Democratic party of Ohio for the office of Governor of the State; that the Democratic party was fully competent to decide whether he is a fit man for that nomination, and that the attempt to deprive them of that right, by his arrest and banishment, was an unmerited imputation upon their intelligence and loyalty, as well as a violation of the Constitution.

Resolved, 17. That we respectfully, but most earnestly, call upon the President of the United States to restore C. L. Vallandigham to his home in Ohio, and that a committee of one from each Congressional District of

Ohio, to be selected by the presiding officer of this convention, is hereby appointed to present this application to the President.

The undersigned, in the discharge of the duty assigned them, do not think it necessary to reiterate the facts connected with the arrest, trial and banishment of Mr. Vallandigham; they are well known to the President and are of public history; nor to enlarge upon the positions taken by the convention, nor to recapitulate the constitutional provisions which it is believed have been contravened; they have been stated at length, and with clearness, in the resolutions which have been recited. The undersigned content themselves with a brief reference to other suggestions pertinent to the subject.

They do not call upon your Excellency as suppliants, praying the revocation of the order banishing Mr. Vallandigham, as a favor, but by the authority of a convention representing a majority of the citizens of the State of Ohio, they respectfully ask it as a right due to an American citizen, in whose personal injury the sovereignty and dignity of the people of Ohio, as a free State, has been offended.

And this duty they perform the more cordially from the consideration that at a time of great national emergency, pregnant with dangers to our Federal Union, it is all-important that the true friends of the Constitution and the Union, however they may differ as to *the mode* of administering the Government, and the measures most likely to be successful in the maintenance of the Constitution and the restoration of the Union, should not be thrown into conflict with each other.

The arrest, unusual trial, and banishment of Mr. Vallandigham have created widespread and alarming disaffection among the people of the State; not only endangering the harmony of the friends of the Constitution and the Union, and tending to disturb the peace and tranquility of the State, but also impairing that confidence in the fidelity of your administration to the great landmarks of free government essential to a peaceful and successful enforcement of the laws of Ohio.

You are reported to have used, in a public communication on this subject, the following language:

> "It gave me pain when I learned that Mr. Vallandigham had been arrested; that is, I was pained that there should have seemed to be a necessity for arresting him, and that it will afford me great pleasure to discharge him so soon as I can by any means believe the public safety will not suffer by it."

The undersigned assure your Excellency, from our personal knowledge of the feelings of the people of Ohio, that the public safety will be far more endangered by continuing Mr. Vallandigham in exile than by releasing him. It may be true that persons differing from him in political views may be found in Ohio and elsewhere who will express a different opinion; but they are certainly mistaken.

Mr. Vallandigham may differ with the President, and even with some of his own political party, as to the true and most effectual means of maintaining the Constitution and restoring the Union; but this difference of opinion does not prove him to be unfaithful to his duties as an American citizen. If a man devotedly attached to the Constitution and the Union conscientiously believes that, from the inherent nature of the Federal compact, the war, in the present condition of things in this country, can not be used as a means of restoring the Union; or that a war to subjugate a part of the States, or a war to revolutionize the social system in a part of the States, could not restore, but would inevitably result in the final destruction of both the Constitution and the Union, is he not to be allowed the right of an American citizen to appeal to the judgment of the people for a change of policy by the constitutional remedy of the ballot-box?

During the war with Mexico many of the political opponents of the Administration then in power thought it their duty to oppose and denounce the war, and to urge before the people of the country that it was unjust, and prosecuted for unholy purposes. With equal reason it might have been said of them that their discussions before the people were calculated to discourage enlistments, "to prevent the raising of troops," and to induce desertions from the army; and leave the Government without an adequate military force to carry on the war.

If the freedom of speech and of the press are to be suspended in time of war, then the essential element of popular government to effect a change of policy in the constitutional mode is at an end. The freedom of speech and of the press is indispensable, and necessarily incident to the nature of popular government itself. If any inconvenience or evils arise from its exercise, they are unavoidable.

On this subject you are reported to have said further:

"It is asserted, in substance, that Mr. Vallandigham was, by a military commander, seized and tried, 'for no other reason than words addressed to a public meeting, in criticism of the course of the Administration, and in condemnation of the military order of the General.' Now, if there be no mistake about this, if there was no reason for the arrest, then I concede that the arrest was wrong. But the arrest, I understand, was made for a very different reason. Mr. Vallandigham avows his hostility to the war on the part of the Union, and his arrest was made because he was laboring with some effect to prevent the raising of troops, to encourage desertions from the army, and to leave the rebellion without an adequate military force to suppress it. He was arrested, not because he was damaging the political prospects of the Administration, or the personal interests of the Commanding General, but because he was damaging the army, upon the existence and vigor of which the life of the Nation depends. He was warring upon the military, and this gave the military constitutional jurisdiction to lay hands upon him. If Mr. Vallandigham was not damaging the military power of the country, then his arrest was made on mistake of facts, which I would be glad to correct on reasonable satisfactory evidence."

In answer to this, permit us to say—*First:* That neither the charge, nor the specifications in support of the charge on which Mr. Vallandigham was tried, impute to him the act of either laboring to prevent the raising of troops or to encourage the desertions from the army. *Secondly:* No evidence on the trial was offered with a view to support, or even tended to support, any such charge. In what instance, and by what act, did he either discourage enlistments or encourage desertions from the army? Who is the man who was discouraged from enlisting? and who encouraged to desert by any act of Mr. Vallandigham? If it be assumed that, perchance, some person might have been discouraged from enlisting, or that some person might have been encouraged to desert, on account of hearing Mr. Vallandigham's views as to the policy of the war as a means of restoring the Union, would that have laid the foundation for his conviction and banishment? If so, upon the same grounds, every political opponent of the Mexican war might have been convicted and banished from the country.

When gentlemen of high standing and extensive influence, including your Excellency, opposed, in the discussions before the people, the policy of the Mexican war, were they "warring upon the military"? and if this "give the military constitutional jurisdiction to lay hands upon" them? And, finally, the charge of the specifications upon which Mr. Vallandigham was tried entitled him to a trial before the civil tribunals, according to express provisions of the late acts of Congress, approved by yourself, July 17, 1862, and March 3, 1863, which were manifestly designed to supersede all necessity or pretext for arbitrary military arrests.

The undersigned are able to agree with you in the opinion you have expressed, that the Constitution is different in time of insurrection or invasion from what it is in time of peace and public security. The Constitution provides for no limitation upon or exceptions to the guarantees of personal liberty, except as to the writ of *habeas corpus*. Has the President, at the time of invasion or insurrection, the right to engraft limitations or exceptions upon these constitutional guarantees whenever, in his judgment, the public safety requires it?

True it is, the article of the Constitution which defines the various powers delegated to Congress declares that "the privilege of the writ of *habeas corpus* shall not be suspended, unless where, in cases of rebellion or invasion, the public safety may require it." But this qualification or limitation upon this restriction upon the powers of Congress has no reference to or connection with the other guarantees of personal liberty.

Expunge from the Constitution this limitation upon the powers of Congress to suspend the writ of *habeas corpus*, and yet the other guarantees of personal liberty would remain unchanged.

Although a man might not have a constitutional right to have an immediate investigation made as to the legality of his arrest, upon *habeas corpus*, yet "his right to a speedy public trial, by an impartial jury of the State and district wherein the crime shall have been committed," will not be altered; neither will his right to the exemption from "cruel and unusual punishments"; nor his right to be secure in his person, houses, papers, and effects, against unreasonable seizures and searches; nor his right not to be deprived of life, liberty or property, without due process of law; nor his right not to be held to answer for a capital or otherwise infamous offense, unless on presentment of indictment of a grand jury be in anywise changed.

And certainly the restriction upon the power of Congress to suspend the writ of *habeas corpus*, in time of insurrection or invasion, could not effect the guarantee that the freedom of speech and of the press shall not be abridged. It is sometimes urged that the proceedings in the civil tribunals are too tardy and ineffective for cases arising in times of insurrection or invasion. It is a full reply to this to say that arrests by civil process may be equally as expeditious and effective as arrests by military orders.

True, a summary trial and punishment are not allowed in the civil courts. But if the offender be under arrest and imprisoned, and not entitled to a discharge on writ of *habeas corpus*, before trial, what more can be required for the purpose of the Government? The idea that all the constitutional guarantees of personal liberty are suspended, throughout the country, at a time of insurrection or invasion in any part of it, places us upon a sea of uncertainty, and subjects the life, liberty, and property of every citizen to the mere will of a military commander, or what he might say that he considers the public safety requires. Does your Excellency wish to have it understood that you hold that the rights of every man throughout this vast country are subject to be annulled whenever you may say that you consider the public safety requires it in time of invasion or insurrection?

You are further reported as having said that the constitutional guarantees of personal liberty have "no application to the present case we have in hand, because the arrests complained of were not made for treason; that is, not for the treason defined in the Constitution, and upon the conviction of which the punishment is death; nor yet were they made to hold persons to answer for capital or otherwise infamous crimes; nor were the proceedings following, in any constitutional or legal sense, criminal prosecutions. The arrests were made on totally different grounds, and the proceedings following accorded with the grounds of the arrests," etc.

The conclusion to be drawn from this position of your Excellency is, that where a man is liable to "a criminal prosecution," or is charged with a crime known to the laws of the land, he is clothed with all the constitutional guarantees for his safety and security from wrong and injustice; but that where he is not liable to "a criminal prosecution," or charged with any crime known to the laws, if the President or any military commander shall say that he considers that the public safety requires it, this man may be put outside of the pale of the constitutional guarantees, and arrested without charge of crime, imprisoned with knowing what for, and any length of time, or to be tried before a court-martial, and sentenced to any kind of punishment unknown to the laws of the land, which the President or military commander may deem proper to impose.

Did the Constitution intend to throw the shield of its securities around the man liable to be charged with treason as defined by it, and yet leave the man not liable to any such charge unprotected by the safeguard of personal liberty and personal security? Can a man not in the military or naval service, nor within the field of the operations of the army, be arrested and imprisoned without any law of the land to authorize it? Can a man thus, in civil life, be punished without any law defining the offense and prescribing the punishment? If the President or a court-martial may prescribe one kind of punishment unauthorized by law, why not any other kind? Banishment is an unusual punishment, and unknown to our laws. If the President has the right to change the punishment prescribed by the court-martial, from imprisonment to banishment, why not from imprisonment to torture upon the rack, or execution upon the gibbet?

If an indefinable kind of constructive treason is to be introduced and engrafted upon the Constitution, unknown to the laws of the land and subject to the will of the President whenever an insurrection or invasion shall occur in any part of this vast country, what safety or security will be left for the liberties of the people?

The constructive treasons that gave the friends of freedom so many years of toil and trouble in England, were inconsiderable compared to this. The precedents which you make will become a part of the Constitution for your successors, if sanctioned and acquiesced in by the people now.

The people of Ohio are willing to co-operate zealously with you in every effort warranted by the Constitution to restore the Union of the States, but they cannot consent to abandon those fundamental principles of civil liberty which are essential to their existence as a free people.

In their name we ask that, by a revocation of the order of his banishment, Mr. Vallandigham may be restored to the enjoyment of those rights of which they believe he has been unconstitutionally deprived.

We have the honor to be, respectfully, yours, etc.,

M. BIRCHARD, *Chairman*, 19th District.
DAVID A. HOUK, *Secretary*, 3d District.
GEORGE BLISS, 14th District.
T. W. BARTLEY, 8th District.
W. J. GORDON, 18th District.
JOHN O'NEILL, 13th District.
C. A. WHITE, 6th District.
W. D. FINCK, 12th District.
ALEXANDER LONG, 2nd District.
J. W. WHITE, 16th District.
JAS. R. MORRIS, 15th District.
GEORGE S. CONVERSE, 7th District.
WARREN P. NOBLE, 9th District.
GEORGE H. PENDLETON, 1st District.
W. A. HUTCHINS, 11th District.
ABNER L. BACKUS, 10th District.
J. F. MCKINNEY, 5th District.
F. C. LE BLOND, 5th District.
LOUIS SCHAEFFER, 17th District.

This address, it will be observed, is purely a technical and constitutional argument against Vallandigham's punishment. It was disingenuous in that it ignored all the facts surrounding the case. Perhaps Lincoln's unanswerable reply to the New York committee had deterred further discussion in that direction. On this committee were very able lawyers, and but few of its members were in sympathy with Vallandigham's extreme views, so it is very probable that they made the best presentation of a bad case. To do this it was necessary to ignore its merits; to forget the legal maxim, *inter arma silent leges*, and to rely entirely on the lawyer's plea.

Lincoln answered in his best argumentative vein, impressively but good-naturedly. Observe his reference to his own record in the Mexican War, which the committee sought to parallel with Vallandigham's. Note his acceptance of the statement that "the people of Ohio are willing to co-operate zealously with you in every effort warranted by the Constitution to restore the Union of the States." The people of Ohio were then doing this very thing in a most zealous way, and the pledge of the committee sounds much like the decree of the "three tailors of Tooley Street." Nevertheless, Lincoln, as his letter shows, was willing to release Vallandigham upon conditions that would do no violence to the patriotism or conscience of any good citizen. His reply was as follows:

WASHINGTON, D. C., June 29, 1863.

GENTLEMEN: The resolutions of the Ohio Democratic State Convention, which you present me, together with your introductory and closing remarks, being in position and argument mainly the same as the resolutions of the Democratic meeting at Albany, New York, I refer you to my response to the latter as meeting most of the points of the former. This response you evidently used in preparing your remarks, and I desire no more than that it be used with accuracy. In a single reading of your remarks, I only discovered one inaccuracy in matter which I suppose you took from that paper. It is where you say, "the undersigned are unable to agree with you in the opinion you have expressed, that the Constitution is different in time of insurrection or invasion from what it is in time of peace and security."

A recurrence to the paper will show you that I have not expressed the opinion you suppose. I expressed the opinion that the Constitution is different in its application in cases of rebellion or invasion, involving the public safety from what it is in times of profound peace, and public security; and this opinion I adhere to, simply because by the Constitution itself, things may be done in the one case which may not be done in the other.

I dislike to waste a word on merely a personal point, but I must respectfully assure you that you will find yourselves at fault, should you ever seek for evidence to prove your assumption that I "opposed in discussions before the people the policy of the Mexican War."

You say, "Expunge from the Constitution this limitation upon the power of Congress to suspend the writ of *habeas corpus*, and yet the other guarantees of personal liberty would remain unchanged." Doubtless if this clause of the Constitution, improperly called as I think a limitation upon the power of Congress were expunged, the other guarantees would remain the same; but the question is, not how those guarantees would stand with the clause out of the Constitution, but how they stand with that clause remaining in it, in case of rebellion or invasion, involving the public safety. If the liberty could be indulged of expunging that clause, letter and spirit, I really think the constitutional argument would be with you.

My general view on this question was stated in the Albany response, and hence I do not state it now. I only add that, as seems to me, the benefit of the writ of *habeas corpus* is the great means through which the guarantees of personal liberty are conserved and made available in the last resort; and corroborative of this view, is the fact that Mr. Vallandigham in the very case in question, under the advice of able lawyers, saw not where else to go, but to the *habeas corpus*. But by the Constitution the benefit of the writ of *habeas corpus* itself may be suspended when in cases of rebellion and invasion the public safety may require it.

You ask in substance whether I really claim that I may override all the guaranteed rights of individuals, on the plea of conserving the public safety—When I may choose to say the public safety requires it. This question, divested of the phraseology calculated to represent me as struggling for an arbitrary personal prerogative, is either a question who shall decide, or an affirmation that nobody shall decide, what public safety does require in cases of rebellion or invasion. The Constitution contemplates the question as likely to occur for decision, but it does not expressly declare who is to decide it. By necessary implication, when rebellion or invasion comes, the decision is to be made from time to time; and I think the man whom, for the time the people have, under the Constitution made the Commander-in-Chief of their army and navy, is the man who holds the power and bears the responsibility of making it. If he uses the power justly, the same people will probably justify him; if he abuses it, he is in their hands, to be dealt with by the modes they have reserved to themselves in the Constitution.

The earnestness with which you insist that persons can only in times of rebellion be lawfully dealt with, in accordance with the rules for criminal trials and punishments in times of peace, induces me to add a word to what I have said on that point in the Albany response. You claim that men may, if they choose, embarrass those whose duty it is to combat a giant rebellion, and then be dealt with only in turn as if there was no rebellion. The Constitution itself rejects this view. The military arrests and detentions which have been made, including those of Mr. Vallandigham, which are not different in principle from the others, have been for prevention and not for punishment—as injunctions to stay injury—as proceedings to keep the peace, and hence, like proceedings in such cases and for like reasons, they have been accompanied with indictments, or trials by juries, nor, in a single case, by any punishment whatever beyond what is purely incidental to the prevention. The original sentence of imprisonment in Mr. Vallandigham's case was to prevent injury to the military service only, and the modification of it was made as a less disagreeable mode to him of securing the same prevention.

I am unable to perceive an insult to Ohio in the case of Mr. Vallandigham. Quite surely nothing of this sort was intended. I was wholly unaware that Mr. Vallandigham was at the time of his arrest, a candidate for the Democratic nomination for Governor, until so informed by your reading to me the resolutions of the Convention. I am grateful to the State of Ohio for many things, especially for the brave soldiers and officers she has given in the present National trial to the armies of the Union.

You claim, as I understand, that, according to my own position in the Albany response, Mr. Vallandigham should be released; and this because, as you claim, he has not damaged the military service, by discouraging enlistments, encouraging desertions, or otherwise; and that, if he had, he should have been turned over to the civil authorities under the recent acts of Congress. I certainly do not know that Mr. Vallandigham has specifically and by direct language advised against enlistments, and in favor of desertion and resistance to drafting. We all know that combinations, armed in some instances, to resist the arrest of deserters, began several months ago; that more recently the like has appeared in resistance to the enrollment preparatory to a draft; and that quite a number of assassinations have occurred from the same animus. These had to be met by military force, and this again has led to bloodshed and death. And now, under a sense of responsibility more weighty and enduring than any which is mere official, I solemnly declare my belief that this hindrance of the military, including maiming and murder, is due to the course in which Mr. Vallandigham has been engaged in a greater degree than to any other cause, and is due to him personally in a greater degree than to any other one man. These things have been notorious, known to all, and of course known to Mr. Vallandigham. Perhaps I would not be wrong to say that they originated with his special friends and adherents. With perfect knowledge of them he has frequently, if not constantly, made speeches in Congress and before popular assemblies, and if it can be shown that with these things staring him in the face, he has ever uttered a word of rebuke or counsel against them, it will be a fact greatly in his favor with me, and one of which, as yet, I am totally ignorant. When it is known that the whole burden of his speeches has been to stir up men against the prosecution of the war, and that in the midst of resistance to it, he has not been known in any instance to counsel against such resistance, it is next to impossible to repel the inference that he has counseled directly in favor of it. With all this before their eyes, the convention you represent have nominated Mr. Vallandigham for Governor of Ohio, and both they and you have declared the purpose to sustain the National Union by all constitutional means. But of course they and you, in common, reserve to yourselves to decide what are constitutional means; and, unlike the Albany meeting, you omit to state or intimate that in your opinion an army is a constitutional means of saving the Union against rebellion, or even to intimate that you are conscious of an existing rebellion being in progress, with the avowed object of destroying that very Union. At the same time your nominee for Governor, in whose behalf you appeal, is known to you and to the world to declare against the use of an army to suppress the rebellion. Your own attitude, therefore, encourages desertion, resistance to the draft, and the like, because it teaches those who incline to desert and escape the draft to believe it is your purpose to protect them, and to hope that you will become strong enough to do so. After a personal intercourse with you, gentlemen of the Union look upon it in this light. It is a substantial hope, and, by consequence, a real strength to the enemy. It is a false hope, and one which you would willingly dispel. I will make the way exceedingly easy. I send you duplicates of this letter in order that you, or a majority of you, may, if you choose, indorse your names upon one of them, and return it thus indorsed to me, with the understanding that those signing are thereby committed to the following propositions, and to nothing else:

1. That there is now a rebellion in the United States, the object and tendency of which is to destroy the National Union; and that, in your opinion, an army and navy are constitutional means for suppressing that rebellion.

2. That no one of you will do anything which, in his own judgment, will tend to hinder the increase or favor the decrease, or lessen the efficiency of the army and navy while engaged in the effort to suppress the rebellion; and,

3. That each of you will, in his sphere, do all he can to have the officers, soldiers, and seamen of the army and navy, while engaged in the effort to suppress the rebellion, paid, fed, clad, and otherwise well provided and supported.

And with the further understanding that upon receiving the letter and names thus indorsed, I will cause them to be published, which publication shall be, within itself, a revocation of the order in relation to Mr. Vallandigham.

It will not escape observation that I consent to the release of Mr. Vallandigham upon terms not embracing any pledge from him or from others as to what he will or will not do. I do this because he is not present to speak for himself, or to authorize others to speak for him, and hence, I shall expect, that on returning he would not put himself practically in antagonism with the position of his friends. But I do it chiefly because I thereby prevail on other influential gentlemen of Ohio to so define their position as to be of immense value to the army—thus more than compensating for the consequences of any mistake in allowing Mr. Vallandigham to return, so that, on the whole, the public safety would not have suffered by it. Still, in regard to Mr. Vallandigham and all others, I must hereafter, as heretofore, do so much as the public service may seem to require.

I have the honor to be respectfully yours, etc.,
A. LINCOLN.

The rejoinder of the committee simply avowed their original position and sought to answer Lincoln's constitutional argument. They rejected his propositions, upon which acceptance he declared he would release

Vallandigham, on the ground that they had no power to make pledges to secure his freedom. They also saw that to accept these positions would be tantamount to supporting Lincoln's administration, which meant the surrender of the Peace Party. The committee's rejoinder to Lincoln was:

NEW YORK, July 1, 1863.

To his Excellency the President of the United States:
SIR: Your answer to the application of the undersigned for a revocation of the order of banishment of Clement L. Vallandigham requires a reply which they proceed with as little delay as possible to make.

They are not able to appreciate the force of the distinction you make between *the Constitution* and *the application* of the Constitution, whereby you assume that powers are delegated to the President at the time of invasion or insurrection, in derogation of the plain language of the Constitution. The inherent provisions of the Constitution remaining the same in time of insurrection or invasion as in time of peace, the President can have no more right to disregard their positive and imperative requirements at the former time than at the latter. Because some things may be done by the terms of the Constitution at the time of invasion or insurrection, which would not be required by the occasion in time of peace, you assume that *any thing whatever,* even though not expressed by the Constitution, may be done on the occasion of insurrection or invasion, which the President may choose to say is required by the public safety. In plainer terms, because the writ of *habeas corpus* may be suspended at time of invasion or insurrection, you infer that all other provisions of the Constitution having in view the protection of life, liberty, and property of the citizen, may be in like manner suspended.

The provision relating to the writ of *habeas corpus* being contained in the first part of the Constitution, the purpose of which is to define the powers delegated to Congress, has no connection in language with the Declaration of Rights, as guarantees of personal liberty, contained in the additional and amendatory articles, and inasmuch as the provision relating to *habeas corpus* expressly provides for its suspension, and the other provisions alluded to do not provide for any such thing, the legal conclusion is that the suspension of the latter is unauthorized. The provision for the writ of *habeas corpus* is merely intended to furnish a *summary* remedy, and not the means whereby personal security is conserved in the final resort; while the other provisions are guarantees of personal rights, the suspension of which puts an end to all pretence of free government. It is true Mr. Vallandigham applied for a writ of *habeas corpus* as a summary remedy against oppression. But the denial of this did not take away his right to a speedy public trial by an impartial jury, or deprive him of his other rights as an American citizen. Your assumption of the right to suspend all the constitutional guarantees of personal liberty, and even of the freedom of speech and of the press, because the summary remedy of *habeas corpus* may be suspended, is at once startling and alarming to all persons desirous of preserving free government in this country.

The inquiry of the undersigned, whether "you hold the rights of every man throughout this vast country, in time of invasion or insurrection, are subject to be *annulled* whenever *you may say* that *you* consider the public safety requires it?" was a plain question, undisguised by circumlocution, and intended simply to elicit information. Your affirmative answer to this question throws a shade upon the fondest anticipations of the framers of the Constitution, who flattered themselves that they had provided safeguards against the dangers which have ever beset and overthrown free government in other ages and countries. Your answer is not to be disguised by the phraseology that the question "is simply a question of who shall decide, or an affirmation that nobody shall decide, what the public safety does require in case of rebellion or invasion." Our Government was designed to be a Government of *law, settled* and *defined,* and not of the arbitrary will of a single man. As a safeguard, the powers were delegated to the legislative, executive, and judicial branches of the Government, and each made co-ordinate with the others, and supreme within its sphere, and thus a mutual check upon each other in case of abuse of power.

It has been the boast of the American people that they had a *written Constitution,* not only expressly *defining,* but also *limiting* the powers of the Government, and providing effectual safeguards for personal liberty, security, and property. And to make the matter more positive and explicit, it was provided by the amendatory articles nine and ten that "the *enumeration* in the Constitution of *certain rights* shall not be construed to *deny* or *disparage* others retained by the people," and that "the powers not delegated to the United States by the Constitution, nor prohibited by it to the States, are reserved to the States respectively or to the people." With this care and precaution on the part of our forefathers who framed our institutions, it was not to be expected that, at so early a day as this, a claim of the President to arbitrary power, limited only by his conception of the requirements of the public safety, would have been asserted. In derogation of the constitutional provisions making the President strictly an executive officer, and vesting all the delegated legislative powers in Congress, your position, as we understand it, would *make your will the rule of action,* and your declaration of the requirements of the public safety the law of the land. Our inquiry was not, therefore, "simply a question *who* shall decide, or the affirmation that *nobody* shall decide, what the public safety requires." Our Government is a Government of *law*, and it is the *law-making power* which ascertains what the public safety requires and prescribes the rule of action; and the duty of the President is simply to execute the laws thus enacted, and not *to make or annul laws*. If any exigency shall arise, the President has the power to convene Congress at any time to provide for it; so that the plea of necessity furnishes no reasonable pretext for any assumption of legislative power.

For a moment contemplate the consequences of such a claim to power. Not only would the dominion of the President be absolute over the rights of individuals, but equally so over the other departments of the Government. If he should claim that the public safety required it, he could arrest and imprison a judge for the conscientious discharge of his duties, paralyze the judicial power, or supersede it by the substitution of courts-martial, subject to *his own will*, throughout the whole country. If any one of the States, even far removed from the rebellion, should not sustain his plan for prosecuting the war, he could, on the plea of public safety, annul and set at defiance the State laws and authorities, arrest and imprison the Governor of the State or the members of the Legislature, while in the faithful discharge of their duties, or he could absolutely control the action, either of Congress or the Supreme Court, by arresting and imprisoning its members, and upon the same ground he could suspend the elective franchise, postpone the elections and declare the perpetuity of his high prerogative. And neither the power of impeachment nor the elections of the people could be made available against such concentration of power.

Surely it is not necessary to subvert free government in this country in order to put down the rebellion; and it *cannot be done* under *the pretence* of putting down the rebellion. Indeed, it is plain that your Administration has been weakened, by the assumption of power not delegated in the Constitution.

In your answer you say to us: "You claim that men may, if they choose, embarrass those whose duty it is to combat a giant rebellion and then be dealt with in terms as if there were no rebellion." You will find yourself in fault, if you will search our communication to you for any such idea. The undersigned believe that the Constitution and the laws of the land, properly administered, furnish ample power to put down an insurrection without the assumption of powers not granted. And if existing legislation be inadequate, it is the duty of Congress to consider what further legislation is necessary, and to make suitable provision by law.

You claim that the military arrests made by your Administration are merely *preventive remedies*, "as injunctions to stay injury, or proceedings to keep the peace, and *not for punishment*." The *ordinary* preventive remedies alluded to are authorized by established law, but the preventive proceedings you institute have their authority merely in the will of the Executive or that of officers subordinate to his authority. And in this proceeding a discretion seems to be exercised as to whether the prisoner shall be allowed a trial or even be permitted to know the nature of the complaint against him, or the name of his accuser. If the proceedings be merely preventive, why not allow the prisoner the benefit of a bond to keep the peace? But if no offence has been committed, why was Mr. Vallandigham tried, convicted, and sentenced by a court-martial? And why the actual punishment by imprisonment or banishment, without the opportunity of obtaining his liberty in the mode usual in preventive remedies, and yet say it is not for punishment?

You still place Mr. Vallandigham's conviction and banishment upon the ground that he had damaged the military service by discouraging enlistments and encouraging desertions, etc., and yet you have not even pretended to controvert our position that he was not charged with, tried, or convicted, for any such offence before the court-martial.

In answer to our position that Mr. Vallandigham was entitled to a trial in the civil tribunals, by virtue of late acts of Congress, you say: *"I certainly do not know that Mr. Vallandigham has specifically and by direct language advised against enlistments and in favor of desertions and resistance to drafting,"* etc., and yet, in a subsequent part of your answer, after speaking to certain disturbances which are alleged to have occurred in resistance of the arrest of deserters and of the enrollment preparatory to the draft, and which you attribute mainly to the course Mr. Vallandigham has pursued, you say that he has made speeches against the war in the midst of resistance to it; that "he has never been known, in any instance, to counsel against such resistance"; and that *"it is next to impossible to repel the inference that he has counselled directly in favor of it."* Permit us to say that your information is most grievously at fault.

The undersigned have been in the habit of hearing Mr. Vallandigham speak before popular assemblages, and they appeal with confidence to every truthful person who has ever heard him for the accuracy of the declaration, that he has never made a speech before the people of Ohio in which he has not counselled submission and obedience to the laws and the Constitution, and advised the peaceful remedies of the judicial tribunals and of the ballot-box for the redress of grievances and for the evils, which afflict our bleeding and suffering country. And, were it not foreign to the purposes of this communication, we would undertake to establish to the satisfaction of any candid person that the disturbances among the people to which you allude, in opposition to the arrest of deserts and the draft, have been occasioned mainly by the measures, policy, and conduct of your Administration, and the course of its political friends. But if the circumstantial evidence exists, to which you allude, which makes "it next to impossible to repel the inference that Mr. Vallandigham has counselled directly in favor" of this resistance, and that the same has been mainly attributable to his conduct, why was he not turned over to the civil authorities to be tried under the late acts of Congress? If there be any foundation in fact for your statements implicating him in resistance to the constituted authorities, he is liable to such prosecution. And we now demand, as a mere act of justice to him, an investigation of this matter before a jury of his country; and respectfully insist that fairness requires either that you retract these charges which you make against him, or that you revoke your order of banishment and allow him the opportunity of an investigation before an impartial jury.

The committee do not deem it necessary to repel at length the imputation that the attitude of themselves or of the Democratic party in Ohio "encourage desertions, resistance to the draft, and the like." Suggestions of that kind are not unusual weapons in our ordinary political contests. They rise readily in the minds of politicians heated with the excitement of partisan strife. During the two years in which the Democratic party of Ohio has been constrained to oppose the policy of the Administration, and to stand up in defence of the Constitution and of personal rights, this charge has been repeatedly made. It has fallen harmless, however, at the feet of those whom it was intended to injure. The committee believe it will do so again. If it were proper to do so in this paper, they might suggest that the measures of the Administration, and its changes of policy in the prosecution of the war, have been the fruitful sources of discouraging enlistments and inducing desertions, and furnish a reason for the undeniable fact that the first call for volunteers was answered by very many more than were demanded, and that the next call for soldiers will probably be responded to by drafted men alone.

The observation of the President in this connection, that neither the convention in its resolutions nor the committee in its communication, intimate that they "are conscious of an existing rebellion being in progress with the avowed object of destroying the Union," needs, perhaps, no reply. The Democratic party of Ohio has felt so keenly the condition of the country, and has been so stricken to the heart by the misfortunes and sorrows which have befallen it, that they hardly deemed it necessary by solemn resolution, when their very State exhibited everywhere the sad evidences of war, to remind the President that they were aware of its existence.

In the conclusion of your communication you propose that, if a majority of the committee shall affix their signatures to a duplicate copy of it, which you have furnished, they shall stand committed to three propositions, therein at length set forth, that he will publish the names thus signed, and that this publication shall operate as a revocation of the order of banishment. The committee cannot refrain from the expression of their surprise that the President should make the fate of Mr. Vallandigham depend upon the opinion of this committee upon these propositions. If the arrest and banishment were legal, and were deserved; if the President exercised a power clearly delegated, under circumstances which warranted its exercise, the order ought not to be revoked, merely because the committee hold, or express, opinions accordant with those of the President. If the arrest and banishment were not legal, or were not deserved by Mr. Vallandigham, then surely he is entitled to an immediate and unconditional discharge.

The people of Ohio were not so deeply moved by the action of the President merely because they were concerned for the personal safety and convenience of Mr. Vallandigham, but because they saw in his arrest and banishment an attack upon their own personal rights; and they attach value to his discharge chiefly as it will indicate and abandonment of the claim to the power of such arrest and banishment. However just the undersigned might regard the principles contained in the several propositions submitted by the President, or how much soever they might, under other circumstances, feel inclined to indorse the sentiments contained therein, yet they assure him that they have not been authorized to enter into any bargains, terms, contracts, or conditions with the President of the United States to procure the release of Mr. Vallandigham. The opinions of the undersigned touching the questions involved in these propositions are well known, have been many times publicly expressed, and are sufficiently manifested in the resolutions of the convention which they represent, and they cannot suppose that the President expects that they will seek the discharge of Mr. Vallandigham by a pledge implying not only an imputation upon their own *sincerity and fidelity* as citizens of the United States, and also carrying with it by implication a concession of *the legality* of his arrest, trial, and banishment, against which they and the convention they represent have solemnly protested. And, while they have asked the revocation of the order of banishment not as a favor, but as a *right* due to the people of Ohio, and with a view to avoid the possibility of conflict or disturbance of the public tranquillity, they do not do this, nor does Mr. Vallandigham desire it, at any sacrifice of their dignity and self-respect.

The idea that such a pledge as that asked from the undersigned would secure the public safety sufficiently to compensate for any mistake of the President in discharging Mr. Vallandigham is, in their opinion, a mere evasion of the grave questions involved in this discussion, and of a direct answer to their demand. And this is made especially apparent by the fact that this pledge is asked in a communication which concludes with an intimation of a disposition on the part of the President to repeat the acts complained of.

The undersigned, therefore, having fully discharged the duty enjoined upon them, leave the responsibility with the President.

In the meantime, since his sentence of exile, the subject of this correspondence had been in the South until June 17, when on the steamer *Cornubia* he ran the blockade, reaching Bermuda on the 20th, and after ten days he left for Halifax, where he arrived on the 5th of July. From thence he proceeded to Quebec and Montreal, receiving at those places cordial and sympathetic receptions; on July 15 he arrived at Niagara Falls, Canada side. Later, at Windsor, Vallandigham established relations with the agents of the southern Confederacy.[85]

Prior to this, however, while in the Confederacy, he was in consultation with its war department.[86]

John Brough, a War Democrat, was nominated as a candidate for governor by the Union Party at its convention, which assembled at Columbus June 17, 1863. This convention met in response to a call to "all loyal citizens who are in favor of the maintenance of the government and the prosecution of the war being carried on for the suppression of the rebellion against it."

Never in the history of the state has there been a campaign of such bitterness. This was due to the momentous issues involved. The election of Vallandigham meant peace when peace meant surrender. It would give powerful impetus to the Confederate cause. The campaign came also at a time when the cause of the Union was at its lowest ebb. The North was discouraged, and Ohio was one of the chief reasons. Vallandigham had aroused a feeling against the draft, and as a result, there was open defiance in Noble County and armed resistance in Holmes County. The Confederate raider, General John H. Morgan, invaded the southern part of the state in July. These conditions were aggravated by the disastrous Union defeat at Chancellorsville, by Lee's invasion of Pennsylvania, and Grant's unsuccessful siege of Vicksburg. This was the gloomy condition confronted by Ohio Unionists in the summer of 1863. It was bettered by the battle of Gettysburg and the surrender of Vicksburg. But these gave little hope to Ohio. The Peace Democracy pursued their campaign with remarkable intensity and enthusiasm.

Their great issue was Vallandigham himself. To them he was an exiled patriot. His sentence was a violation of free speech, personal liberty, and the rights of Magna Charta. Not a word about the preservation of the Union. On the other hand, the Unionists denounced him as an "unhung traitor" and declared that his election would prolong the war and possibly give success to the Confederacy. This was the view not only of the Union Party of Ohio, but throughout the country.[87]

Brough was an eloquent and logical orator and was rugged and point-blank in his discussions. George E. Pugh, candidate for lieutenant-governor with Vallandigham, was the principal spokesman for his absent chief. He declared that if his candidate were elected, there would be "fifty thousand fully armed and equipped freeman of Ohio to receive their governor-elect at the Canadian line and escort him to the State House to see that he takes the oath of office." Brough replied that Vallandigham's election would precipitate civil war in Ohio, "for," said he, "I tell you there is a mighty mass of men in this state whose nerves are strung up like steel, who never will permit this dishonor to be consummated in their native state."

This generation has no conception of the intense bitterness of the campaign. It can only be obtained by recourse to the newspapers, pamphlets, and speeches of that period. The campaign of 1840—"Tippecanoe and Tyler Too"—was one of thrilling excitement. Songs, hard cider, and political camp meetings were its features, but the voters were good-humored, yet earnest. Now there was all the enthusiasm of 1840, but mixed with such bitter feelings that lifelong friends parted, and attachments, even of family ties, were severed. From the words of the great Democrat, Stephen A. Douglas, the Unionists took the rule by which they measured the loyalty of their friends and neighbors: "there are only two sides to this question. Every man must be for the United States or against it. There can be no neutrals in this war; only patriots or traitors."[88]

The meetings and processions of both parties were of huge proportions. The Vallandigham following were inspired with a fanatical devotion to their exiled chief, which resulted in a series of demonstrations of such magnitude as to give the appearance of coming victory. On the other hand, the Brough meetings, while on a large scale, were dominated by a feeling of earnestness, yet not lacking in enthusiasm. The noise and glamour of the campaign were with Vallandigham; the serious labor and undefatigable work of organization were with Brough. Both sides were confident of victory; one claimed it with confidence, the other expected Brough's election by about five thousand majority.

John Brough[89] was elected governor of Ohio by over 101,000 majority. It was difficult to say which party was the most surprised.

There was an element which the leaders, wiseacres, and political diviners could not measure, because they could not see it. This was the silent vote. An analysis shows that fully twenty-five thousand of Vallandigham's party voted for Brough. This was composed of Democrats who preferred to remain with their party organization rather than follow the War Democrats into the Union Party. They were represented by Democratic leaders like Rufus P. Ranney, Hugh J. Jewett, and Henry B. Payne, all men of great ability and high character. They favored the war but did not approve of many acts of Lincoln's administration. As for Vallandigham, they regarded him as a mountebank and demagogue, with selfishness as his ruling spirit.

Lincoln received the result in Ohio with a joy that he did not suppress. For months he had watched anxiously its growing disaffection, as well as its rising tide of pacifism. He knew that the defeat of Brough would break the back of the Union and that a victory would be as valuable as that of Gettysburg or Vicksburg.

All night long he was beside the telegraph in Washington, receiving information from Ohio.[90] Brough was at his residence in Cleveland furnishing it. A little past midnight, Lincoln wired, "What is your majority now?" and Brough's reply was, "About 50,000." At five o'clock in the morning, in response to a final inquiry, Brough wired that he thought his majority would be over 100,000, to which there came this answer: *"Glory to God in the Highest. Ohio has saved the Nation. A. Lincoln."*[91]

Lincoln was next brought into contract with Ohio affairs under what must have been to him very unpleasant circumstances, because there was involved a disagreement with his party friends. This was due to the defection of one of the leading members of his cabinet, Salmon P. Chase, secretary of the treasury. Ultimately the tension became so intolerable that the secretary resigned under circumstances equivalent to dismissal.

Some peculiarities of Chase's temperament have been referred to, and it will be necessary to resort to a further consideration of that subject in order to understand the unfortunate conditions that developed his inharmonious relations with Lincoln. The trouble commenced when Chase failed to receive the nomination at Chicago. He never could forgive Fate for overlooking him for the unhewn and rugged Illinois lawyer. By common consent, including Lincoln's, Chase was one of the great statesmen of that time, and with Seward and Sumner formed the triumvirate of the rising Republican Party. Chase would not have objected to have been beaten by Seward—but by Lincoln it was a disappointment. That this should have been accomplished by his own state added bitterness to his soul, for he firmly believed that Ohio alone deprived him of attaining his great ambition. We have read his reference to this in his letter of congratulation to Lincoln.

This thought never left his mind. "Nobody doubts," he said, in writing to a friend who had been a delegate,[92] "that had the Ohio delegation manifested the same disregard of personal preferences, which was exhibited by the New York, Illinois and Missouri delegations and given me, as the nominee of Ohio, the same earnest and genuine support which was given to Mr. Seward, Mr. Lincoln and Mr. Bates, by those delegates respectively, that my vote on the first ballot would have largely exceeded Mr. Lincoln's; and there are those who felt themselves constrained to vote for the other candidates in consequence of the division of the Ohio delegation, who do not hesitate to give it as their judgment that had our delegation acted toward me in the same generous spirit that was manifested by the other delegations towards the candidates presented by their states, the nomination would have been given to Ohio."

Chase regarded Lincoln's choice as unfortunate for the country; he was honest about this, although really it was pure envy which worked in his soul without his knowledge. He believed that in the trying time that everybody saw was coming, a man of great experience in public life, of pronounced and accepted intellectual standing, and who had trod the heights of leadership, should be president of the United States. So did Senator Seward, and both were bitterly disappointed at the failure of the Republicans to recognize either as the man for the hour.

The manner in which each of these men received his blow—for such it was to them—is typical of his nature and worthwhile of a passing reference. Seward was a practical statesman, and withal an experienced politician. He was fearlessly antislavery, although he was slow in joining the Republican Party. He waited to be sure that it contained the seeds of success. This shows that he was not a "rainbow chaser" and wanted realities, thus exhibiting his practical mind. He was shocked at his defeat, but after a temporary depression, he adjusted himself to the situation. He entered the cabinet with a willing and loyal spirit. He felt that he was necessary to Lincoln's success. After he accepted the place, he wrote to his wife: "I have advised Mr. L. that I will not decline. It is inevitable, I will try to save freedom and my country."

Like Chase, he was satisfied that Lincoln's job was too big for him. He was not secretary of state a month before wrote the president an outline of what the foreign and domestic policies should be, and intimated that he, as premier, was the man to carry them out. An average president would have been angered and insulted. It was an intimation to the chief executive that he was unable to appreciate, or to perform his duties. Seward did this in good faith and in a spirit of helpfulness. Up to this time he did not know Lincoln. He replied to his secretary that the policy of the administration was in the president's hands, and whatever "must be done, I must do it." And this correspondence, which would have made a laughingstock of Seward, was hid away, and the public never read it until after the death of both of these great men. It took Seward's just and practical mind but a short time to see that Lincoln was the real leader of his cabinet, and he had the honesty to say so. From this time, he was Lincoln's most useful and loyal friend.

In Chase his defeat produced an entirely different effect. It became a grievance constantly fanned by feelings that he was unappreciated and betrayed. He had a sensitive mind and great personal pride. He was an idealist. When these things are remembered, we can understand and forgive his failings. His politics were altogether influenced by the traits of his temperament. He advocated the cause of the lowly bondsman from a sense of moral duty. To him slavery was wicked and unchristian. Thus convinced of its immorality, he deemed it his duty to himself and his country to do what he could to abolish it. It shocked his nature to feel that of all the nations of Christendom, his alone maintained human slavery.

The sacrifices that he made in his young manhood in fighting slavery were those which only come from one whose heart and soul were in the cause. The catalog of his suffering reminds of us Paul's in his fight for Christianity. But young Chase kept the faith, and neither "rotten-egging" nor being hissed from the platform, nor the frowning of churches, nor the social condemnation, nor loss of business prevented him from championing the poor slave in political conventions, the courts, and in the press. In course of time this young man, increasing in strength and winning greater confidence, entered the United States Senate. It was the Augustan era of American statesmen. Among his colleagues were

Webster, Clay, Benton, Calhoun, Cass, Corwin, Bell, Douglas, Jefferson Davis, William H. Seward, and Hannibal Hamlin. Here he took rank among the leaders, and eventually acting with the Republican Party, he became a national character; then came 1860, and disappointment.

On December 31, Lincoln wrote Chase saying, "In these troublous times, I would much like a conference with you. Please visit me here at once." Chase immediately proceeded to Springfield, arriving there January 3, and Lincoln, hearing of his presence, waived all formality, and called upon him at his hotel. Lincoln had a special feeling of kindness for Chase, because he was the only one of the Republican leaders outside of Illinois that came into that state and gave him active support in the Lincoln–Douglas campaign. After a two days' conference Lincoln conditionally offered to appoint Chase secretary of the treasury. The matter was not determined until two days after Lincoln's inauguration, when he sent Chase's name to the Senate without consulting him. Chase even then wanted to decline, but pressed by friends and a sense of duty, he accepted. He entered the cabinet in a disturbed mood and was an irritant from thenceforward.

Chase tendered his resignation to Lincoln more than once because of differences over appointments. It seems a very trivial cause and unworthy of the greatness and dignity of the secretary of the treasury. If such results followed a difference over state policy, we could understand it; but in the midst of a great war, for the finance minister, upon whom so much depended, to quit his post because he could not have a favorite politician appointed, is almost incredible. But an understanding of Chase's character makes such actions clear. Of practical politics and men he knew little and was therefore an easy prey to designing friends, who appealed to his pride as well as to his vanity. Upon these known weaknesses they worked, with such results as eventually brought his humiliation.

There was a growing dissatisfaction in certain quarters at this time to the renomination of Lincoln. A powerful coterie of Republican senators and representatives who were opposed to his conservatism made up their minds that he should not be renominated. There was also a group of conservatives who were of the same opinion. New York papers—*The Tribune, Herald,* and *Times*—were either openly opposed to his candidacy or were negatively unfriendly.

This element was composed of the congressional bosses, augmented by every element of dissatisfaction engendered by the war. In its ranks were crooked and thwarted contractors, disappointed office-seekers, both in civil and military life, and newspapers that failed to "run" Lincoln. All were laboring under the impression that Washington furnished the public opinion of the country, a fallacy still believed in by some. Chase, in his vanity, encouraged this movement against Lincoln, finally agreeing to become the opposition candidate. On February 22, 1864, he wrote Lincoln thus:[93]

> A few weeks ago, several gentlemen called on me and expressed their desire, which, they said, was shared by many earnest friends of our common cause, that I would allow my name to be submitted to the consideration of the people, in connection with the approaching election for Chief Magistrate. I replied that I feared such use might impair my usefulness as head of the Treasury Department, and that I much preferred to continue my labors where I am, and free from disturbing influences, until I could honorably retire from them. We had several interviews. After consultation and conference with others, they expressed their united judgment that the use of my name as proposed would not effect my usefulness in my present position; and that I ought to consent to it. I accepted their judgment as decisive; but at the same time told them, distinctly, that I could render them no help, except what might come incidentally from the faithful discharge of public duties; for these must have my whole time. I said also that I desired them to regard themselves as not only entirely at liberty, but as requested, to withdraw my name from consideration, whenever in their judgment the public interest would be promoted by so doing.
>
> The organization of the committee, I presume, followed these conversations; but I was not consulted about it, nor have I been consulted as to its action; nor do I even know who composed it. I have never wished that my name should have a moment's thought in comparison with the common cause of enfranchisement and restoration, or be continued before the public a moment after the indication of a preference, by the friends of that cause, for another.
>
> I have thought this explanation due to you as well as to myself. If there is anything in my action or position which, in your judgment, will prejudice the public interest under my charge, I beg you to say so; I do not wish to administer the Treasury Department one day without your entire confidence. For yourself I cherish sincere respect and esteem; and, permit me to add, affection. Differences of opinion as to administrative action have not changed these sentiments; nor have they been changed by assaults upon me by persons who profess themselves the special

representatives of your views and policy. You are not responsible for acts not your own; nor will you hold me responsible except for what I do or say myself.

Chase now had ample reason to resign; the manly course, after determining to be a candidate against his chief, would have been to leave the cabinet, as, for instance, James G. Blaine did from that of President Harrison under similar circumstances. On this question, however, he followed the judgment of his sponsors. They knew the value of the treasury department in a political campaign; they knew that in its army of spies, special agents, and deputies there was already a splendid Chase organization.

Lincoln made no objection to his secretary of the treasury being a candidate against him, for he wrote him, February 29:[94]

> Whether you shall remain at the head of the Treasury Department is a question which I do not allow myself to consider from any standpoint other than my judgment of the public service; and in that view, I do not perceive occasion for a change.

With Chase's candidacy in full swing and all his supporters, departmental and otherwise, Lincoln at once displayed the hand of the politician. He had equally good men for helpers—men who had spent their lives in the political fields. These also proceeded to work. Notably among them were Montgomery Blair and Simon Cameron. Lincoln was satisfied that the people were with him; his purpose was to have them speak before the politicians could control the national convention. New Hampshire, the native state of Chase, declared "Abraham Lincoln to be the people's choice for re-election." Montgomery Blair had the Maryland legislature declare for the renomination of Lincoln, and a similar resolution, through Cameron's influence, was passed by the Pennsylvania legislature. Then Rhode Island, a state supposedly controlled by Senator Sprague, Chase's son-in-law, declared for Lincoln. But the deathblow to Chase's candidacy came from his own state of Ohio. Here the Republicans in the legislature ended the Chase candidacy by adopting unanimously a resolution offered by John M. Connell of Fairfield County, senator from the Ninth District, declaring that "the people of Ohio and her soldiers in the field demand the renomination of Abraham Lincoln to the Presidency." Amidst cheering and enthusiasm the resolution was adopted.[95]

Immediately followed the withdrawal of Chase, and again he had failed in the greatest and controlling ambition of his life. He had a restless desire for the presidency; it became an obsession and destroyed his judgment and even his high sense of honor. Leaving this subject, it may be well to record that he was an aspirant for the presidential nomination in 1856, 1860, 1864 on the Republican ticket, 1868 on the Democratic, and in 1872 on the Liberal Republican.

In time came another resignation; of course, this was after Lincoln's renomination at Baltimore. It grew out of the vacancy in the assistant treasurership at New York. It is immaterial to go into details.

The resignation of the secretary was on June 29; and the country, being in a strained condition financially, it was regarded as a calamity. Chase's friends came forward urging Lincoln to refuse to accept the resignation. Governor Brough made an earnest effort in this direction; his associate in office, William Henry Smith, secretary of state, gives an interesting account of Brough's efforts in this matter:[96]

> Before the President accepted the resignation of Mr. Chase, he had a conference with Governor Brough, who was then at the Capital. An account of this, as related by the Governor, may throw some light on this interesting imbroglio. It is given here as written down on Governor Brough's return to Columbus.
>
> On his way to the War Department Governor Brough met the President, who insisted on his entering the Executive Mansion with him. "The truth is," said Mr. Lincoln, "I have a little matter on hand which concerns the State of Ohio, and which I have a notion to tell you, though you must remember that it is not public until tomorrow." The Governor assured Mr. Lincoln that he never desired such confidences as they usually proved troublesome, but he inquired: "What is it—another Treasury imbroglio?"
>
> *Mr. Lincoln.* "Right. Hit it the first time; it is a Treasury imbroglio."
>
> *Governor Brough.* "Well, Mr. President, before going further, I have a question to ask: Is it beyond mediation?"
>
> *Mr. L.* "Well," (hesitatingly), "perhaps and perhaps not. What do you propose?"
>
> *Gov. B.* "First tell me the nature of the difficulty."
>
> *Mr. L.* "It's about the Cisco business."
>
> *Gov. B.* "I don't wish to intrude, but for the interest of the country, and it being nothing more serious than that, if you will delay action until tomorrow morning when I can get the Ohio men together, I think it can be arranged."

Mr. L. "But this is the third time he has thrown it at me, and I don't think I am called on to continue to beg him to take it back, especially when the country would not go to destruction in consequence."

Gov. B. "This is not simply a personal matter. The people will not understand it. They will insist there is no longer any harmony in the counsels of the Nation, and the retiring of the Secretary of the Treasury is a sure indication that the bottom is about to fall out. Therefore, to save the country from this backset, if you will give me time, I think Ohio can close the breach and the world be none the wiser."

Mr. L. "You doctored the business up once, but on the whole, Brough, I reckon you had better let it alone this time."

The conversational form is followed as preserved in the diary of the writer, July 12, 1864.

The mediation of friends was useless; Lincoln wrote Chase accepting his resignation. "Of all I have said in commendation," he wrote, "of your ability and fidelity, I have nothing to unsay; and yet you and I have reached a point of mutual embarrassment in our official relations which, it seems to me, cannot be overcome or longer sustained consistently with the public service."

Lincoln's estimate of Chase's ability had always been high, and his opinion was not affected by personal differences. So when Chief Justice Taney died the October following, Lincoln made up his mind to appoint Chase to the vacancy. To a committee who objected to the appointment, Lincoln said:[97] "Mr. Chase is a very able man. He is a very ambitious man, and I think on the subject of the presidency a little insane. He has not always behaved very well lately, and people say to me, 'now is the time to *crush him out*'. Well, I'm not in favor of crushing anybody out. If there is anything a man can do, and do it well, I say let him do it. Give him a chance."

At another time he said of Chase:[98] "Of all the great men I have ever known, Chase is equal to about one and one-half of the best of them."

On December 6, 1864, Lincoln wrote out with his own hand the appointment of Chase for chief justice of the United States, and the Senate confirmed unanimously the nomination without reference.

CHAPTER 8

THE LINCOLN OBSEQUIES IN OHIO; CEREMONIES AT CLEVELAND AND COLUMBUS[99]

When on the morning of April 15, 1865, the nation learned the death of Lincoln at the hand of an assassin, the people were at first dazed; then came a feeling of profound grief, and a pall of gloom overshadowed the land. As his loss became a fact in the hearts of the people, they seemed to appreciate him the more. They realized now his greatness. As they looked back over the four years of war, they appreciated how he had stood out in that terrible period like an inspired prophet, guiding his people through storms such as never swept over a civilized nation before, guiding them often against the will of their leaders, against their complaints and criminations. But all this time he had the unbroken confidence of his people—"the plain people" as he used to say. Their faith in him came as a benediction to him; it gave him joy even in his tribulations. These people, now that he had left them, could see in their sorrow his power to grasp momentous questions of state; how his mind pierced the clouds that their minds saw through but darkly; and how his penetrating wisdom had saved the Union, and with it freedom for all the land.

The transfer of Lincoln's remains from Washington to his home at Springfield was, in sad solemnity and moral grandeur, the most impressive pageant in the history of mankind. The cities through which the funeral procession passed, with great depth of feeling and sad decorum, gave their most profound homage of respect to the remains.

When the funeral train entered Ohio, Governor Brough, on behalf of the state, received it at Wickliffe, Lake County. Here his staff joined him, consisting of General B. R. Cowen, adjutant general; General Merrill Barlow, quartermaster general; General R. N. Barr, surgeon general; Col. Sidney D. Maxwell, aide-de-camp; Lt.-Col. John T. Mercer, assistant adjutant general; F. A. Marble, Esq., private secretary.

Major General Joseph Hooker, commanding the Northern Department of Ohio, also joined the funeral party at Wickliffe, under orders from the war department to accompany the president's remains to Springfield with his staff, including Colonel Swords, assistant quartermaster general; Lieutenant Simpson, U.S. Engineers; Lieutenant Colonel Lathrop, assistant inspector general; Major Bannister, chief paymaster; Major MacFeely, commissary, U. S. A.; and Captain Taylor. United States Senator Sherman, Hon. Samuel Galloway, Octavius Waters, and Major Montgomery also met the remains at Wickliffe; together with a number of the prominent citizens of northern Ohio, who had been appointed at Cleveland a committee to attend the funeral procession from the state line to that city.

There was a special feature about the running of the train from Erie to Cleveland that deserves notice. As far as possible, everything connected with the train was the same as on the occasion of Lincoln's journey over that road in 1861. The locomotive (the *William Case*) was the same. The engineer, William Congden, was dead, and the engine was run by John Benjamin. The fireman in 1861, George Martin, was engineer, but asked and obtained the privilege of again acting as fireman on the train. The same conductor, E. D. Page, had control of the train. Superintendent Henry Nottingham, as before, had the complete management. The pilot engine, *Idaho*, which preceded the train ten minutes, was run by engineer J. McGuire and fireman Frank Keehen.

As soon as it was definitely ascertained that the remains of President Lincoln would pass through Cleveland on their way to Springfield, measures were taken to extend to them the honor due from a grateful people to their beloved chief magistrate. The first movement originated in the city council, in the shape of a series of resolutions introduced by Amos Townsend, appropriate to the occasion, authorizing the appointment of a committee, with the mayor as chairman, to make the necessary preparations. This committee consisted of George B. Senter, mayor; Thomas Jones, Jr., president of the council, and Joseph Sturges, Ansel Roberts, and Amos Townsend, trustees. It held its first meeting at the mayor's office on Wednesday evening, April 19, when George B. Senter was chosen permanent chairman and Thomas Jones, Jr., permanent secretary.

The Board of Trade took action on Thursday, April 27, and appointed Philo Chamberlin, R. T. Lyon, J. F. Freeman, S. F. Lester, W. Murray, and A. J. Begges, a committee to cooperate with a committee from the city council in all matters pertaining to the reception of the remains of the president. This committee met with the council committee on Saturday evening, and on motion was incorporated with that committee.

The council committee in the meantime had added to their number several prominent citizens, and the augmented committee took the name of the General Committee of Arrangements, and consisted of the following gentlemen:

Hon. George B. Senter, chairman; Thomas Jones, Jr., and J. C. Sage, secretaries; Ansel Roberts, Hon. R. P. Spaulding, Colonel W. H. Hayward, W. B. Castle, R. T. Lyon, W. Murray, S. F. Lester, A. Stone, Jr., L. M. Hubby, Joseph Sturges, Amos Townsend, Hon. H. Payne, Colonel Jas. Barnett, Wm. Bingham, Philo Chamberlin, J. F. Freeman, A. J. Begges, H. M. Chapin, M. Barlow, A. S. Sanford.

At the meeting of the General Committee of Arrangements on Saturday evening, April 22, the following subcommittees were named, and the mayor authorized to designate the names of the gentlemen to fill them: On Location of Remains, Reception, Procession, Military Entertainment, Music, Decoration, and Carriages. As filled by Mayor Senter, the subcommittees were as follows:

On Location of Remains—Philo Chamberlin, H. B. Payne, Ansel Roberts, Wm. Bingham, A. S. Sanford, and Amasa Stone, Jr.

On Reception—George B. Senter, chairman, Thomas Jones, Jr., Ansel Roberts, Joseph Sturges, Amos Townsend, Hon. David Tod, Wm. B. Castle, Hon. H. B. Payne, Hon. H. M. Chapin, Amasa Stone, Jr., Hon. E. S. Flint, Hon. R. C. Parsons, Hon. H. V. Willson, General M. Barlow, M. R. Keith, Hon. S. O. Griswold, Hon. F. J. Dickman, S. D. McMillen, Anson Stager, Hon. George Mygatt, Hon. John Brough, Hon. R. P. Spaulding, Hon. S. Williamson, C. W. Palmer, Philo Chamberlin, Hon. F. T. Backus, Stillman Witt, W. H. Truscott, George A. Benedict, Hon. A. Everett, T. P. Handy, D. B. Sexton, T. M. Kelley, L. A. Pierce, Hon. Samuel Starkweather, Hon. John A. Foot.

On Procession.—Colonel James Barnett, William Bingham, Colonel John P. Ross, Silas Merchant, Amos Townsend, Colonel W. H. Hayward, Captain F. W. Pelton, Captain B. L. Spangler.

On Military.—General A. S. Sanford, Colonel Charles Whittlesey, Colonel W. H. Hayward, Major J. D. Palmer, William Bingham.

On Entertainment.—Thomas Jones, Jr., Earl Bill, John A. Wheeler, Joseph Sturges, E. Cowles.

On Music.—B. Seymore, R. T. Lyon, R. Crawford, Daniel Stephan.

On Decoration.—John M. Sterling, Peter Thatcher, B. Butts, F. R. Elliott, T. Ross, Dr. E. Sterling, William Beckenbach, Capt. Spaulding, George Howe.

On Carriages.—Nelson Purdy, William Murray, David Price, Peter Goldrick.

To Meet the Remains.—Hon. R. P. Spaulding, Gov. David Tod, Thomas Jones, Jr., Col. Anson Stager, Amasa Stone, Jr., Hon. H. B. Payne, Hon. John A. Foot, Hon. H. V. Willson, Stillman Witt, Ansel Roberts, William Bingham, Hon. William B. Castle, Charles Hickox, John Martin, Hon. William Collins, H. N. Johnson, Dr. G. C. E. Weber, Dr. Proctor Thayer, E. Cowles, H. B. Hurlbut, Jacob Hovey, James Worswick, George Willey, Lemuel Crawford.

At a subsequent meeting of the General Committee of Arrangements, the following gentlemen were selected to act as a civic guard of honor:

Fayette Brown, chairman, H. F. Brayton, E. Simms, Charles Pettingell, John Bousfield, George W. Woodworth, C. L. Russell, George W. Gardner, M. B. Clark, James Worswick, A. T. Brinsmade, E. Cowles, O. N. Skeels, Allayne Maynard, Samuel Starkweather, T. S. Beckwith, C. S. McKenzie, E. Chester, H. J. Herrick, K. Hays, George Presly, J. W. Fitch, L. M. Pitkin, H. D. Ruggles, E. Rockwell, Charles Glasser, John Hartness, A. E. Burlison, E. R. Perkins, John Huntington, S. H. Benedict, F. T. Wallace, Harvey Rice, Jacob Hovey, S. H. Mather, George C. Dodge, D. W. Cross, James Parnell, James J. Tracy, R. K. Winslow, John E. Carey, G. W. Calkins, E. J. Estep, J. P. Bishop, William Jones, H. K. Reynolds, F. C. Keith, H. C. McFarland, V. C. Taylor, George B. Ely, S. Hyman, J. H. Morley, A. J. Wenham, L. L. Lyon, W. P. Fogg, J. C. Calhoun, Charles Whitaker, E. J. Gorham, Moses Kelley, T. W. Leek, H. N. Raymond, M. L. Brooks, B. F. Peixotto, S. Thorman, Frank W. Parsons, E. S. Root, A. B. Stone, A. Chisholm, G. A. Hyde, H. C. Hawkins, R. E. Mix, C. C. Rogers,

Augustus Thieme, Jacob Schroeder, William Hart, C. A. Read, Reuben Becker, J. P. Robinson, S. M. Carpenter, James Hill, S. W. Crittenden, H. S. Davis, G. B. Murphey, C. A. Brayton, W. M. Crowell, Peter Thatcher, N. M. Standard, William Melbinch, S. M. Strong, J. M. Perkins, T. J. Burrin, G. Herrick, J. C. Buell, William J. Smith, Henry Blair, J. V. Painter, E. S. Willard, Thomas Quayle, James Mason, Joseph Perkins, William Collins, J. F. Clark, Thomas Burnham, John H. Gorham, W. J. Boardman, Arthur Quinn, Charles Hickox, H. G. Hitchcock, Robert F. Paine, William Edwards, H. Harvey, S. L. Mather, H. B. Hurlbut, W. F. Otis, C. W. Coe, M. C. Younglove, A. G. Colwell, H. C. Blossom, W. V. Craw, B. Lampson, E. M. Peck, Frank Kelly, George F. Marshall, E. P. Morgan, E. W. Sackrider, J. B. Glenn, C. S. Hobbs, J. A. Reddington, J. A. Harris, H. G. Abbey, John F. Warner, D. P. Eells, John C. Grannis, George H. Burt, C. W. Noble, F. J. Prentiss, C. A. Crumb, Addison Hills, George A. Stanley, George F. Armstrong, Joseph Randerson, Charles Evatt, O. C. Scoville, P. Roeder, H. W. Leutkemeyer, C. J. Ballard, A. Rettberg, Louis Smithknight, B. Steadman, I. Buckingham, W. Lawty, W. Wellhouse, L. A. Benton, H. J. Hoyt, T. D. Eells.

The guard was divided into six squads, under the direction of the following gentlemen:

First aid—J. Ensworth; second aid—Louis Smithknight; third aid—Robert Hanna; first assistant—Peter Thatcher; second assistant—H. F. Brayton; third assistant—F. T. Wallace; fourth assistant—J. P. Robinson; fifth assistant—George F. Marshall; sixth assistant—Thomas Quayle.

The Committee on Location of Remains found no room or building in which to place the remains, suitable to accommodate the vast crowd that would be present and wish to take the last look at their late president. The committee, therefore, decided to erect upon the east side of the park a proper structure. The Committee of Arrangements authorized the erection, and the building was immediately commenced, and on Thursday night was completed. It stood directly east of the monument and was an oblong structure twenty-four by thirty-six feet, and fourteen feet high. The roof was pagoda-shaped, and over the center of the main roof was a second roof, raised about four feet, and forming a canopy over the catafalque. The sides and ends of the building were open above the low breastwork, which was covered with a black cloth. The roof was supported by pillars shrouded in black and white, and the open sides were elegantly draped with festoons of white and black, looped up with rosettes of white and black. The roof was of white canvas, the ribs supporting it being shrouded in black. The ends of the building were heavily draped with black cloth. Over each end of the building was a large golden eagle with the national shield. The sides supporting the second roof were covered with black cloth on the outside, on which were fastened evergreen wreaths and floral devices. At the east end of the building, where the procession entered, were six splendid regimental flags of silk. Eight immense plumes of black crape surmounted the sides of the building. Slender flag poles bearing crape streamers and mourning flags were ranged along the top of the building. Evergreen and floral wreaths were used to loop up the drapery and crown the capitals of the columns. Directly over the upper roof was a streamer stretched between two flag poles, bearing the inscription from Horace: *Extinctus amabitur idem* ("Dead, he will be loved the same").

The inside of the building was in admirable keeping with the exterior decorations. Heavy drapery of black cloth, festoons of evergreen, and floral wreaths and bouquets completely shrouded the pillars and roof. In the center was the catafalque, a raised dais, twelve feet long, four feet wide, and about two feet high to the underside of the coffin. The floor and sides of the dais were covered with black cloth and velvet. The floor was so inclined that, on entering the building, the visitors were able at once to see the remains and keep them in sight until nearly leaving the building. From the corners of the dais sprang four slender columns supporting a canopy draped with black cloth with silver fringe, and the corners of the canopy hung with silver tassels. The capitals of the pillars were wreathed with flowers. At the head and foot of the dais were several seats covered with black cloth, designed for the use of the guard of honor. The floor of the building was covered thickly with matting, so as to deaden every sound. The building was well lit with gas at night. The people entered from the east and passed through the broad passages on each side of the dais, going out on the west side. Cleveland was the first place on the route of the funeral cortege where a special building had to be erected for the reception of the remains.

Mayor Senter appointed the following gentlemen as pallbearers:

Hon. John Brough, Hon. David Tod, Hon. John Sherman, Hon. James M. Ashley, Hon. J. C. Deven, Hon. Horace Foot, Hon. John Crowell, Hon. J. P. Robinson, Hon. D. R. Tilden, Gen. R. P. Buckland, Gen. O. M. Oviatt, Hon. R. P. Spaulding.

Every train that arrived on the railroads during Thursday and Thursday night, was filled; all the hotels were crowded, and hundreds of persons were unable to procure even a sleeping place upon the floor.

The symbols of mourning were universal. Men, women, and children, of all classes and conditions, wore some badge or symbol of sorrow. Toward evening of Thursday the citizens on Superior, Euclid, Prospect, Bank, and other streets, and around the square, commenced to drape their dwellings and places of business. Along the line designated for the passing of the procession, the draping was very elaborate, tasteful, and almost universal.

The following was the order of proceedings for the day, as promulgated by Colonel James Barnett, chief marshal:

> The following programme of arrangements is announced for the solemnization of the obsequies of Abraham Lincoln, late President of the United States, in this city, on Friday, the 28th inst.
>
> The bells of the city will be tolled during the moving of the procession.
>
> The shipping in the harbor, and the proprietors of public houses and others, are requested to display their colors at half-mast during the day.
>
> It is earnestly requested that all places of business or amusement be closed during the day.
>
> Vehicles of all kinds will be withdrawn from the streets through which the procession will pass, and none will be allowed in the procession except those designated.
>
> Delegations will be promptly at their places of rendezvous, prepared to march at the appointed time, failing in which, they will be excluded from their positions, and will take their places on the left.
>
> A national salute of thirty-six guns will be fired by the 8th Independent Battery, at 7 o'clock A. M., and half-hour guns thereafter until sunset.
>
> The procession will move from the Euclid street station at 7:30 A. M., through Euclid street to Erie, down Erie to Superior, down Superior to the Park, where the remains will be deposited in the building erected for that purpose, and exposed to view until 10 o'clock P. M.

At daybreak on Friday morning, the citizens were startled from their slumbers by a salute of artillery, and in a very short time the whole city was astir. By six o'clock the streets were crowded with people, some wending their way down to the Union Depot, to the park, or to other advantageous positions on the line of march, whilst throngs of people started for the Euclid Street Depot, from which the procession was to start. Thousands of people from the country and from other cities had arrived during the preceding days of the week, and all night the streets had been crowded. The weather was gloomy and threatened rain, and by the time the train arrived, the rain began to fall steadily but not heavily. The city could scarcely have looked to better advantage, in spite of the rain, as the dust was laid, and the partly opened foliage, with its delicate green tint, lent beauty to the elegant dwellings and grounds along the avenues through which the procession was to pass.

The importance and solemnity of the occasion was evidently appreciated by everyone. The dense crowds that lined the streets from the Euclid Street Depot to the public square, the numerous badges of mourning worn, the heavily-draped buildings, and the uniform stillness and decorum of the immense gathering of people, testified to the respect and love borne to the deceased by the people of Cleveland and the surrounding country. The immense crowd was hourly added to by the trains and steamers arriving from different points.

Punctually at seven o'clock the funeral train ran into the Union Depot. The sight as it passed down the Lake Shore track was impressive and was witnessed by a great crowd of people on the bank. On reaching the depot, the locomotive of the Cleveland and Pittsburgh Railroad, tastefully draped, took the engine in its reversed position and drew it to the Euclid Street station, arriving there about twenty minutes after seven o'clock. As the train moved up, a national salute of thirty-six guns was fired. As the train came up the Lake Shore track, a very beautiful incident took place. Miss Fields, of Wilson Street, had erected an arch of evergreens on the bank of the lake near the track, and as the train passed, appeared in the arch as the Goddess of Liberty in mourning.

On arriving at the Euclid Street Depot, the train was stopped so that the funeral car lay nearly across the road. The depot was heavily draped with mourning and flags, and a draped flag hung from a line stretched directly across the road. The Veteran Reserve Corps were drawn up around the funeral car, eight of them being ready to carry the coffin, whilst the others formed in line on either side with drawn swords presented. The guard of honor stood on one side, and Governor Brough and staff, with the leading members of the committees and the pallbearers on the other. The Camp Chase band stood in front of the depot, and the hearse was drawn up a few yards distant. The hearse was surmounted with large black and white plumes, and the national colors draped. The hangings were of black velvet, with heavy silver fringe and silver tassels, fastened up with crape rosettes, each with a silver star in the center. A beautiful wreath of flowers hung at the head of the hearse, and the bed on which the coffin was to rest was strewn thickly with white blossoms. Six white horses, decorated with festoons of crape, looped up with crape rosettes and silver stars, drew the hearse and were attended by six colored grooms, wearing crape and mourning rosettes. The decorations were arranged and executed by Mrs. R. F. Paine.

At a signal given, the band played a solemn dirge, and the coffin was taken out of the car and borne to the hearse on the shoulders of the Veteran Reserves, the other Veteran Reserves marching by its side with drawn swords, attended by the pallbearers and guard. On the head of the coffin was a cross of white flowers and a wreath of similar flowers at the foot.

The hearse, surrounded by the Veteran Reserve Guard, with the pallbearers on either side, the guard of honor, mounted, following, and preceded by the band playing a dirge, passed up Wilson Avenue.

The 29th O. N. G. was drawn up in line and saluted the cortege as it passed. The civic guard of honor met the hearse on Prospect Street and saluted it when the cortege turned, and went back to Euclid Street, when the procession was formed according to program.

The crowd around the station was exceedingly large, but owing to the excellent police arrangements and the orderly character of the people, there was no trouble or confusion. The large space reserved was kept perfectly clear. When the coffin was brought from the car, so great was the anxiety of the people to see it, that a number—most of them women—got under the train and remained there until warned off by the police to save their lives. The scene when the procession started was very solemn. A slight rain fell, dripping like tears on the remains of the good man in whose honor the crowd had gathered, but not enough to be heeded by the people assembled. The street was lined with a continuous wall of people, and the yards and houses were also crowded. The long perspective of Euclid Street stretched away in unrivaled beauty, and the procession, with its solid column, great length, and imposing display, made up a scene never equaled in Cleveland. There was scarcely any variation from the published order of the chief marshal in the formation of the procession.

First came the military escort, Colonel Hayward commanding, led by the Camp Chase band. The escort consisted of the 29th Regiment,

Ohio National Guard, and the 8th Independent Battery, under the command of Lieutenant Grenninger. The escort was followed by Major General Hooker and staff, and officers of the army on horseback. Then came Governor Brough and staff, and the pallbearers in carriages. The hearse came next, followed by the escort of honor that accompanied the remains from Washington to Springfield. The General Committee of Arrangements, civic guard of honor, and clergy followed on foot. This closed the first division, which was under the direction of Colonel O. H. Payne, assistant marshal.

The second division, under the direction of Amos Townsend, Esq., assistant marshal, was led by the Detroit City Band. In this division were the following societies and bodies: United States civil officers, Earl Bill, marshal; a large number of returned veteran soldiers under command of Captain James K. O'Reilly; city council and other city officers; Cleveland Board of Trade, and members of boards of trade from other cities; a delegation of citizens from Meadville, Captain Derrickson acting as marshal.

George H. Burt, Esq., had charge of the third division, which was led by the Detroit Light Guard Band. The Knights Templar followed the band, dressed in full regalia with their banners draped in mourning. They acted as an escort to the Order of Free and Accepted Masons, some in regalia and others wearing a sprig of evergreen on their breasts. Bigelow Lodge, West Side, turned out eighty strong, in full regalia with banners and emblems of the order all appropriately draped. Following the Masons came the Order of Odd Fellows, about a thousand strong, also with regalia and banners dressed with weeds of sorrow. Among the Odd Fellows from outside the city were Cataract Lodge No. 295, from Newburgh, and members from other places.

The fourth division was under direction of Major W. P. Edgarton, assistant marshal. Next to the Temperance Band, which was at the head of this division, came the Father Matthew Temperance Society, very strong in numbers, wearing their sashes and carrying their banners, all clothed in mourning. The Fenian Brotherhood followed the Temperance Society, and after them came the Laboring Men's Union, carrying a banner with the motto:—"We mourn the loss of our President; Labor is the wealth of the Nation; United we Stand, Divided we Fall." The St. Bonifacius Society came next, followed by the Aurora Band, from the West Side. Following the band were the St. Joseph Society, St. Vincent Society, St. Andrew's Society, St. George's Society, and Mona's Relief Society. All these societies were in full ranks, bearing their distinctive banners and emblems.

The fifth division, in charge of assistant marshal Major Seymour Race, embraced the members of the Ancient Order of Good Fellows; Ohio City Lodge of Good Fellows; the Hungarian Association, with their national badges and colors; and Solomon and Montefiore Lodges I. O. B. B., under the marshalship of B. F. Peixotto, grand master of the order in the United States. Leland's Band led the fifth division.

The sixth division was under the direction of Captain Basil L. Spangler, assistant marshal. The first society represented in this division was the German Benevolent Mutual Society. This society was followed by Eureka Lodge No. 14 of Colored Masons; 1,188 G. U. O. O. F., also colored. This society carried a banner, on which was inscribed: "We mourn for Abraham Lincoln, the True Friend of Liberty." The Colored Equal Rights League followed. Cleveland Division No. 275 and Forest City Temple No. 52, Sons of Temperance, came next, and the Seamen's Union closed the organized procession. The union carried a small full-rigged bark, with flag at half mast.

The chief marshal, Colonel James Barnett, and his valuable assistants, Colonel J. P. Ross, Silas Merchant, Colonel O. H. Payne, Amos Townsend, George H. Burt, Major W. P. Edgarton, Major S. Race, and Captain B. L. Spangler, formed and conducted the long procession with the most perfect order. There was no confusion, no noise, and all the different societies and bodies fell into the places in the procession allotted to them on time and with the precision of clockwork.

After the procession started from the depot, it moved slowly and solemnly, without stop or detention, until it reached the square. As it neared the western end of Euclid Street, the number of people began to increase until the sidewalks and far into the street became a solid mass; but there was no noise or confusion in the crowd that lined the streets on the line of march. All seemed impressed with the deep solemnity of the occasion.

The draping of the houses and buildings in mourning along the route of the procession was general. There was not a house on Euclid Street, from the square to the Euclid Street Depot, which did not display some symbol of grief. Prospect and many other streets were also very generally draped. The greatest display, however, was on Superior and Euclid streets, and around the square. On City High School building was a large shield, surrounded by flags, intertwined with white and black mourning. At the residence of A. B. Stone, Esq., on Euclid Street, was the following truthful motto: "His aims were for God, his Country, and Truth. He died a blessed Martyr." At Rouse's Block, corner of Superior Street and the square, was a profuse display of festoons of white and black with flags, and on the square front the motto: "An Honest man—the noblest work." The county courthouse, city council hall, the government building, and other places around the square near the pavilion in which the remains reposed during the day, were all tastefully and appropriately dressed in mourning.

The entire front of E. I. Baldwin's store was covered with black, on which was the motto: "A glorious career of service and devotion is crowned with a martyr's death." All the other prominent business buildings were tastefully and elaborately decorated. The ladies connected with the Soldiers' Aid Society displayed much taste in the draping of the front of their rooms. Their windows were covered on the inside with a white background, on which was neatly arranged folds of black, and on the outside were many rosettes and small flags, also appropriately arranged. All the hotels, telegraph offices, and express offices were appropriately draped.

There were over six thousand in the procession of organized societies. After the main procession passed a given point, the citizens fell in behind and followed it through the pavilion, in the same good order as characterized the proceedings. There was a considerable crush at the entrance gates on Superior Street, but no boisterous actions. The admirable arrangements of the committee for preserving order in the neighborhood of the building where the remains were to be placed prevented confusion. The procession entered the enclosure by the east gate, and after the removal of the body to the building filed out at the Rockwell Street gate. The 29th O. N. G. occupied positions inside the enclosure and were stationed as sentinels at numerous points. The hearse was driven up to the south side of the pavilion, and the coffin borne on the shoulders of Veteran Reserves to the place prepared for it under the canopy. As the body passed, the band played a dirge. As soon as the coffin was placed on the dais, a committee of ladies advanced and placed on it a number of floral ornaments and evergreens, wreathed in the forms of crosses and coronals. The embalmer and undertaker opened the coffin and inspected the remains. The Right Reverend Charles Pettit McIlvaine, bishop of the Diocese of Ohio, advanced to the coffin and read from the Burial Service of the Episcopal Church:

"I am the resurrection and the life, sayeth the Lord; he that believeth in me, though he were dead, yet shall he live; and whosoever liveth and believeth in me shall never die.

"We brought nothing into the world, and it is certain we can carry nothing out. The Lord gave, and the Lord hath taken away; blessed be the name of the Lord.

"Man that is born of a woman, hath but a short time to live, and is full of misery. He cometh up, and is cut down, like a flower; he fleeth as it were a shadow and never continueth in one stay.

"In the midst of life we are in death; of whom may we see for succor, but of Thee, O Lord, who for our sins are justly displeased?"

Bishop McIlvaine then offered an eloquent prayer, in which he prayed that this great affliction may be of good to the people. He prayed for blessing on the family of the deceased, and for health and blessing on Secretary Seward, whom the assassin tried, but failed to destroy. For President Johnson he asked that he might be led to follow the great example set him by his illustrious predecessor.

The religious services being concluded, the procession filed through the pavilion, passing through both aisles. Many were affected to tears. The invalid soldiers from the military hospital, who were drawn up inside the enclosure previous to the arrival of the procession, passed through, and many a bronzed veteran's eyes were wet as he gazed upon him who had laid down his life for his country. After the procession had passed through, the public were admitted, and thousands poured in a steady stream, without haste or confusion.

The heavy rain, which continued to fall from the first start of the procession down to the removal of the body from the building to the cars, seemed to have no effect in damping the eagerness of the people to take a last look at the remains of their beloved president. All day long the endless procession marched through without a break or pause, and when the lamps were lit the crowd thickened rather than diminished. The crowds seeking admission were formed by the police outside the enclosure into a column four deep, and those desiring of seeing the remains had to fall into the rear of the column and await their turn to enter. The column, on entering the enclosure, passed up to the east end of the pavilion, where it separated into two columns, each of two abreast, and marched on either side of the catafalque, passing along, on emerging to the monument, where they either went westward forward toward Superior, or southward toward Ontario Street. The military guard of officers appointed by General Hooker stood at the foot of the coffin and at the corners. One of the guard of honor of general officers stood or sat at the head of the coffin, Rear Admiral Davis occupying that position in the forenoon. The civic guards of honor were arranged along the sides of the building to pass the visitors on in proper order. A squad of the 29th O. N. G. was stationed at different points in the enclosure.

The most reverent silence and deep feeling were exhibited by all who passed through. The passageway being ample, there was abundant facility for obtaining a good view of the remains. The features were but slightly changed from the appearance they bore when exposed in the Capitol at Washington.

At different times in the day an accurate count of those passing through within a certain length of time was taken. In the first four hours, the rate of nine thousand per hour; then it fell to between seven and eight thousand, and increased in the evening and night. Until evening the visitors were nearly all from abroad, the city people holding back to give those a chance who would have to leave by the evening trains. At ten o'clock at night, when the gates were shut, over one hundred thousand people had visited the remains, and this without noise, disorder, or confusion of any kind.

A distinguished feature of the ceremonies and testimonials of the day was the profusion and beauty of the floral decorations and floral offerings. Besides the great number of flowers woven into the decorations of the pavilion, a large number of beautiful floral devices were laid on the coffin. Among them were the floral offerings made by the ladies of the Soldiers' Aid Society of northern Ohio, consisting of an anchor of white roses, azaleas, and other white flowers, each fluke of the anchor being made of magnificent calla; a cross of beautiful red blossoms; and a wreath of blue flowers. The ladies decided to place the anchor in charge of Lieutenant Colonel Simpson, U. S. Engineers, for presentation to Captain Stephen Champlin, one of the survivors of the Battle of Lake Erie. The cross and wreath accompanied the remains from Cleveland.

A salute was fired on the arrival of the remains at the square, and another at sunset. Half-hour guns were also fired during the day by the 8th Independent Battery, O. N. G. Five large and beautiful flags, draped in mourning, floated from the staff in the park all day.

During the afternoon the bands from abroad and those belonging to Cleveland were stationed on the balconies of the hotels and other prominent buildings, and played dirges, adding to the solemnity and impressiveness of the occasion.

A delegation of two hundred came from Meadville and joined in the procession, under the marshalship of Captain Derrickson. They wore a large badge upon the lapel of the coat with the word "Meadville." Also a delegation of about five hundred came from Detroit to do honor to the memory of the president. Two bands, the Detroit City and Light Guard, escorted them.

By invitation of Governor Brough, the Illinois delegation and the general officers of the escort paid him a visit at his residence.

The following officers were detailed as a guard of honor to the remains of the president, while in the Forest City:

First Relief—Rear Admiral Davis; Major D. Bannister, paymaster, U.S.A.; Captain Mix, U.S. Cavalry; Captain Meisner, V. R. C.; Major Perry, U. S. A.; Sergeant Sternburg, U.S.A.

Second Relief—Captain Taylor, U.S.N.; Lieutenant Colonel Simpson, U.S. Engineers; Lieutenant Colonel De La Vergne, U.S.V.; Captain Rower, Veteran Guard; Lieutenant Robinson, Veteran Guard.

Third Relief—Major General Barnard, U.S. Engineers; Colonel Swords, A. Q. M.; Captain J. J. Upham, U.S.A.; Captain Voges, A. Q. M.; Captain DeForest, N. G.; Captain Tibbitts, N. G.

At ten minutes past ten the coffin was closed. Up to the very last moment there was a stream of people passing through the pavilion, and if the remains had been exposed until twelve o'clock there would undoubtedly have been the same interest manifested to take one last look. At ten minutes past eleven o'clock the coffin was taken from the beautiful resting place of the day and placed in the hearse, preparatory to being conveyed to the funeral car. The escort was as follows: The 29th Regiment, O. N. G., Colonel Hayward; the general committee of arrangements; the military guard of honor in carriages; the civic guard of honor bearing flambeaux; the Father Matthew Temperance Society; the Eureka Lodge of Masons. The cortege proceeded down Superior Street, preceded by three bands playing a dirge, thence down Vineyard Street, at the foot of which the funeral train had been placed. The coffin was placed in the funeral car, and at precisely twelve o'clock the train started for Columbus, under the direction of Superintendent Flint with Charles Gale as conductor.

About the time the remains were being removed from the pavilion the rain poured down in torrents and continued until after the train started. Notwithstanding this, the streets the whole length of the line of march were crowded with people, many of whom were ladies. Everything was conducted with the greatest order and decorum, and the citizens of Cleveland returned to their homes with the consciousness that they had paid the last tribute of respect to a great and good man in a proper manner.

The correspondent of the *New York Times* writing from Cleveland said: "Everywhere deep sorrow has been manifested, and the feeling seems, if possible, to deepen, as we move Westwards with the remains to their final resting place."

The funeral train was preceded, between Cleveland and Columbus, by the pilot engine *Louisville*, in charge of assistant superintendent Blee and master mechanic W. F. Smith, with E. Van Camp as engineer and C. Van Camp as fireman. The engine of the funeral train was the *Nashville*, with George West as engineer and Peter Hugo as fireman. Mr. T. J. Higgins, the superintendent of telegraph, accompanied the train with necessary telegraph instruments, to be used in case of accident. General McCallum, who had temporary military possession of all railroads from Washington to Springfield, had an efficient aid in G. P. Duke, of the Baltimore and Ohio Railroad Company, who carried out his superior's orders as to the time of starting, with a fidelity which commanded general admiration.

Evidences of grief were manifested along the entire line between the Forest City and the Capital. The people gathered at the depots and at other points in throngs, eager to pay tribute to the memory of him whom they had loved. From the time the train left Cleveland until it reached Crestline, the rain fell in torrents, notwithstanding which bonfires and torches were lit, the principal buildings draped in mourning, bells tolled, flags floated at half mast, and the sorrowing inhabitants stood in groups, uncovered and with saddened faces gazing with awe and veneration upon the cortege as it moved slowly by.

After daybreak, the rain having ceased, the demonstrations were more general but of a less impressive character. At Cardington an immense crowd of citizens assembled to do the customary honors. Bells were tolled, minute guns fired, and the station was tastefully festooned with the national flag draped with rosettes of crape. In front and over the doors and windows was a white banner on which was inscribed, "He sleeps in the blessings of the poor, whose fetters God commanded him to break." At other villages similar devices were exhibited, and sadness and mourning, deep and solemn, prevailed in town and hamlet. Beside the track, about five miles above Columbus, stood an aged woman, bare-headed, her gray hairs disheveled, tears coursing down her furrowed cheeks, holding in her right hand a sable scarf and in her left a bouquet of wildflowers, which she stretched imploringly toward the funeral car.

In accordance with a call signed by a large number of the prominent and influential citizens of Columbus, a public meeting was held at the city hall on the evening of April 17, for the purpose of making arrangements for the suitable observance of the day appointed for the funeral of the assassinated president, at Washington, and to properly receive the remains at the Capital of Ohio. Hon. Samuel Galloway was selected as chairman, and H. T. Chittenden as secretary. Prayer was offered by Rev. C. E. Felton. The chairman set forth, in a few appropriate remarks, the object for which the people had assembled. On the motion of L. J. Critchfield, Esq., a committee of five was appointed to draft resolutions expressive of the sense of the meeting. The following gentlemen were appointed by the chair: L. J. Critchfield, George M. Parsons, C. N. Olds, B. F. Martin, and Peter Ambos.

Rev. J. M. Trimble, Hon. Samuel Galloway, and Hon. Chauncey N. Olds addressed the meeting. The committee on resolutions reported a series declaring that treason embraced murder and all other crimes necessary to accomplish its ends; expressing grief and indignation at the assassination of the president; tendering to his stricken family heartfelt condolence; avowing confidence in Andrew Johnson, and resolving:

> That, in token of the public sorrow on account of this great calamity, and to the honor of the illustrious dead, the citizens of Columbus be requested to close their places of business on tomorrow, between the hours of eleven o'clock A. M. and three o'clock P. M., the hours of the funeral services at Washington, and that those having charge of the bells in this city, cause them to be tolled during that time.

The following resolution was then offered by W. G. Deshler and adopted unanimously:

> *Resolved,* That a committee of nine be appointed to co-operate with the committee of the City Council, in any appropriate ceremonies, should the body of our late President be brought to our city; and also in conjunction with the City Council committee, to arrange for a public oration upon the life and services of Abraham Lincoln.

The chair appointed the following committee in pursuance of this resolution: W. G. Deshler, David S. Gray, J. E. St. Clair, W. Failing, Isaac Eberly, Rev. K. Mees, L. Kilbourne, C. P. L. Butler, and S. Loving. On motion, Hon. Samuel Galloway was added to the committee.

The city council cordially cooperated with the citizens in the movement thus inaugurated. On motion of Cyrus Field, it was agreed that the mayor, city officers, and members of the city council join in the procession to escort the remains of the late president, and, on motion, Messrs. Donaldson and Ross were appointed a committee to make the necessary arrangements for that purpose.

The council had previously

Resolved, That a committee of nine (one from each Ward) be appointed to act in conjunction with such committees as may be appointed by the State authorities, and the citizens generally, to make suitable preparations for the reception of the remains of the late President.

On the 24th of April, the adjutant general of Ohio promulgated the following order:

GENERAL HEADQUARTERS, STATE OF OHIO,
ADJUTANT GENERAL'S OFFICE,
COLUMBUS, April 23, 1865.

GENERAL ORDER,
 NO. 5.

Major John W. Skiles, 88th O. V. I., is hereby appointed Chief Marshal of the ceremonies in honor of the remains of the late President Lincoln, in the city of Columbus, on the 29th inst. He will appoint his own aids, and will have entire control of the ceremonies and procession attending the transfer of the remains from and to the depot.

All societies, delegations, or other organizations, wishing to participate in the ceremonies, will report, by telegraph, or letter, to the Chief Marshal, on or before 10 o'clock A. M. of Friday, 28th inst.

The headquarters of the Chief Marshal, during Thursday and Friday, 27th and 28th inst., will be at the Adjutant-General's office in the Capitol.

By order of the Governor:
B. R. COWEN,
Adjutant-General of Ohio.

James Patterson, chairman of the city council committee, and W. G. Deshler, chairman of the citizens' committee, announced that the funeral train would arrive at Columbus on the morning of April 29, at half-past seven o'clock—that the remains of the president would be escorted to the Capitol by a military and civic procession, where they would lie in state until six o'clock p.m., and that at three o'clock an oration would be delivered on the terrace on the east side of the Capitol Square. The committee requested the general suspension of business and described the general order of exercises, cordially invited societies and associations to join the procession, and announced the following officers of the day:

Chief Marshal—Major John W. Skiles.
Aids—Charles Scarrett, Ed. Fields, Carl Bancroft, Ed. Fitch, A. Greenleaf, W. W. Bailey, Theo. Butler, Capt. Jas. Grover, C. S. Dyer, John W. Doherty, C. W. Douty, R. S. Neil, Maj. L. S. Sullivant, Jno. Radebaugh.
Pall-Bearers—Dr. John Andrews, Robert Neil, F. C. Kelton, John Field, Augustus Platt, Christian Heyl, E. W. Gwynne, W. B. Hubbard, Judge Taylor, Jno. Brooks, Wm. B. Thrall, D. W. Deshler, L. Goodale, Jos. R. Swan, Wm. T. Martin, Wm. M. Awl, G. W. Moneypenny, John M. Walcutt, F. Stewart, John Noble, F. Jaeger, Sr., Amos S. Ramsey.
Executive Committee—W. G. Deshler, C. P. L. Butler, James Patterson, S. N. Field, F. Jaeger.
Finance Committee—B. Gilmore, W. Failing, Isaac Eberly, S. N. Field.
Escort Committee—Samuel Galloway, L. Kilbourne, S. Loving, James Patterson, John Miller, J. Reinhard.
Committee on Catafalque, Decoration, Etc.—D. S. Gray, A. B. Buttles, Wm. Gaver.
Committee on Music and Printing—A. B. Buttles, Rev. K. Mees, B. Gilmore, Wm. Naughton.
Committee on Reception of Escort and Guests—W. Failing, B. Gilmore, J. E. St. Clair.
Committee on Carriages—C. P. L. Butler, Wm. Gaver.

As soon as committees and associations had made report to him, the chief marshal advertised the following:

ORDER OF PROCESSION

COLUMBUS, O., April 27, 1865.

1st. The remains of Abraham Lincoln, late President of the United States, will arrive in the city of Columbus, O., at 7 o'clock A. M., Saturday, the 29th instant, at the Union Depot.

2nd. The funeral escort will consist of the 88th O. V. Infantry.

3rd. Officers of the army, not on duty with troops, are respectfully invited to participate in the obsequies. They will report to Major James Van Voost, 18th U. S. Infantry, at Headquarters, Tod Barracks, at 6 o'clock A. M., Saturday.

4th. Detachments of the army and volunteer organizations, not on duty with the escort, will be assigned positions on application to Captain L. Nichols, Tod Barracks. They will appear with side arms only, and will report at 6 o'clock A. M., Saturday.

5th. All military officers to be in uniform, and with side arms. The usual badge of mourning will be worn on the left arm and sword hilt.

6th. In order to prevent confusion at the entrance gate, all who are not in line of procession will form after the left of the procession has entered the Capitol Square in two ranks, on the outside of the Square fence, on High street, running north to Broad, south to State, thence east on Broad and State streets, for extent. They will enter the west gate four abreast, in regular order, by inward march of each rank, and in no other way.

It is desired to pass all through the Capitol, and in order to accommodate each person the public must preserve order and follow the programme as adopted.

A sufficient guard, composed of the 18th U. S. Infantry, will be stationed at the depot to prevent any delay or confusion in transferring the remains to the catafalque, and in seating the escort accompanying the remains.

7th. All delegations who have reported and have been assigned to positions in line of procession, will report promptly at their designated places, and will be moved by Assistant Marshals in charge.

MILITARY ESCORT

Eighty-eighth O. V. Infantry, under command of Lieutenant-Col. Webber.

ORDER OF PROCESSION

1st. Officiating clergyman and orator in open carriage.
2nd. Undertaker in buggy.
3rd. Pall bearers in carriages; carriages three abreast.

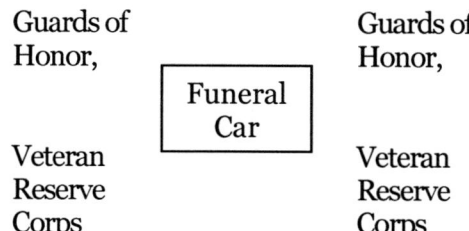

4th. Pall bearers in carriages; carriages three abreast.

5th. Escort accompanying remains from Washington in open carriages, three abreast, in charge of Assistant Marshals Theodore Comstock and Henry Wilson.

6th. Major-General Hooker and staff, mounted.

7th. Brevet Brigadier-General W. P. Richardson and staff, mounted.

8th. A. A. Provost-Marshal General Col. Wilcox and staff, mounted.

9th. Brigadier-General Wager Swayne and staff, in open carriage.

10th. Officers of the army on duty, and temporarily at this post, on foot, Major James Van Voost, 18th U. S. Infantry, commanding.

11th. Soldiers at this post not on duty with escort, Capt. Levi. T. Nichols commanding.

12th. Governor Brough and suite.

13th. Camp Thomas Band.

14th. Committee of Arrangements on foot.

15th. Chief Marshal John W. Skiles, and Special Aids Charles Scarrett and Theo. H. Butler.

FIRST DIVISION

Assistant Marshals—E. G. Field and John Radebaugh.

16th. Reverend Clergy, City and State, will form on Depot street, right resting on Exchange Hotel.

17th. Heads of Departments, State of Ohio, will form north of railroad track, in open carriages, right resting opposite of Exchange Hotel.

18th. Mayors of Cincinnati and Columbus, and Presidents of City Councils of said cities, in open carriages.

19th. City Councils of Cincinnati and Columbus on foot, forming on north Public Lane, right resting on High street.

20th. Judges and officers of Supreme Court of State of Ohio, in carriages.

21st. Judges and officers of Supreme Court of State of Ohio, in carriages.

22nd. Judges and officers of Franklin and other County Courts, on foot, forming with right resting north of railroad track, in rear of carriages.

SECOND DIVISION

Assistant Marshals—Carl Bancroft and E. A. Fitch.

23d. Masonic Order will form on West North street, right resting on High, left extending north on Front street.

THIRD DIVISION

Assistant Marshals—A. Greenleaf and J. W. Doherty.

24th. Independent Order of Odd Fellows, right resting on East North and High, left extending on South Front street.

FOURTH DIVISION

Assistant Marshals—C. W. Douty and S. H. Olmsted.

25th. United Ancient Order of Druids, right resting on corner of High and West Spring streets, left extending on North Front street.

26th. Tod Barracks Band. Fenian Brotherhood, right resting on corner of East Spring and High streets, left extending south on Third street.

27th. Mechanics' Association will form with right resting on the left of Fenian Brotherhood. Third street.

28th. St. Martin's and St. John's Benevolent Associations, right resting on corner of West Long and High streets, left extending north on Front.

The Butcher's Association will form with their right resting on the left of the St. Martin's and St. John's Benevolent Associations.

FIFTH DIVISION

Assistant Marshals—Colonel J. Wing and W. W. Bagley.

29th. Fire Department, right resting on corner of East Long and High streets, left extending on Long. Colored Masonic Orders, right resting on corner of East Gay and High streets, extending east on Gay. Colored Benevolent Association will form with their right resting on left of Colored Masonic Fraternity.

30th. All delegations from a distance will form with right resting on West Gay and North, left extending on North Front.

The different delegations are hereby directed to form in four ranks.

ROUTE OF PROCESSION

The procession will move promptly from south of the depot at 7:30 A. M., south on High street to Broad, east on Broad to Fourth, south on Fourth to State, east on State to Seventh, south on Seventh to Town, west on Town to

High, north on High to west front of the Capitol.

A mounted cavalry force will be stationed at all the intersections of High street north of Town street, for the purpose of preventing all vehicles from entering on High street—that it must be kept clear during the movements of the procession.

At 6 P. M. the Capitol will be closed. The procession will re-form in the following order to escort the remains to the depot.

Military escort.

Escort accompanying the remains.

Pall bearers.

Masonic Fraternity will form on East State street, the right resting on High.

Independent Order of Odd Fellows will form on East Broad street, right resting on High.

All other organizations will form on West Broad street, right resting on High.

All carriages, except those appropriated to the Escort Committee, will be under the charge of Assistant Marshals C. S. Dyer and H. M. Neil.

The guard at the Capitol will be under charge of Captain M. C. Wilkinson, 15th V. R. C.

JOHN W. SKILES,
Major and Grand Marshal.

Fourteen days from that on which the American people were shocked by the intelligence that a president, honored and loved for services more precious than any rendered by a chief magistrate since Washington retired to private life, had been assassinated, the remains of that president were brought to the capital of Ohio. A heavy rain fell on the night previous, and the early morning was gloomy, but about the hour appointed for the arrival of the funeral train the clouds broke away and the rain ceased. At the appointed hour the funeral train entered the Union Depot, amid the ringing of muffled bells, and stopped so that the funeral car lay nearly across High Street. An immense crowd of spectators was congregated in the vicinity of the depot. Bands of music, assembled with the military in procession, played solemn dirges while the coffin was taken from the car and laid in the hearse by a portion of the Veteran Reserve Corps, the other Veteran Reserves marching by its side with drawn sabers, attended by the pallbearers and military guard of honor.

The procession was then formed according to the program and was the most imposing and the most impressive which ever marched through the streets of Columbus. The slow, measured tread of the troops, the muffled drum, the dead march, the enshrouded colors, told their own tale of the fearfully solemn occasion on which they were passing in review before the assembled thousands as witnesses.

The hearse was the great center of attraction. All along the line of march it was preceded and followed by hundreds of all ages, sexes, and conditions, striving to keep as near as possible to the somber structure. It was seventeen feet long, eight and a half feet wide, and seventeen and a half feet from the ground to the apex of the canopy. The main platform was four feet from the ground, on which rested a dais for the reception of the coffin, twelve feet long by five wide, raised two and a half feet above the platform. The canopy resembled in shape a Chinese pagoda. The interior of the roof was lined with silk flags, and the outside covered with black broadcloth, as were the dais, the main platform, and the entire hearse. Black cloth, festooned, depended from the platform within a few inches of the ground, fringed with silver lace, and ornamented with heavy tassels of black silk. Surrounding the cornice of the canopy were thirty-six silver stars, and on the apex and the four corners were five heavy black plumes. The canopy was appropriately curtained with black cloth, lined with white merino. On each side of the dais was the word *Lincoln* in silver letters. The hearse was drawn by six white horses, covered with black cloth, which was edged with silver fringe. The heads of the horses were surmounted with large black plumes, and each was led by a groom dressed in black, with white gloves and a white band around his hat. On the dais, nearly in the center of the hearse, the coffin was placed in full view of the multitudes on the streets.

Every window, housetop, balcony, and every inch of the sidewalk on either side of High Street was densely crowded with a mournful throng, assembled to pay homage to departed worth. In all the enormous crowd profound silence reigned. Conversation was carried on in whispers. The completeness of every detail of the procession was remarked by all, and much praise awarded the committee of arrangements. The display made by the various orders and associations in the procession elicited universal commendation. The fire department was the subject of especial notice and praise. The neat, clean uniforms of the officers and men, the splendid condition of the steamers and hose-carts, and the decorated car filled with forty-two young ladies habited in deep mourning, were among the noticeable incidents of the day. A very impressive feature of the occasion was the singing by the young ladies in the mourning car of the fire department, of 1027th hymn of the Methodist Episcopal collection, commencing with:

"Great Ruler of the earth and skies,"

and the 1018th hymn, commencing with

"Behold, O Lord, before Thy Throne."

The route of the procession was south on High Street to Broad; east on Broad to Fourth; south on Fourth to State; east on State to Seventh; south on Seventh to Town; west on Town to High; north on High to the west front of the Capitol. Along the entire line of march, dwelling houses, shops, stores, and other places of business, as well as all public buildings, were tastefully and solemnly decorated. It is proper to mention, on East Broadway, the offices of the Adams and American Express companies, and the military offices in the Buckeye block. The seminary hospital was adorned with mottoes in wreaths of evergreens, a draped picture of President Lincoln, and draped flags; and when the procession passed it, the invalid soldiers strewed flowers before the hearse. The headquarters of provost marshal General Wilcox, on State Street, were very handsomely decorated. The north end and east front of the Market House, the Odd Fellows' Hall, and the Gwynne block were each appropriately dressed in mourning. On the large front of Kelton, Bancroft & Co.'s wholesale dry goods house, the national colors hung in rich heavy folds from the top of each of the windows, shrouded in black, and most tastefully arranged with President Lincoln's initial letters in the center. The various engine houses of the fire department were draped and adorned with appropriate mottoes. The towers, gable, offices, baggage rooms, and lamps of the Union Depot were heavily draped, as was also the office of the Little Miami Railroad Company. Among the most noticeable displays on High Street, we mention the First National Bank building, the store rooms of Bain & Son, Blynn, Smith & Conrad, Randall & Aston, Thrall & Benham, F. D. Clark, Griffin & Champion, Naughton, Fay, and J. D. Osborn & Co. The great feature of the decoration was found at the clothing house of Marcus Childs, in the Neil House building. Thousands of persons were attracted by the beauty and appropriateness of the designs and the very elegant manner in which they were carried out. Beginning at the south window we find them each draped with black cloth, relieved by white stars at regular intervals, and in established order. This window was adorned with the following mottoes:

"Servant of God, well done.
Thy race is o'er, thy victory won."

"The last Martyr for Freedom."

"Heaven but tries our virtues by affliction."

"East, West, North, and South mourn,
The greatest friend of suffering humanity is gone."

The President dies, we mourn;
The Nation lives, we rejoice."

The next window north:

"Our Country, Washington, Lincoln, Memoriori Eterna!"

"Memento Mori, Born Feb. 12th, 1809, Died April 15th, 1865."

"Too good for earth, to Heaven thou art fled,
And left the Nation in tears."

"He was a good man, and a just one."

The third window:

"Our Chief has fallen."

"In mourning tears the Nation's grief is spent,
Mankind has lost a friend, we a President."

"The Nation mourns."

"His memory, like the Union he preserved, is not for a day, but for all time."

"Weep, nature, weep, put on thy mourning garb."

The north window:

"We mourn our loss."

"We loved him, yes, no tongue can tell
How much we loved him, and how well."

"Fear not, Abraham, I am thy shield; thy reward shall be exceeding great."

"Only the actions of the just
Smell sweet and blossom in the dust."

"His noblest motive was the public good."

At the base of the front windows a draped portrait of Lincoln was exhibited, and each doorway was hung in heavy festoons of black cloth. Over all, a draped flag was extended.

The west gateway of the Capitol Square was arched and bore the simple inscription "Ohio Mourns." The columns at the west front of the Capitol were tastefully draped in spiral turns of mourning cloth from top to bottom. Immediately over the entrance (west front) was placed the inscription "God Moves in a Mysterious Way," and over the cornice of the columns was placed a quotation from President Lincoln's last inaugural address: "With Malice toward none; with Charity for all." Each of the windows in the west front was heavily draped.

At about nine o'clock the head of the procession arrived at the west entrance of Capitol Square. The 88th O. V. I., acting as special escort, passed in immediately, forming lines in two ranks on each side of the passway from the gate to the steps of the Capitol. During the momentary delay, the silence and deep feeling manifested by the people in the procession, by those crowding the streets in every direction, and by those gazing from every available window was without precedent. The gaze seemed to alternate between the coffin being removed from the hearse containing the man dead and his striking living utterance, "With malice toward none, with charity for all," looking down upon them from the architrave of the Capitol. As the coffin, borne upon the shoulders of eight of the sergeants constituting the Veteran Guard, passed toward the archway, the band gave expression to the solemn emotions of the hour in a dirge, the high officials in attendance assumed their places as escort, and thousands of bowed heads said as plainly as the letters arching the entrance, "Ohio Mourns." Slowly and solemnly the escort, headed by General Hooker and staff, and Governor Brough and staff, passed to the Capitol entrance, and reverently the coffin was lowered from the shoulders of the veterans to the flowery bed awaiting it. The officers named, with their attendants, Major General Hunter and staff, the general officers in charge of the corpse from Washington, General Wager Swayne and staff, and members of committees, assumed their proper places around the catafalque with uncovered heads; the guard from the Veteran Reserve Corps formed in line on each side, and, as soon as the corpse was in place, Rev. C. E. Felton offered an appropriate prayer. Impressive as was this scene, it was surpassed by the one that followed immediately on the opening of the coffin. Amid silence almost painful, the lid was raised—a sigh from those present—a slight movement by the undertaker—and for minutes all was again as still as death. The veteran officers and soldiers, with bowed heads, seemed immovable as statues; unconsciously every face mirrored the contending emotions of the heart, and the grouping around the dead of citizens and soldiers, seen by those forming the head of the procession at the foot of the western stairway, formed a scene never to be forgotten and not to be described. Mrs. Hoffner, representing the Horticultural Society of Cincinnati, the only lady present, stepped softly forward and placed at the foot of the coffin an anchor composed of delicate white flowers and evergreen boughs, a wreath of the same upon the breast of the dead, and a cross at the head. Instructions were given more by signs than words and arrangements made for the people to look upon the remains.

The rotunda of the Capitol, well calculated for display, grand in its loftiness, and much the resort of our people, was transformed into a gorgeous tomb. The column of light streaming down from the lofty dome made distinct and impressive each feature of the solemn scene below. There was no stiffness to jar with softened feeling, no unwonted display to mar the solemnity, but beautifully and simply grand as was the character of him whose mortal remains were to repose therein, the rotunda of Ohio's Capitol emblemed the sorrow of Ohio's people. The entranceways and the corresponding panels were uniformly draped with black cloth, falling in heavy folds from the arches to the floor. In the panels the drapings were gathered to the sides equidistant from arch to floor, and then allowed to fall in full volume, and closing at the bottom as at the top. In three of these central spaces thus formed were grouped the war-worn battle flags of veteran Ohio regiments. In the other panel, the one between the north and east entrances, tastefully mounted and appropriately draped, was Powell's painting, "Perry's Victory"; the grouping of the characters and the sublimity of the scene represented, adding much to the general and impressive beauty of the rotunda. Above the panels, entirely round the dome, were three rows of festoons with black and white pendants, the whole joining appropriately the general drapings below.

On a platform with a base of twenty-one and a half by twenty-eight feet, rising by five steps until it presented a top surface perhaps one-half as large, was placed the dais for the reception of the coffin. This platform, tastefully carpeted, the rise of each step dressed in black, was ornamented with emblematical flowers and plants in vases so arranged as to present, with their impression of beauty, the sorrow for the dead. At the corners facing the west entrance were large vases containing beautiful specimens of amaranth, and midway between them a grand central vase glowing with the richness and beauty of the choicest flowers of the season. A similar disposition of vases faced the east entrance, from the corner ones the flowers of the emblematical Justitia, reaching to the height of the dais. Around these large vases were grouped smaller ones, rising in gradations of beauty with the steps of the platform. The dais was most properly the crowning beauty of the structure, and in a brief description it is impossible to do it justice. Rectangular in form, with a side elevation of two feet, it was without canopy and beautifully ornamented. The sides were covered with black broadcloth, over which drooped from the top festoons of white merino and tassels of white silk. The end facing the west entrance bore inscribed, on a black panel with white border, in silver letters, the word "Lincoln." From the festooning at the top rose in graceful swell a bed of white roses, immortelles, and orange blossoms, the pure white relieved only by the deep fresh green of the leaves and sprigs accompanying.

The guard of honor was relieved by the following named officers, acting in the same capacity and under the immediate charge of Colonel J. A. Wilcox and Major L. S. Sullivant: Captain Douglas, 13th O. V. I.; Captain Stivers, U.S.A.; Captain Walker, 5th O. V. C.; Captain A. T. Wikoff, 91st O. V. I.; Captain McGroat, Captain Hull, 18th O. V. I.; Captain H. P. Wands, 22d Mich.; Captain Davis, 18th O. V. I.; Captain Hannal, 124th O. V. I.; Lieutenant Horringer, 2nd O. V. C.; Lieutenant J. H. Orr, 109th O. V. I.; Lieutenant H. B. Freeman, 18th O. V. I.;

Adjutant D. C. Patrick, and Lieutenants J. B. Dague, G. I. Davison, J. D. Wilson, and Norris Killen, of the 88th O. V. I.

The officers, pallbearers, and committees, after looking upon the remains, retired, excepting those having the body in charge. The officers forming the guard were assigned their positions, and without delay the people commenced moving in the rotunda. First came the various military organizations of the procession, the men formed in four ranks, marching without noise upon a carpet to the catafalque, passing by twos on each side of the coffin—the face and upper part of the body being brought in full view of each individual—and then those on the right passing out at the south and those on the left turning to the north. Then followed in order the various delegations of the procession, succeeded by the people *en masse*; the same order being preserved throughout the day.

The impressive solemnity with which the ceremonies were inaugurated continued without interruption. The officers on duty firmly but courteously enforced every rule, and the people seemed imbued with such a spirit that they all moved on as one person. Not an indecorous action, not a whispered word, not a frowning countenance marred the scene. The marked order, the seemliness of action, and the subdued demeanor of the multitude, composed of every class, age, and color, during the entire day, form a feature of this more than pageant that speaks louder than the most eloquent and pathetic words the people's love for Abraham Lincoln.

By actual count it was found that over eight thousand passed in and out every hour from half after nine until four o'clock, and, making due allowance, it is thought that over fifty thousand people viewed the remains in that time. The unparalleled good order prevailing at all times must remain ever a source of pride to all participating.

Many scenes during the day were affecting and impressive, but to chronicle them all would fill a volume. All felt the sorrow, and countenance and act mirrored it with striking plainness. Thousands of persons stood in line on High Street, four abreast; the lines extending in either direction, north from the west gateway to Long Street, and south from the west gateway to Rich Street, patiently awaiting their opportunity. Fore more than six hours a steady stream of humanity poured through the channel, all eager to gaze at the martyred president on his bier.

Long before the hour appointed for the delivery of the funeral oration, the east terrace of the Statehouse was crowded with men and women, who had gathered to hear the lessons which might be suggested from the exemplary life and violent death of Abraham Lincoln. A platform had been erected immediately in front of the entrance to the Capitol, and upon this platform, at three o'clock, appeared Major General Hunter, Major General Hooker, Major General Barnard, Brigadier General Townsend, Brigadier General McCallum, Colonel Swords, Colonel Simpson, Colonel Lathrop, Captain Taylor, Hon. T. B. Shannon of California, Hon. T. W. Terry of Michigan, Hon. Mr. Clarke of Kansas, the orator, Hon. Job E. Stevenson of Chillicothe, and Revs. E. P. Goodwin and C. E. Felton of Columbus. After appropriate music by military bands and the singing of a hymn by a choir, under the direction of J. A. Scarritt, a prayer, impressive in thought and earnest in manner and word, was offered by the pastor of the Congregational Church of Columbus, Mr. Goodwin. A solemn hymn was then sung by the choir. When Mr. Stevenson began his oration, a mournful quiet pervaded the large assembly. It was broken during the delivery of the oration only when the orator, alluding to the great crime which rebellion had instigated, demanded that justice be done the criminals and declared that conciliation of those who had murdered Mercy was condemned by the cries to heaven of thousands of soldiers murdered in rebel prisons—by bereaved homes in all loyal States. Mr. Stevenson's oration follows:

> *My Fellow Citizens:*—Ohio mourns, America mourns, the civilized world will mourn the cruel death of Abraham Lincoln, the brave, the wise, the good; bravest, wisest, best of men.
>
> History alone can measure and weigh his worth, but we, in parting from his mortal remains, may indulge the fullness of our hearts in a few broken words of his life and his death and his fame; his noble life and martyr's death, and matchless fame. A western farmer's son, self-made, in early manhood he won, by sterling qualities of head and heart, the public confidence, and was entrusted with the people's power. Growing with his growing State, he became a leader in the West.
>
> Elected President, he disbelieved the threats of traitors and sought to serve his term in peace. The clouds of civil war darkened the land. The President pleaded and prayed for peace, "long declined the war," and only when the storm broke in fury on the flag, did he arm for the Union.
>
> For four years the war raged, and the President was tried as a man was never tried before.
>
> Oh, "with what a load of toil and care" has he come, with steady, steadfast step, through the valley and shadow of defeat, over the bright

mountain of victory, up to the sunlit plain of peace.

Tried by dire disaster at Bull Run, where volunteer patriots met veteran traitors; at Fredericksburg, where courage contended with nature; at Chancellorsville, that desperate venture; in the dismal swamps of the Chickahominy, where a brave army was buried in vain; by the chronic siege of Charleston; the mockery of Richmond, and the dangers at Washington—through all these trials the President stood firm, trusting in God and people, while the people trusted in God and in him.

There were never braver men than the Union volunteers; none braver ever rallied in Grecian phalanx or Roman legion; none braver ever bent the Saxon bow, or bore barbarian battle-ax, or set the lance in rest; none braver ever followed the crescent or the cross, or fought with Napoleon, or Wellington, or Washington. Yet the Commander-in-Chief of the Union army and navy was worthy of the men filling for four years the foremost and most perilous post unfaltering.

Tried by good fortune, he saw the soldiers of the west recover the great valley, and bring back to the Union the Father of Waters, and all his beautiful children; he saw the legions of Lee hurled from the heights of Gettysburg; he saw the flag of the free rise on Lookout Mountain and spread from the river to the sea, and rest over Sumter; he saw the Star Spangled Banner, brightened by the blaze of battle, bloom over Richmond, and he saw Lee surrender. Yet, he remained wise and modest, giving all the glory to God and our army and navy.

Tried by civil affairs, which would have taxed the powers and tested the virtue of Jefferson, Hamilton and Washington, he administered them so wisely and well, that after three years no man was found to take his place. He was re-elected and the harvest of success came in so grandly, that he might have said; "Now Lord lettest thou thy servant depart in peace, for mine eyes have seen thy salvation." Yet he was free from the weakness of vanity.

Thus did he exhibit, on occasion, in due proportion and harmonious action, those cardinal virtues, the trinity of true greatness—courage, wisdom and goodness;—goodness to love the right, and courage to do the right. Tried by these tests and by the touch-stone of success, he was the greatest of living men.

He stood on the summit, his brow bathed in the beams of the rising sun of peace, singing in his heart the angelic song of "Glory to God in the highest; peace on earth; good will to man."

"With malice toward none, and charity for all," he had forgiven the people of the South, and might have forgotten their leaders—covering with the broad mantle of his charity their multitude of sins.

But he is slain—slain by slavery. That fiend incarnate did the deed. Beaten in battle, the leaders sought to save slavery by assassination. Their madness presaged their destruction.

Abraham Lincoln was the personification of Mercy. Andrew Johnson is the personification of Justice.

They have murdered Mercy, and Justice reigns alone—and the people, with one voice, pray to heaven that justice may be done. The mere momentum of our victorious armies will crush every rebel in arms, and then may our eyes behold the majesty of the law. They have appealed to the sword;—if they were tried by the laws of war, their barbarous crimes against humanity would doom them to death.

The blood of thousands of murdered prisoners cries to heaven. The shades of sixty-two thousand starved soldiers rise up in judgment against them. The body of the murdered President condemns them. Some deprecate vengeance. There is no room for vengeance here. Long before justice can have her perfect work the material will be exhausted, and the record closed.

Some wonder why the South killed her best friend. Abraham Lincoln was the true friend of the people of the South; for he was their friend as Jesus is the friend of sinners—ready to save when they repent. He was not the friend of rebellion, of treason, of slavery—he was their boldest and strongest foe, and therefore they slew him—but in his death they die; the people have judged them, and they stand convicted, smitten with remorse and dismay—while the cause for which the President perished, sanctified by his blood, grows stronger and brighter. These are some of the consequences of the death of Abraham Lincoln. Ours is the grief—theirs the loss, and his is the gain. He died for Liberty and Union, and now he wears the martyr's glorious crown. He is our crowned President. While the Union survives—while the love of Liberty warms the human heart, Abraham Lincoln will hold high rank among the immortal dead.

The nation is saved and redeemed. She needs no aid from rebel hands to reconstruct the Union. The Union needs no reconstruction. It was not made by man; it was created by the God of Nations. It is vital and immortal. If it has wounds in members of its body, they will heal, and leave no scar, without the opiate of compromise with treason. Let us beware of the Delilah of the South, who has so lately betrayed our strong man. Let the "Prodigals" feed on the husks till they come in repentance, and ask to be received in their father's house—not as the equals to their faithful brethren, but on a level with their former servants. Then we can consider their petition, and discuss the question, not of the reconstruction of the Union, but of the formation of free States from the national domain. Until then let the sword which reclaimed their territory rule it, tempered by national law. Some cry conciliation, and say there can be no true peace by conquest. On the contrary, there is no enduring peace but the peace that is conquered. The peace of France is a conquered peace; the peace of England was conquered and conquered again; the peace of our fathers was a conquered peace; the peace of the world is a conquered peace; the peace of Heaven is a conquered peace; and thanks be to God, our peace is to be a conquered, and therefore a lasting peace. For a thousand years shall the people enjoy Liberty and Union in peace and security. The nation revived through all her members by the hand of free labor, prosperity shall fill and overflow the land—roll along the railways—thrill the electric wires—pulsate on the rivers—blossom on the lakes, and whiten the seas; and the imperial free Republic, the best and strongest Government on earth, will be a monument of the glory of Abraham Lincoln—while over and above all, shall rise and swell the great "dome of his fame."

When the orator took his seat, earnest and solemn manifestations of approval testified that he had appropriately and impressively spoken for the people.

Immediately there were cries for Hooker. Major General Hooker rose from his seat when the band began to play a dirge. He stood until the music stopped and then administered those who called for him a just rebuke.

General Hooker said: "My friends, I thank you very much for the compliment you pay me by your call. If I do not respond by remarks, you will ascribe it to the inappropriateness of the occasion. You call was dictated by curiosity as much as to hear a speech from me; that I grant you. Further you must excuse me."

This frank speech was received in the spirit which dictated it. The ceremonies were then concluded by the singing of the ode written by William Cullen Bryant, which formed a part of the funeral ceremonies in New York.

The hour for the removal of the coffin from the rotunda having nearly arrived, a majority of the people who had listened to the funeral oration quietly wended their way toward High Street, which was densely thronged, until the cortege was reformed and moved to the depot.

At six o'clock in the evening the doors of the Capitol were closed, the bugle sounded the assembly, the soldiers took arms, and the procession began reforming for the final escort to the depot. As the body was being borne out to the funeral car at the west gateway of the Capitol grounds, a national salute was fired. Soon after, the procession moved, and the remains of the president were transferred to the funeral car at the depot of the Indiana Central Railway for transportation to Indianapolis.

The committee superintending the catafalque in the rotunda determined to allow it to remain until the remains of Lincoln were consigned to the tomb at Springfield; and it is to be recorded as a memorable deed for the citizens of Columbus, that every morning until that of the 4th of May, fresh flowers were placed around the dais where the president's coffin had rested, and thousands of men, women, and children visited and revisited the catafalque, and again and again with sad emotion viewed the symbols of grief which decorated the rotunda of Ohio's Capitol, in which, in February, 1861, Mr. Lincoln had been given the most enthusiastic reception ever bestowed by the people of Ohio upon a citizen of the Republic.

The funeral train left Columbus at eight o'clock. B. E. Smith, Esq., president, and J. M. Lunt, Esq., superintendent of the Columbus and Indianapolis Central Railway, accompanied it, giving personal attention to the wants and wishes of the passengers. They had with them Messrs. Blemer and Cummings, chief track men, and William Slater, telegraphic operator, with all the necessary implements for immediate repair. S. A. Hughes, Esq., as conductor, and Mr. James Gounley, engineer, were in charge of the train.

At Pleasant Valley, bonfires lit up the country for miles. A large concourse of citizens assembled around the depot. Two American flags, draped in mourning, were held in hand by two ladies. At Unionville about two hundred persons present, most of them sitting in wagons— the people having come from the country. At Milford, assembled around bonfires, four or five hundred people waved flags and handkerchiefs slowly. About two miles from that place a farmer and his family were standing in a field by a bonfire, waving a flag. At Woodstock about five hundred people greeted the train. The ladies presented bouquets; one by Miss Villard, Miss Lucy Kimble and Miss Mary Cranston, on the part of the ladies of Woodstock; another by Miss Ann Currier; and another by Mrs. G. Martin and Miss Delilah Beltz, two sisters. These ladies were permitted to enter the president's car and strew flowers on the coffin. The Woodstock Cornet Band, U. Cushman, leader, played a dirge and hymn—"Dreaming, I Sleep, Love," and Pleyel's Hymn. The village bells slowly rang; men stood silent with uncovered heads. A soldier stood in the center of an assemblage holding a flag. All men stood uncovered.

Urbana was reached at ten o'clock, forty minutes. Not less than three thousand people had gathered near the depot. On the platform was a large cross, entwined with circling wreaths of evergreens, which was worked under the direction of Mrs. Milo G. Williams, president, Ladies' Soldiers' Aid Society. From the top of the cross, and shorter arms, were hung illuminated colored transparencies. On the opposite side of the track was an elevated platform, on which were forty gentlemen and ladies, who sang with patriotic sweetness the hymn entitled, "Go to Thy Rest." The singing represented the Methodist, Baptist, Episcopalian, and Presbyterian churches. Large bonfires made night as light as day. Minute guns were fired. Ten young ladies entered the car and strewed flowers on the martyr's bier. One of the ladies was so affected that she cried and wept in great anguish.

At St. Paris were brilliant illuminations, by which could be seen a number of drooped flags, a large assembly present, who stood in silence as they looked on the moving train. A bouquet was presented and placed on the coffin by Mrs. Purron. The bouquet was a most artistic one made by Stoutey Meyer. At Westville Station crowds were gathered to pay respect to the dead. At Conover a long line of people two deep stood in file; on the right little boys and girls, then young men and women, and on the left the elderly people. In the center, supporting a large American flag, were three young ladies, Miss Eliza Throckmorton, Miss Nora Brecount, and Miss Barnes. A patriotic religious song, with a slow and mournful air, was chanted by the flag-bearers.

At twenty minutes past twelve o'clock the train reached Piqua. Not less than ten thousand people crowded about it. The Troy Band and the Piqua Band played appropriate music, after which a delegation from the Methodist churches, under Rev. Granville (Colonel) Moody, sang a hymn. Rev. Moody repeated the first line, when it was sung by the entire choir. Think of such actions at the midnight hour, when humanity is supposed to lay by its cares and take its rest in the arms of repose. At Gettysburg was a large number of people around huge bonfires. Drooping flags and other evidences of mourning were displayed. There were like scenes at Richmond Junction and Covington.

At Greenville, Ohio, thirty-six young ladies dressed in white, slowly waving the star spangled banner, greeted the cortege. Lafayette's Requiem was sung with thrilling effect by a number of ladies and gentlemen. About five hundred people were congregated on the platform. Company C, 28th Ohio Infantry, was drawn up in line with firearms reversed. The depot was tastefully decorated. On either side of the depot were two bonfires fifteen feet high, which shed most brilliant light all around the train and depot.

At New Paris great bonfires lit up the skies. A crowd was gathered about, who stood with uncovered heads. A beautiful arch of evergreens was formed above the track, under which the train passed. The arch was twenty feet high and thirty feet in circumference. At Wiley's, New Madison, and Weaver's Stations, hundreds of mourners were congregated.

The funeral train was delivered just across the line, at Richmond, by the Ohio officials to Governor Morton of Indiana and his suite.

Thus Ohio, honoring Lincoln in his lifetime, gave him her supreme homage at his death.

NOTES

¹Thomas Corwin, born in Bourbon County, Kentucky, July 29, 1794; served as a wagon-boy in the war of 1812; elected to the Ohio legislature in 1822 and in 1829; member of Congress 1831–1841; governor, 1841–43; United States senator, 1845; secretary of the treasury under President Fillmore, 1850–52; member of Congress, 1859–61; minister to Mexico from March 1861 to May 1864; died in Washington, D. C., December 18, 1865.

²Joshua Reed Giddings, born in Athens, Pennsylvania, October 6, 1795; in 1805 came with his parents to Wayne Township, Ashtabula County, Ohio; volunteer in the War of 1812; admitted to the Bar, 1820; elected to the Ohio legislature, 1826; member of Congress, 1839–59; conspicuous as an anti-slavery leader; consul general in Canada from 1861 until he died in Montreal, Canada, May 27, 1864.

³Peter Hitchcock, born in Cheshire, Connecticut, October 19, 1781; died in Painesville, Ohio, May 11, 1853; graduated from Yale, 1801; removed to Geauga County, Ohio, 1806; served in the Ohio legislature, 1810–1816; elected to Congress, 1816; served as judge of the Supreme Court twenty-eight years, retiring in 1852; delegate to Constitutional Convention in 1850.

⁴Timothy D. Lincoln was born in Brimfield, Massachusetts, May 11, 1815; educated at Wesleyan University, Middletown, Connecticut; settled in Cincinnati, 1841; admitted to the Bar by the state Supreme Court, 1842; had an extensive practice in admiralty, insurance, and patent law; ranked high at the Ohio Bar; died April 1, 1890.

⁵Samuel Galloway, born in Gettysburg, Pennsylvania, March 20, 1811; died in Columbus, Ohio, April 5, 1872; removed to Ohio in 1819; graduated at

Miami, 1833; taught until 1842; admitted to the Bar, 1842; practiced law at Chillicothe until 1844; elected secretary of state, 1844, served eight years; elected to Congress, 1854; defeated by S. S. Cox in 1856 and 1858; was active in organizing the Republican Party.

[6]Edwin M. Stanton, born in Steubenville, Ohio, December 19, 1814; died in Washington, D. C., December 24, 1869; admitted to the Bar, 1833; reporter of Ohio Supreme Court, 1842–1845; attorney general under President Buchanan; appointed secretary of war by President Lincoln, January 15, 1862, served throughout the administration and part of Johnson's administration; appointed by President Grant as justice of the Supreme Court four days before his death.

[7]William L. Dickson was born in Scott County, Indiana, September 19, 1827; he was a distinguished member of the Cincinnati Bar for thirty years; was an uncompromising abolitionist; organized the first colored regiment during the Civil War; was the confidant of Lincoln, Stanton, and Chase; died, October 15, 1889.

[8]Nicholas Longworth was born at Newark, New Jersey, January 16, 1782; in 1803 settled in Cincinnati and admitted to the Bar; after twenty-five years experience at the Bar, he devoted himself to the cultivation of the grape, upon which he became the greatest authority in America; he is known as the father of American grape culture; died in Cincinnati, 1863.

[9]William Dennison, born in Cincinnati, Ohio, November 23, 1815; graduated from Miami University, 1835; admitted to the Bar, 1840, and removed to Columbus; elected to state Senate, 1845; governor, 1860–1862; postmaster general in President Lincoln's cabinet, 1864–1866; died in Columbus, Ohio, June 15, 1882.

[10]Rufus P. Ranney, born in Blandford, Massachusetts, October 13, 1813; family removed to Portage County, Ohio, 1827; admitted to the Bar, 1838; was member of the state Constitutional Convention of 1850; elected under the Constitution to the Supreme Court, and served until 1857; in 1859 was defeated as Democratic candidate for governor; elected judge of the Supreme Court in 1862; resigned in 1864; died, December 6, 1891.

[11]Allen G. Thurman, born at Lynchburg, Virginia, November 13, 1813; came with his parents to Chillicothe, Ohio, 1819; admitted to the Bar, 1835; member of Congress, 1845–47; served as judge of the Supreme Court, 1851–56; declined reelection to the bench and resumed the practice of law; unsuccessful candidate for governor, 1867; United States senator, 1869–81; Democratic candidate for vice president, 1888; died at Columbus, Ohio, December 12, 1895.

[12]Thomas Ewing, born at West Liberty, Virginia, December 28, 1789; died at Lancaster, Ohio, October 26, 1871; removed with his family in 1792 to what is now Athens County, Ohio; entered Ohio University at Athens, where in 1815 he received the first degree of B. A. that was ever granted in the Northwest; admitted to the Bar in 1816; served as United States senator, 1831–1837, and 1850–1861; secretary of the treasury under President Harrison, 1841; secretary of the interior under President Taylor, 1849; in the Supreme Court he ranked among the leading lawyers of the nation.

[13]Henry Stanbery, born in New York City, February 2, 1803; removed with his parents to Zanesville, Ohio; admitted to the Bar, 1824; attorney general of Ohio, 1846; member of the Constitutional Convention, 1850; attorney general of the United States under President Johnson, 1866–67; resigned that office to serve as counsel for the president in the impeachment trial; was afterward nominated to the Supreme Court of the United States, but not confirmed; died in New York City, June 26, 1881.

[14]Stephen A. Douglas, born in Brandon, Vermont, April 23, 1813; died in Chicago, Illinois, June 3, 1861; settled in Illinois, 1833; admitted to the Bar, 1834; became prominent in the Democratic Party of his state and remained so until his death; served as judge of the Supreme Court of Illinois, member of Congress, and United States senator, and in 1860 was candidate of his party for president being defeated by Lincoln.

[15]James Ford Rhodes: *History of the United States*, Vol. I, p. 496.

[16]*Ex Parte Bushnell*, 9 *Ohio State Reports*, pp. 77–325.

[17]Randall and Ryan: *History of Ohio*, Vol. IV, pp. 135–138.

[18]Salmon P. Chase, born in Cornish, New Hampshire, January 13, 1808; admitted to the Bar and established himself in Cincinnati in 1830; elected United States senator in 1849, and governor in 1855 and 1857; secretary of the treasury under Lincoln from 1861 to June 30, 1864; chief justice of the Supreme Court of the United States from December 6, 1864, until his death in New York City, May 7, 1873.

[19]John Sherman, born at Lancaster, Ohio, May 10, 1823; admitted to the Bar, 1844; elected to Congress, 1854; served until he entered the Senate March 4, 1861; reelected in 1867 and 1873; resigned to become secretary of the treasury under President Hayes in 1877; returned to the Senate, 1881; served until March, 1897, when he resigned to become secretary of state under President McKinley; resigned that position in 1898; died in Washington, D.C., October 22, 1900.

[20]George E. Pugh, born in Cincinnati, November 28, 1822; served in the Mexican War; served in the Ohio legislature, 1848–49; was attorney general of Ohio 1852–54; United States senator from December 1855 to March 1861; defended Clement L. Vallandigham in *habeas corpus* proceedings in 1863; died in Cincinnati, July 19, 1876.

[21]Samuel S. Cox, born in Zanesville, Ohio, September 30, 1824; member of Congress from Ohio, 1857–65, and from New York, 1869–1885, and 1886–89; served for a short time as minister to Turkey; author: *Eight Years in Congress*; *Why We Laugh*; *Diversion of a Diplomat in Turkey*; *A Buckeye Abroad*; *Arctic Sunbeams*; *Orient Sunbeams*; *Search for Winter Sunbeams*; etc.; died in New York, September 10, 1889.

[22]George H. Pendleton, born in Cincinnati, Ohio, July 25, 1825; served in state Senate, 1854–55; member of Congress, 1856–65; opposed the Lincoln administration during the war; candidate for vice president on the Democratic ticket in 1864; elected United States senator 1878; in 1882 introduced the Civil Service bill, which was passed in 1883; appointed minister to Germany, 1885; died at Brussels, Belgium, November 24, 1889.

[23]William Allen, born in Edenton, North Carolina, December 1803; walked in winter from Lynchburg, Virginia, to Chillicothe, Ohio, where his half-sister, mother of Allen G. Thurman, was living; in 1832 elected member of Congress and served 1833–35; served in United States Senate, 1837–49; governor of Ohio 1874–76; died July 11, 1879.

[24]George H. Porter: *Ohio Politics During the Civil War Period*, p. 26.

[25]The speech of Douglas at Columbus was telegraphed in full to the *New York Times*; this was regarded at the time as a remarkable piece of newspaper enterprise.

[26]*Lincoln–Douglas Debates*. Columbus, O., 1860, pp. 240–254.

[27]Mrs. Alice Corner Brown in *History of Columbus*, by Osman C. Hooper, p. 44.

[28]Addison Peale Russell, born in Wilmington, Ohio, September 8, 1826; served in Ohio legislature, 1855–57; secretary of state, 1857–61. Author: *Half Tints*, 1867; *Library Notes*, 1884; *A Club of One*; *In a Club Corner*, 1890; *Sub-Coelum*, 1893; died July 24, 1912.

[29]Rutherford Birchard Hayes, born in Delaware, Ohio, October 4, 1822; graduated from Kenyon College, 1842; admitted to the Bar, 1845; became city

solicitor of Cincinnati, 1858; served with distinction during the Civil War, rising to brevet major general, March 13, 1865; member of Congress, 1865-67, and reelected; governor, 1868-1872; reelected for third term, 1875; nineteenth president of the United States, 1877-81; died at Fremont, Ohio, January 17, 1893.

30Moncure Daniel Conway: *Autobiography, Memories and Experiences*, Vol. I, p. 317.

31Charles Richard Williams: *Life of Rutherford Birchard Hayes*, Vol. I, p. 3.

32*Lincoln–Douglas Debates*, p. III.

33*Political Debates between Hon. Abraham Lincoln and Hon. Stephen A. Douglas in the Celebrated Campaign of 1858, in Illinois, Including the Preceding Speeches of Each at Chicago, Springfield, etc.; Also the Two Great Speeches of Mr. Lincoln in Ohio in 1859, as Carefully Prepared by the Reporters of Each Party, and Published at the Times of Their Delivery.* Columbus: Follett, Foster and Company, 1860. Very scarce and usually quoted as *Lincoln–Douglas Debates*.

34James Ford Rhodes: *History of the United States*, Vol. II, p. 343.

35James Ford Rhodes: *History of the United States*, Vol. II, p. 458.

36Since the days of Clay and Webster no man has spoken to a larger assemblage of the intellect and mental culture of our city. . . . No man ever before made such an impression on his first appeal to a New York audience—*New York Tribune*, February 23, 1860.

37The original is in the autograph collection of former Governor James E. Campbell, president of the Ohio State Archaeological and Historical Society.

38*Proceedings of the First Three Republican National Conventions of 1856, 1860, and 1864, Including Proceedings of the Antecedent National Convention Held at Pittsburgh in February 1856, as Reported by Horace Greely.* Published and Copyrighted by Charles W. Johnson, Minneapolis, Minn., p. 173.

39*Caucuses of 1860. A History of the National Political Conventions of the Current Presidential Campaign: by M. Halstead, an Eye Witness of Them All*. Columbus: Follett, Foster and Company, 1860, p. 143.

40*Proceedings of the First Three Republican National Conventions, etc.*; p. 148.

[41] Murat Halstead: *Caucuses of 1860, etc.*; p. 145.

[42] Joseph P. Smith: *History of the Republican Party in Ohio*, Vol. I, pp. 116–118. Remarkable for its accuracy and comprehensiveness.

[43] Norton S. Townshend, alternate for James Monroe of Oberlin, delegate from the 11th district, who was absent.

[44] *Proceedings of the First Three Republican National Conventions, etc.*, p. 153. Note the discrepancy between Cartter's announcement and the fact; only three of the votes were changed from Chase. See also William Henry Smith: *A Political History of Slavery*, Vol. I, p. 292. Joseph P. Smith: *History of the Republican Party of Ohio*, Vol. I, pp. 116–118.

[45] Murat Halstead: *Caucuses of 1860, etc.*, p. 149.

[46] Robert B. Warden: *An Account of the Private Life and Public Services of Salmon Portland Chase*, p. 363.

[47] I saw Lincoln on this occasion. I had just entered upon my seventh year, when one cold sunshiny morning my mother, wrapping me up snugly said, "We are going to see Abe Lincoln." What this name stood for I did not then know, but I had heard it for months in the home; we children shouted it shrilly day by day, and I heard marching men cheer for it. But I knew he was a great big man, and that he was on his way to be President. So far as the events of this day are concerned, they stand out in my memory with certainty. I remember as well as if it were yesterday my excited mother tying a "comforter" about my neck, of her putting on her shawl and bonnet, and finally of her cutting slices of bread, buttering them and wrapping them in paper. Before the day was over I saw her wisdom in this. Then almost on a run we started for the depot, which was only two squares away. We found seats on a lumber pile, and there sat for hours. Late in the afternoon the train came. The crowd surged and almost pushed us from our position. My mother stood firm, and to save me from being crushed she lifted me upon her head, and there I sat, she looking between my legs. We were close to where Lincoln passed. I could see him plainly. His figure is now historic, made so by his eventful life and tragic death, but even then to a boy in his seventh year he was impressive in form and bearing. I remember his face was such as would naturally attract a child; while it was grave, it was kind, and had nothing of repelling solemnity about it. I saw his tall form step into his carriage which was driven off amidst a pageantry of colors and beauty. Thus was given to a boy the inestimable privilege, which has been a lifetime pride and satisfaction of seeing Lincoln, one of the greatest characters God has given to the human race.—D. J. R.

[48]Cincinnati *Daily Gazette*, February 13, 1861.

[49]Cincinnati *Daily Gazette*, February 13, 1861.

[50]William Henry Smith, born in Austerlitz, New York, December 1, 1833. He was editorial writer on the Cincinnati *Daily Gazette* at the opening of the Civil War; was active in raising troops; elected secretary of state of Ohio in 1864, and reelected in 1866; appointed collector of the port of Chicago in 1877; became manager of Associated Press in 1883; was an authoritative writer on historical subjects. Compiled *The St. Clair Papers*, 2 volumes, wrote *A Political History of Slavery*, 2 volumes, a biography of Charles Hammond, and many historical essays and addresses. Died at Lake Forest, Illinois, July 27, 1896.

[51]Francis E. Browne: *The Every-Day Life of Lincoln*, pp. 271–273.

[52]Lincoln stopped at this hotel on his last visit in 1859. Judge Dickson tells this incident concerning it: When Lincoln was about to depart he asked for his bill and was informed that it was paid. After he was nominated a letter and bill came to him requesting payment, which evidently was neglected by the committee, and the hotel proprietor shrewdly surmised that this was a good time to collect. Lincoln was indignant at this seeming imputation against his honor, and especially so at one item, of which he wrote, "as to wines, liquors, and cigars, we had none—absolutely none. These last may have been in Room 15 by order of the committee, but I do not recollect them at all." Needless to say, he did not pay the bill.

[53]Cincinnati *Daily Gazette*, February 12, 1861.

[54]Charles Richard Williams: *The Life of Rutherford Birchard Hayes*, Vol. I, p. 118.

[55]Cincinnati *Daily Gazette*, February 13, 1861.

[56]Cincinnati *Daily Gazette*, February 14, 1861.

[57]William T. Coggeshall: *The Journeys of Lincoln*, published by the *Ohio State Journal*, Columbus, 1865, p. 42.

[58]*Journal of the House of Representatives*. Second Session, Fifty-Fourth General Assembly, Columbus, Ohio, 1861, p. 173.

[59]*Ohio State Journal*, February 14, 1861.

⁶⁰William T. Coggeshall, born in Lewiston, Pennsylvania, September 6, 1824; connected with Cincinnati *Commercial Gazette*, 1854–6; state librarian, 1856–62; served on staff of Governor Dennison; in charge of *Ohio State Journal*, 1865; had resigned from army on account of ill health; served on the staff of Governor Cox, 1866; minister to Ecuador. Author of *The Genius of the West, Poets and Poetry of the West, The Journeys of Lincoln, Stories of Frontier Adventure*, and contributed much to periodical literature. Died at Quito, Ecuador, August 6, 1867.

⁶¹William T. Coggeshall: *The Journeys of Lincoln*, pp. 49–50.

⁶²William T. Coggeshall: *The Journeys of Lincoln*, pp. 56–58.

⁶³Cincinnati *Daily Gazette*, February 16, 1861.

⁶⁴The late William G. Deshler of Columbus, one of the leading bankers of Ohio, told me that he, with Governor Dennison, stood by Lincoln at the library steps when he received the immense crowd on the occasion of his inaugural visit. Mr. Deshler said that many of the crowd openly expressed disapproval of his speech on the west front of the Statehouse. Some did so graciously, some rudely, some with regret. One, enthusiastic from refreshments, said, "Abe, you've got to give them rebels hotter shot than that before they're licked." Lincoln laughed and passed his visitor on. Mr. Deshler said Governor Dennison and many prominent Republicans in the legislature were disappointed with Lincoln's speeches in Columbus.—D. J. R.

⁶⁵If the Cotton States shall decide that they can do better out of the Union than in it, we insist on letting them go in peace.—New York *Tribune*, November 9, 1860.

⁶⁶Edward McPherson: *The Political History of the United States of America During the Great Rebellion*, p. 60, note.

⁶⁷J. P. Usher, assistant secretary and secretary of the interior, in: *Reminiscences of Abraham Lincoln by Distinguished Men of His Time*. Edited by Allen Thorndyke Rice, p. 211.

⁶⁸At first these editorials puzzled me very much; they were against all the traditions of the *Journal*. A Whig organ from the founding of that party, it became an active force in the organizing of the Republican Party. It had none of the motives of the other papers herein quoted. As its constituency was not interested in Southern trade, nor was the paper of Abolition antecedents. Upon reading W. D. Howells' "Years of My Youth" written fifty-seven years

after these editorials, I began to see light. In this work, the last of his life, he dwells upon the days when he was on this paper. The editor and part proprietor was Henry D. Cooke of Sandusky (a brother of Jay Cooke) who came to Columbus to "rehabilitate" the *Journal*. He was a busy man and finally turned over the editorial work to two young men in their early twenties—Joseph Price and W. D. Howells. "We both wrote leading editorials, which our chief supervised and censored for a while, and then let them go as we wrote them, perhaps finding no great mischief in them." Thus in these perilous and critical days the policy of the *Journal* was in the hands of these two boys, one an opinionated doctrinaire and the other what Senator Chandler used to call "one of them damn literary fellows." There were a good many views floating around those days, emotional and otherwise, even in the Republican Party. Howells says his chief had no well defined policy. If the young editors had understood that it was unnecessary in a paper that had helped elect Lincoln to have any policy other than that of supporting him, this would have saved their chief worry. But it was otherwise, and he writes a confession and apology: "If his subordinates had any settled policy, it was to get what fun they could out of the sentimentalists, and if they had any fixed belief it was that if we had a war peace must be made on the basis of disunion when the war was over. In our wisdom we doubted if the sections could ever live together in a union which they had fought for and against. But we did not say this in print, though as matters grew more hopeless Price one day seized the occasion of declaring that the Constitution was a rope of sand. I do not remember what occasion he had for saying this, but it brought our chief actively back to censorship; Price's position was somewhat explained away, and we went on much as before, much as everybody else went on. I will not, in the confession of our youthful rashness, pretend that there were any journalists who seemed then or seem wiser now or acted with greater forecast; and I am sure that we always spoke from our consciences, with a settled conviction that the South was wrong."

The editorials on secession, on the expulsion of South Carolina, and the failure of the Union, did great harm at the time, as the *Journal*, next to the Cincinnati *Gazette*, was the most influential Republican paper in the state. — D. J. R.

[69] George H. Porter: *Ohio Politics During the Civil War Period*, p. 52.

[70] James Ford Rhodes: *History of the United States*, Vol. III, p. 302.

[71] 58 *Ohio Laws*, pp. 89, 107, 132.

[72] Clement Laird Vallandigham was born at New Lisbon, Ohio, July 29, 1820; admitted to Bar, 1842; in Ohio House of Representatives, 1845–46;

edited *Dayton Empire*, 1847–49; candidate for Congress against Lewis D. Campbell in 1847; defeated, but seated on a contest; served from May 25, 1858 until March 3, 1863; nominated for governor of Ohio, June 11, 1863; defeated by John Brough, Union candidate; delegate to Democratic conventions of 1864 and 1868; died at Lebanon, Ohio, June 17, 1871; his death resulted from the accidental discharge of a pistol in his own hands while illustrating his theory of how a certain homicide occurred in which he was defending the accused.

[73]*A Life of Clement L. Vallandigham, by His Brother, Rev. James L. Vallandigham*, 1872, pp. 141–142.

[74]*The Record of Hon. C. L. Vallandigham on Abolition, the Union and the Civil War*, 1863, pp. 88, 91.

[75]*A Life of Clement L. Vallandigham, by His Brother, Rev. James L. Vallandigham*, p. 161.

[76]On this subject: *Ohio Politics During the Civil War Period*; George H. Porter, 1911; Randall and Ryan's *History of Ohio*, 1912, Vol. IV, chaps. 7, 8, 9, 10; *The Civil War Literature of Ohio, A Bibliography with Explanatory Notes*; Daniel J. Ryan, 1911.

[77]*The Record of Hon. C. L. Vallandigham*, pp. 173–204. Daniel J. Ryan: *The Civil War Literature of Ohio*, pp. 433–434.

[78]*The Record of Hon. C. L. Vallandigham*, pp. 168–204. Daniel J. Ryan: *The Civil War Literature of Ohio*, pp. 434–435.

[79]*Report of the Judge Advocate General on "The Order of American Knights," alias "The Sons of Liberty," A Western Conspiracy in Aid of the Southern Rebellion.* Washington, D.C., 1864.

In *The Civil War Literature of Ohio*, pp. 329–330, the report is summarized thus: "Under the instruction of the Secretary of War, Joseph Holt, Judge Advocate General, made an investigation in regard to the Secret Associations and Conspiracies against the Government. On October 8, 1864, this report was filed; it is based on testimony furnished from different sources. It forms one of the most important documents of the war, and has a decided connection with military and political affairs in Ohio during the years 1863 and 1864. In this report the Judge Advocate General exposes the origin, extent, organization, history, purposes, ritual, members, and operation of the various secret political bodies existing in the North, but sympathizing with the Southern Confederacy. They were located in nearly every Northern state, but were most numerous in Ohio, Indiana, Illinois, Missouri, and Kentucky. It is declared that the scene of operations in Ohio was in Cincinnati, Dayton, and Hamilton, and that C. L. Vallandigham was the founder of the order. The force of the order in Ohio is stated at from 80,000 to 108,000.

"The report declares that the purposes of the 'Order of American Knights,' or 'Sons of Liberty,' were: To aid desertions from the Union Armies; to circulate disloyal publications; to give intelligence to the enemy; to aid recruiting for the Confederates within the Union lines; to furnish the enemy with arms and supplies; to co-operate in Confederate raids and invasions; to destroy government property; to persecute and impoverish Union men; to assassinate those of special influence or in high authority; and to set up a Northwestern Confederacy.

" 'While the capacity of this order for fatal mischief,' said Judge Holt, 'has, by means of the arrest of its leaders, the seizure of its arms, and the other vigorous means which have been pursued, been seriously impaired, it is still busy with its secret plottings against the government, and with its perfidious designs in aid of the Southern Rebellion. It is reported to have recently issued new designs and passwords, and its members assert that foul means will be used to prevent the success of the Administration at the coming election, and threaten an extended revolt in the event of the re-election of President Lincoln.'

"This report contains much that is important and valuable, and a knowledge of it is necessary to a proper conception of the political condition of Ohio and the North at this period."

[80]*The Trial of Hon. Clement L. Vallandigham by a Military Commission; and the Proceedings under His Application for a Writ of Habeas Corpus in the Circuit Court of the United States for the Southern District of Ohio*, Cincinnati, 1863, pp. 7, 11, *et seq.*

[81]Edward McPherson: *The Political History of the United States of America During the Great Rebellion*, 1865, pp. 163–167.

[82]James Ford Rhodes: *History of the United States*, Vol. IV, p. 257. Herein is quoted testimony of General Joseph E. Hooker before a Joint Committee on the Conduct of the War, stating that great quantities of civilian clothing were shipped to his camps from families in the North to aid the young soldiers in deserting.

[83]On the day before Vallandigham was nominated, June 10, General Lee in a letter to President Jefferson Davis wrote, "Under these circumstances we should neglect no honorable means of dividing and weakening our enemies, that they may feel some of the difficulties experienced by ourselves. It seems to

me that the most effectual mode of accomplishing this object, now within our reach, is to give all the encouragement we can, consistently with truth, to the rising peace party of the North." *War of the Rebellion: A Compilation of the Official Records of the Union and Confederate Armies,* Washington, 1880–1901, Vol. XXVII, Part III, p. 881.

84   Washington, May 29, 1863.
Major General Burnside,
Cincinnati, Ohio.
   Your dispatch of today received. When I shall wish to supersede you I will let you know. All the cabinet regretted the necessity of arresting, for instance, Vallandigham, some perhaps doubting there was a real necessity for it; but being done, all were for seeing you through with it.
   A. Lincoln.

[85] For a history of Vallandigham's negotiations with the Confederate government in Canada, see Randall and Ryan's *History of Ohio,* Vol. IV, pp. 265–71.

[86] *A Rebel War Clerk's Diary at the Confederate States Capital,* by J. B. Jones, clerk in the war department of the Confederate States government, 1866, Vol. I, pp. 334, 351, 353, 357, 358.
   An extremely interesting and reliable view of the inside workings of the Confederacy at Richmond covering the whole period of the war. The authors states in his preface, "This diary was written with the knowledge of the President and Secretary of War." In the summer of 1863 are the following entries:
   May 27th.—Vallandigham has been sent to Shelbyville, within our lines. I think our people ought to give him a friendly greeting.
   June 17th.—A sealed envelope came today, addressed by the President to the Secretary of War, marked "Highly important and confidential," which, of course, I sent to the Secretary immediately without breaking the seal, as it is my duty to do to all letters not private or confidential. I can as yet only conjecture what it referred to. It may be of good, and it may be of bad import.
   June 18th.—I have good reason to suppose that the package marked "important," etc., sent from the President's office yesterday to the Secretary of War, was the substance of a conversation which took place between Mr. Ould and Mr. Vallandigham. What Mr. V. revealed to Mr. O., perhaps supposing the latter, although employed here, friendly to ultimate reconstruction there is no means of conjecturing. But it was deemed "highly important."
   June 22d.—Today I saw the memorandum of Mr. Ould, of the conversation held with Mr. Vallandigham, for file in the archives. He says if we *can only hold out* this year that the peace party of the North would sweep the Lincoln dynasty out of political existence. He seems to have thought that our

cause was sinking, and feared we would submit, which would, of course, be ruinous to his party! But he advises strongly against any invasion of Pennsylvania, for that would unite all parties of the North, and so strengthen Lincoln's hands that he would be able to crush all opposition and trample upon the constitutional rights of the people.

Mr. V. said nothing to indicate that either he or the party had any other idea than that the Union would be reconstructed under Democratic rule. The President indorsed, with his own pen, on this document, that, in regard to invasion of the North, experience proved the contrary of what Mr. V. asserted. But Mr. V. is for restoring the Union, amicably, of course, and if it cannot be so done, then possibly he is in favor of recognizing our independence. He says any reconstruction which is not voluntary on our part, would soon be followed by another separation, and a worse war than the present one.

[87]Not on the people of the loyal, but those of the disloyal States, and of England, feel that the fate of the Union rests upon the result of the election in Ohio.—*New York Tribune*, October 3, 1863.

[88]Speech in Wigwam at Chicago, May 1, 1861. Louis Howland: *Stephen A. Douglas*, p. 369.

[89]John Brough, born in Marietta, Ohio, September 17, 1811; read law but decided to engage in journalism; elected to the legislature in 1838; in 1839 was appointed auditor of state; made great reforms in that office; while auditor of state he established the *Cincinnati Enquirer*. After his term expired he retired to private life and was engaged in the railroad business; nominated for governor on the Union ticket as a War Democrat in 1863; died in Cleveland, Ohio, August 29, 1865.

[90]Francis E. Brown: *The Every-Day Life of Abraham Lincoln*, p. 510.

[91]Extracts from *Diary of Gideon Welles, Secretary of the Navy under Lincoln and Johnson*: Vol. I, pp. 469–70.

Oct. 13, 1863.—The elections in Ohio absorb attention. The President, says he feels nervous.

Oct. 14.—I stopped in to see and congratulate the President, who is in good spirits and greatly relieved from the depression of yesterday. He told me he had more anxiety in regard to the election results of yesterday than he had in 1860 when he was chosen. He could not, he said, have believed four years ago, that one genuine American would, or could, be induced to vote for such a man as Vallandigham, yet he has been made the candidate of a large party, their representative man, and has received a vote that is a discredit to the country. The President showed a good deal of emotion as he dwelt on the subject.

⁹²Letter to Joseph H. Barrett, May 20, 1860, in *Diary and Correspondence of Salmon P. Chase: Annual Report of the American Historical Association for the Year 1902*, Vol. II, p. 287.

⁹³J. W. Schuckers: *The Life and Public Services of Salmon Portland Chase*, pp. 500–1.

⁹⁴J. W. Schuckers: *The Life and Public Services of Salmon Portland Chase*, p. 502.

⁹⁵Joseph P. Smith: *History of the Republican Party in Ohio*, Vol. I, p. 172.

⁹⁶William Henry Smith: *A Political History of Slavery*, Vol. II, note pp. 183–184.

⁹⁷James Ford Rhodes: *History of the United States*, Vol. V, p. 46.

⁹⁸J. W. Schuckers: *The Life and Public Services of Salmon Portland Chase*, p. 509.

⁹⁹I have adopted almost all of this chapter from *Journeys of Lincoln*, by W. T. Coggeshall, who compiled it from newspapers of Cleveland and Columbus. This little book is one of the rarest items of *Lincolniana*. It was published by the *Ohio State Journal* in 1865, for the benefit of a fund to be devoted to the erection of a monument in Capitol Square at Columbus in memory of Abraham Lincoln, and of the Ohio soldiers fallen in battle. The object however was never accomplished.—D. J. R.

INDEX

2nd Cincinnati Battalion 114
2nd O. V. C. 209
5th O. V. C. 209
8th Independent Battery 187, 190, 194
13th Ohio Volunteer Infantry 209
15th Veteran Reserve Corps 203
18th Ohio Volunteer Infantry 209
18th U.S. Infantry 200, 201
22nd Michigan 209
28th Ohio Infantry 216
29th Ohio National Guard 189, 190, 192, 194, 195
88th Ohio Volunteer Infantry 198, 200, 207, 210
91st Ohio Volunteer Infantry 209
109th Ohio Volunteer Infantry 209
124th Ohio Volunteer Infantry 209
131st Regiment Ohio 60
Abbey, H. G. 185
Akron, OH 128
Alabama, secession of 132
Allbright, C. J. 103, 105, 106
Allen, C. M. 100
Allen, William 31, 222
Alliance, OH 128
Ambos, Peter 19, 197
American Party 27, 64
Ammis, ____ 114
Anderson, ____ 114

Andress, C. O. 66
Andrews, John 199
Andrews, G. W. 122
Andrews, Sherlock J. 128, 129–130
Applegate, Daniel 103, 105, 106
Armstrong, George F. 185
Arter, D. 103, 106
Articles of Confederation 31
Ashley, James M. 186
Ashtabula, OH 132
Ashtabula County, OH 111, 219
Ashtabula Sentinel 140
Athens, OH 102, 221
Athens, County OH 122, 221
Athens, PA 219
Auglaize County, OH 122
Austerlitz, NY 225
Awl, William M. 199
Backus, Abner L. 159
Backus, F. T. 183
Bagley, W. W. 202
Bailey, W. W. 199
Baker, L. H. 66
Baldwin, E. I. 192
Ballard, C. J. 185
Baltimore, MD 20, 60, 178
Baltimore and Ohio Railroad 196
Bancroft, Carl 199, 202
Bannister, ____ 182, 195
Barlow, Merrill 128, 182, 183
Barnard, ____ 195, 211
Barnes, ____ 216

Barnett, James 129, 183, 184, 187, 191
Barr, R. N. 182
Barrere, John M. 102, 106
Barret, ____ 19, 20
Barrett, Joseph 102, 105, 106, 232
Bartley, T. W. 159
Bartlow, ____ 60
Bascom, W. T. 32
Bates, ____ 100, 173
Bates, ____ 114
Beckenbach, William 184
Becker, Reuben 185
Beckett, William 102, 105, 106
Beckwith, T. S. 184
Beebe, H. Y. 103, 105, 106, 107
Begges, A. J. 183
Bell, John 110, 175
Bellefontaine, OH 102
Belmont County, OH 95
Beltz, Delilah 215
Benedict, George A. 183
Benedict, S. H. 184
Benjamin, John 182
Benton, Thomas H. 175
Benton, L. A. 185
Bermuda 170
Bigelow, O. D. 95
Bill, Earl 102, 105, 106, 107, 184, 190
Bingham, William 183, 184
Birchard, M. 159
Bishop, J. P. 184
Bishop, R. M. 113, 114, 118
   welcomes Lincoln 115–116

Blaine, James G. 12, 110, 177
Blair, Henry 185
Blair, Montgomery 177
Blandford, MA 220
Blee, ____ 196
Blemer, ____ 215
Bliss, George 159
Bloomington, IL 96
Blossom, H. C. 185
Boardman, W. J. 185
Borden, H. C. 66
Bosley, ____ 114
Boston, MA 27, 150
Bourbon County, KY 219
Bousfield, John 184
Boyce, James S. 66
Brandon, VT 221
Brayton, C. A. 185
Brayton, H. F. 184, 185
Breckinridge, John 78, 110, 116
Brecount, Nora 216
Brimfield, MA 219
Brinsmade, A. T. 184
Brodbeck, Conrad 101, 102, 105, 106, 107
Brooks, Jno. 199
Brooks, M. L. 184
Brough, John 11, 195, 231
  gubernatorial run 170–172, 228
  interaction with Lincoln 172, 178–179
  role in funeral honors 182, 183, 186, 188, 190, 201, 208
Brown, Alice Comer 222
Brown, Fayette 184
Brown, John 15
Brown, S. E. 122
Brussels, Belgium 222
Bryant, William Cullen 97, 214
Buchanan, James 108, 135, 220
Buckingham, I. 185
Buckland, R. P. 186
Bucyrus, OH 102
Buell, Don Carlos 143
Buell, J. C. 185
Bull Run, battle of 212
Burgess, G. D. 102, 106
Burlison, A. E. 184
Burnham, Thomas 185

Burnside, Ambrose 148, 149, 150, 151, 230
Burrin, T. J. 185
Burroughs, ____ 60
Burt, George H. 185, 190, 191
Butler, C. P. L. 198, 199
Butler, J. C. 66
Butler, Theo. 199, 201
Buttles, A. B. 122, 199
Buttles, Lucian 123
Butts, B. 184
Calhoun, J. C. 184
Calhoun, John 175
Calkins, G. W. 184
Cambridge, OH 103
Cameron, Simon 177
Campbell, James E. 223
Campbell, Lewis D. 228
Canton, OH, Zouaves 128
Cardington, OH 196
Carey, John E. 184
Carpenter, S. M. 185
Carr, Amos 95
Carroll County, OH 95
Carroll, N. W. 95
Carrollton, OH 103
Carson, Enoch T. 66
Cartter, David Kellogg 101, 102, 103, 104, 105, 106, 107, 108, 224
Casey, C. N. 66
Cass, Lewis 175
Castle, William B. 183, 184
Chamberlin, Philo 183
Champaign County, OH 95
Champlin, Stephen 194
Chancellorsville, battle of 170, 212
Chandler, ____ 227
Chapin, H. M. 183
Charleston, SC 65, 68, 77, 87, 212
Chase, Salmon P. 9, 29, 33, 97, 98, 99, 220, 221
  correspondence with Lincoln 30–31, 109–110, 176–177
  in Lincoln's cabinet 143, 144, 172–179
  presidential aspirations 94, 100–101, 103–104, 105–110, 176–178, 224
  on slavery 103–104, 174

Cheshire, CT 219
Chester, E. 184
Chesterfield, OH 103
Chicago, IL 12, 18, 19, 21, 26–27, 67, 96, 98, 221, 225
  Republican convention 9, 99–108, 135, 172, 231
Chicago Tribune 107
Chickahominy River 212
Childs, Marcus 205
Chillicothe, OH 102, 147, 211, 220, 222
Chisholm, A. 184
Chittenden, H. T. 197
Cincinnati, Hamilton, and Dayton Railroad 65
Cincinnati, OH 56, 60, 99, 102, 107, 108, 113, 132, 140, 201, 208, 219, 220, 221, 222, 223, 229, 230
  Douglas speech 32
  Lincoln's early visits 17–18, 20–23
  Lincoln speeches 32–33, 56–58, 63–90, 93, 94, 116–117, 119–120
  and slavery 103
  welcomes Lincoln 113–116, 121
Cincinnati *Commercial* 86, 87, 105, 138, 139, 226
Cincinnati *Enquirer* 86, 87–89, 231
Cincinnati *Gazette* 86–88, 118, 225, 226, 227
Cincinnati Zouaves 114
Circleville, OH 102
Clark, F. D. 205
Clark, J. F. 185
Clark, M. B. 184
Clark, Milton L. 102, 106
Clarke, ____ 211
Clarke, Reeder W. 102, 105, 106
Clay, Henry 53, 64, 110, 116, 175, 223
Cleveland Greys 129
Cleveland Light Dragoons 129
Cleveland, OH 27, 60, 102, 103, 107, 127, 132, 172, 176, 231, 232
  Lincoln's speech 130–131
  Lincoln's visit 128–131
  obsequies 182–196

Cleveland *Herald* 127
Cleveland and Pittsburgh Railroad 128, 188
Cleveland Regiment Light Artillery 129
Clifton, George 95
Clifton, OH 22
Clipper 17, 18
Coe, C. W. 185
Coffin, ___ 17
Coggeshall, William T. 126, 226, 232
Collins, William 184, 185
Columbus and Indianapolis Central Railway 215
Columbus, OH 17, 18, 19, 64, 96, 110, 121, 122, 132, 140, 178, 220, 222, 226, 227, 232
  Democratic state convention 150–151
  Douglas speech 32, 55, 72, 80
  Lincoln speeches 32–57, 64, 93, 94, 95, 124–125, 125–126
  obsequies 195–215
  Republican state convention 27, 29, 101
  Union Party convention 170
  and Vallandigham 144, 145, 146, 150, 152
Columbus Machine Manufacturing Company 19
Columbus *Ohio State Journal* 54, 110, 111, 137–139, 225, 226, 232
Colwell, A. G. 185
Comstock, Theodore 201
Congden, William 182
Conneaut, OH 132
Connecticut, Lincoln's visit 97
Connell, John M. 177
Conover, OH 216
Continental Battalion 114
Converse, George S. 159
Conway, Moncure D. 89, 223
Cooke, Henry D. 227
Cooke, Jay 227
Cooper Institute, NY 97, 145, 146
Cornish, NH 221
Cornubia 170

Corwin, Thomas 13, 14, 16, 31, 33, 102, 103, 104, 106, 107, 175, 219
Corwine, Richard M. 66, 99, 100, 101, 102, 104, 106, 107
Coshocton, OH 127
Covington, OH 216
Cowen, B. R. 182, 198
Cowles, E. 184
Cox, Jacob D. 143, 226
Cox, Samuel S. 31, 151, 220, 222
Cox, William 66
Craighead, Samuel 59
Cranston, Mary 215
Craw, W. V. 185
Crawford, Lemuel 184
Crawford, R. 184
Crestline, OH 196
Cridland, ___ 59
Critchfield, L. J. 197
Crittenden, John 14, 78, 89
Crittenden, S. W. 185
Crook, George 143
Cross, D. W. 184
Crowell, John 186
Crowell, W. M. 185
Crumb, C. A. 185
Cummings, ___ 215
Cummings, John E. 102, 106
Cunard, S. T. 95
Cunningham, J. F. 66
Cuppy, F. P. 122
Currier, Anne 215
Cushman, U. 215
Custer, George A. 143
Cutter, Alfred 66
Cuyahoga County, OH 27, 95, 101
Dague, J. B. 210
Darke County, OH 95
Davis, ___ 209
Davis, Charles 194, 195
Davis, David 100
Davis, H. S. 185
Davis, J. S. 66
Davis, Jefferson 52, 132–133, 134, 135, 147, 149, 175, 229
Davison, G. I. 210
Day, T. C. 66
Dayton Daily Empire 58, 228

Dayton, OH 56, 59, 60, 86, 98, 102, 145, 147, 148, 229
Dayton, William L. 63
Defiance, OH 102
DeForest, ___ 195
De La Vergne, ___ 195
Delano, Columbus 10, 103, 105, 106
Delaware, OH 222
Dennison, William 25, 64, 90, 94, 95, 103, 122, 123, 127, 131, 144, 220, 226
Derrickson, ___ 190, 195
Deshler, W. G. 197, 198, 199, 226
Detroit, MI 60, 190, 195
Deven, J. C. 186
Dickman, F. J. 183
Dickson, William 21, 22, 220, 225
Dodge, George C. 184
Doherty, John W. 199, 202
Donaldson, ___ 198
Douglas, ___ 209
Douglas, Stephen A. 31, 57, 64, 108, 116, 117, 125, 131, 175, 221
  debates Lincoln 16, 26, 31, 33–35, 63, 91, 93, 95–96, 110
  Ohio speeches 32, 222
  "Popular Sovereignty" 26–27, 36–56, 57–58, 60–61, 73–74, 83
  presidential race 65–89, 98, 110
  on Union 135, 171
Douty, C. W. 199, 202
Dresden, OH 127
Dred Scott decision 36, 43, 47–54, 75–76, 95
Dubois, Jesse K. 100
Duke, G. P. 196
Dunlap, C. N. 66
Dyer, C. S. 199, 203
Edenton, NC 222
Eberly, Isaac 198, 199
Edgar, ___ 59
Edgarton, W. P. 190, 191
Edmonson, ___ 59
Edwards, William 185
Eells, D. P. 185
Eells, T. D. 185

Egbert, Jacob 95
Eggleston, Benjamin 66, 102, 105, 106
Elliot, James 66
Elliott, F. R. 184
Ely, George B. 184
Ennis, ___ 105, 106
Enos, R. K. 103
Ensworth, J. 185
Ephesus 136
Erie, PA 182
Estep, E. J. 184
Evatt, Charles 185
Everett, Edward 110
Everett, A. 183
Ewing, Thomas 25, 221
Failing, W. 198, 199
Fairfield County OH 177
Felton, C. E. 197, 208, 211
Field, Cyrus 198
Field, E. G. 201
Field, John 199
Field, S. N. 199
Fields, ___ 188
Fields, Ed 199
Fillmore, Millard 219
Finck, W. D. 159
Fitch, Ed. A. 199, 202
Fitch, J. W. 184
Flagg, W. G. 122
Flint, ___ 195
Flint, E. S. 183
Florida, secession of 132
Fogg, W. P. 184
Follett, Foster & Co. 96, 111, 223
Foot, Horace 186
Foot, John A. 183
Fort Sumter 121, 144, 145, 212
Fort Warren 150, 151
Fosdick, Chas. E. 66
Fox, ___ 17, 18
Franklin County, OH 125, 201
Freeman, ___ 66
Freeman, H. B. 209
Freeman, J. F. 183
Freeport, IL 47, 48, 76
Free Soil Party 27, 104
Fremont, OH 223
Fugitive Slave Law 27, 28–31, 84, 97, 103, 104, 131, 139
Galbreath, Charles B. 7, 12

Gale, Charles 195
Galloway, Samuel 19, 30, 55, 97, 98, 101, 110, 111, 182, 197, 198, 199, 219
Gano, John S. 66
Gardner, George W. 184
Garfield, James A. 143
Gaver, William 199
Geauga County, OH 95, 219
Geiger, Levi 102, 106
Geneva, OH 131
German Yagers 114
Gettysburg, battle of 170, 172, 212
Gettysburg, OH 216
Gettysburg, PA 219
Giddings, Joshua R. 13, 14, 15, 16, 29, 31, 103, 105, 107, 140, 219, 220
Gilmore, ___ 143
Gilmore, B. 199
Glasser, Charles 184
Glenn, J. B. 185
Goepper, M. 66
Goldrick, Peter 184
Goodale, L. 199
Goodwin, E. P. 211
Gordon, W. J. 159
Gorham, E. J. 184
Gorham, John H. 185
Gounley, James 215
Graham, E. 102, 105, 106, 107
Grannis, John C. 185
Grant, Ulysses 143, 170, 220
Gray, David S. 198, 199
Greeley, Horace 133, 136, 146
Greene County, OH 95
Greenleaf, A. 199, 202
Green, John K. 66
Greenville, OH 216
Greenwood, Miles 66, 114
Grenninger, ___ 190
Griswold, S. O. 183
Grover, James 199
Gurley, John A. 60
Gurley, John J. 102, 105, 106
Gwynne, E. W. 199
Halifax, Canada 170
Hall, Oakey 134
Halstead, Murat 105, 108, 223, 224
Hamilton, Alexander 143, 212

Hamilton, OH 60, 102, 229
Hamilton County, OH 32, 101, 122
Hamlin, Hannibal 109, 110, 115, 175
Hammond, Charles 225
Handy, T. P. 183
Hancock County, OH 95
Hanna, Robert 185
Hannal, ___ 209
Harding, ___ 20, 21
Harn, G. U. 102, 105, 106
Harper's Monthly 21, 37, 43, 55, 94
Harris, J. A. 185
Harrison, William Henry 100, 104, 221
Harrison, Benjamin 177
Hart, William 185
Hartness, John 184
Harvey, H. 185
Hassaurek, Fred 66, 102, 105, 106, 107, 121
Hawkins, H. C. 184
Hayes, Rutherford B. 64, 66, 89, 99, 113, 120–121, 221, 222–223, 225
Haynes, Daniel 95
Hays, ___ 66
Hays, K. 184
Hayward, W. H. 183, 184, 189, 195
Haywood, W. H. 128
Hazen, William 143
Hechman, ___ 129
Herrick, G. 185
Herrick, H. J. 184
Heyl, Christian 199
Hickman, ___ 39, 77
Hickox, Charles 184, 185
Higgins, T. J. 196
Hill, James 185
Hiller, Charles 66
Hills, Addison 185
History of Butler County 60
Hitchcock, H. G. 185
Hitchcock, Peter 17, 219
Hitchcock, R. 103, 105, 106, 107
Hivling, A. 102, 106
Hobbs, C. S. 185
Hoffner, ___ 208

Hogan, M. B. 66
Holmes County OH 170
Holmes, G. W. 122
Holt, Joseph 228, 229
Holtnorth, ___ 129
Hooker, Joseph 182, 190, 194, 201, 208, 211, 214, 229
Horace 186
Horringer, ___ 209
Horton, Valentine 101, 102, 105, 106, 107
Houk, David A. 159
Hovey, Jacob 184
Howard, ___ 111
Howe, George 184
Howells, W. C. 140
Howells, William Dean 111, 140, 226, 227
Hoy, John 95
Hoyt, H. J. 185
Hubbard, W. B. 199
Hubbell, ___ 114
Hubby, L. M. 183
Hudson, OH 128
Hughes, S. A. 215
Hugo, Peter 196
Hull, ___ 209
Hunter, David 208, 211
Huntington, John 184
Hurlbut, H. B. 184, 185
Hutchins, W. A. 159
Hyde, G. A. 184
Hyman, S. 184
Idaho 182
Illinois, Lincoln's speeches 140
Illinois State Journal 93
Independence Hall 140
Independent Guthrie Greys Battalion 114
Indiana, Lincoln's speech 140
Indianapolis, IN 60, 113, 118, 214
Indianapolis and Cincinnati Railroad 113
Jackson, ___ 114
Jackson, Andrew 104, 145
Jaeger, Sr., F. 199
Jefferson, OH 103
Jefferson County, OH 95
Jefferson, Thomas 41, 44, 79, 117, 145, 212

Jewett, Hugh H. 150, 172
Jobson, Frank 66
Johnson, Andrew 193, 197, 213, 220, 221
Johnson, E. M. 66
Johnson, H. N. 184
Johnson, Herschel 110
Johnson, Reverdy 20
Johnson, Richard M. 35
Johnson, Samuel C. 95
Jones, ___ 114
Jones, J. B. 230
Jones, Jr., Thomas 183, 184
Jones, William 184
Judd, N. B. 91, 104
Kansas–Nebraska Act 26, 42, 63
Kansas statehood 41, 61
Katz, G. W. S. 66
Keck, J. L. 66
Keehen, Frank 182
Keith, F. C. 184
Keith, M. R. 183
Kelley, Moses 184
Kelley, T. M. 183
Kelly, Frank 185
Kelton, F. C. 199
Kennedy, John P. 93, 99
Kennett, ___ 114
Kenyon College 222
Kilbourne, L. 198, 199
Killen, Norris 210
Kimble, Lucy 215
Kinsey, ___ 87
Kirk, Robert C. 123
Klotter, George 66
Ladd, James H. 95
Lafayette Guards 114
Lake County OH 182
Lake Erie, battle of 194
Lake Forest, IL 225
Lake Shore Railroad 188
Lampson, B. 185
Lancaster, OH 221
Lane, Joseph 110
Lathrop, ___ 182, 211
Lawrence County, OH 95
Lawty, W. 185
Leavitt, H. H. 150
Lebanon, OH 102, 107, 228
LeBlond, F. C. 159
Lee, Robert E. 170, 212, 229

Leek, T. W. 184
Leggett, Mortimer 143
Lester, S. F. 183
Leutkemeyer, H. W. 185
Lewiston, PA 226
Liberty Party 103
Licking County, OH 95
Lincoln, Abraham
  and children 115
  correspondence of 17–18, 19–20, 30–31, 32, 96, 97–98, 98–99, 99–100, 111, 122, 135–136, 150, 160–163, 172, 177, 230
  dealings with Chase 30–31, 98, 99, 109–110, 172–179
  debates Douglas 16, 26, 31, 33–34, 47, 63–86, 91–92, 93, 94–95, 96, 110
  relations with Vallandigham 11, 147–172, 230, 231
  depression 21, 91, 118, 231
  downplays crisis 131, 132
  Emancipation Proclamation 10
  faith of 118, 124, 127, 212
  funeral ceremonies 12, 182, 187–217
  legal practice 17–20
  legislator 13–16
  on peace movement 151
  physical appearance 22, 60, 88, 125, 194
  and "Popular Sovereignty" 36–54, 54–56, 60–61, 73–74, 83, 98
  as presidential candidate 92, 104–112
  on slavery 30, 34, 57–58, 66–86, 92, 120, 121
Lincoln, Mary 21, 131
Lincoln, Robert 121
Lincoln, Tad 122
Lincoln, T. D. "Tim" 18, 219
Lincoln, Willie 122
Little Miami Railway 121, 205
Logan County, OH 95
Logan, Linus 17, 18
Long, Alexander 159
Longworth, Nicholas 22, 121, 220
Looker, N. R. 66

Lookout Mountain 212
Lorain County, OH 95, 122
Louisiana Purchase 26
Louisiana, secession of 132
Louisville (locomotive) 196
Loving, S. 198, 199
Lowe, P. P. 102, 105, 106
Lunt, J. M. 215
Lynchburg, VA 220, 222
Lyon, L. L. 184
Lyon, R. T. 183, 184
Lytle, ___ 114
Macaulay, ___ 145
MacFeely, ___ 182
Mack, ___ 129
Mack, Henry 66
Madison, James 79, 117
Madison, OH 131
Magill, C. M. 66
Mahoning County, OH 95
Mail (steamboat) 18
Manchester, OH 18
Manny, John H. 20
Mansfield, OH 92–93, 99, 105
Marble, F. A. 182
Marietta, OH 231
Marshall, George F. 185
Martin, B. F. 197
Martin, Mrs. G. 215
Martin, George 182
Martin, John L. 95, 184
Martin, William T. 199
Martin's Ferry, OH 103
Mason, James 185
Massillon, OH 103
Masters, I. U. 128, 129
Mather, S. H. 184
Mather, S. L. 185
Maxwell, Sidney D. 182
Maynard, Allayne 184
McCallum, Daniel 196, 211
McClellan, George B. 143, 150
McCook, ___ 143
McCormick, Cyrus H. 20
McCrea, Will 60
McCullough, S. W. 95
McDonald, William 95
McDowell, Irvin 143
McFarland, H. C. 184
McGroat, ___ 209
McGuire, J. 182

McIlvaine, Charles Pettit 192, 193
McKenzie, C. S. 184
McKinley, William 221
McKinney, J. F. 159
McLean, John 21, 99, 100, 103–107
McMillen, S. D. 183
Meadville, PA 190, 195
Medill, Joseph 107
Mees, K. 198, 199
Meigs County, OH 101
Meisner, ___ 195
Melbinch, William 185
Mercer, John T. 182
Merchant, Silas 184, 191
Mexican War 13–14, 16, 155, 156, 159, 160, 222
Mexico City 13
Meyer, Fred 66
Meyer, Stoutey 216
Miami County, OH 122
Miami University 220
Miami Valley 60
Middletown, CT 219
Milford, OH 215
Miller, ___ 114
Miller, John 199
Millersburg, OH 103
Mills, ___ 122
Mississippi River 19
Mississippi, secession of 132
Missouri Compromise 26, 44, 75
Mitchel, Ormsby 143
Mix, ___ 195
Mix, R. E. 184
Molliter, Stephen 66
Moneypenny, G. W. 199
Monroe, James 102, 122, 224
Monroe, James (president) 104
Monterey, Mexico 13
Montgomery County, OH 98, 101, 122
Montgomery, ___ 182
Montreal, Canada 170, 219
Moody, Granville 216
Moore, Amos 66
Morgan, E. P. 185
Morgan, John Hunt 170
Morley, J. H. 184

Morris, Jas. R. 159
Morrow County, OH 95
Mount Auburn, OH 22
Mount Gilead, OH 102
Mount Vernon, OH 10, 103, 148, 149
Murphey, G. B. 185
Murray, W. 183
Murray, William 184
Mygatt, George S. 131, 183
Nashville (locomotive) 196
Naughton, William 199
Neil, H. M. 203
Neil, R. S. 199
Neil, Robert 199
Nesbitt, B. 95
Newark, NJ 220
Newark, OH 102, 127
Newburgh, OH 190
Newcomerstown, OH 127
New Jersey, Lincoln's visits 140
New Lisbon, OH 227
New Madison Station, OH 217
New Market, OH 102
New Paris, OH 217
New York, Lincoln's visits 97, 140
New York City 59, 97, 134, 145, 148, 164, 214, 221, 223
New York Herald 93, 99, 175
New York Times 175, 196, 222
New York Tribune 133, 146, 175, 223, 226, 231
Niagara Falls, Canada 170
Nichols, Levi T. 200, 201
Nickum, Mrs. Charles W. 59, 60
Noble County OH 170
Noble, C. W. 185
Noble, John 199
Noble, Warren P. 159
Northrup, A. L. 95
Norwalk, OH 102
Nottingham, Henry 182
Oberkleine, Frederick 119
Oberlin, OH 102, 224
Oberlin–Wellington Rescue Case 27, 29
O'Bannon, P. N. 95
Ogden, S. E. 122
O'Hara, George 131

Ohio River 18, 44, 70, 73, 139
Ohio State Journal 54, 110, 111, 137, 225, 226, 232
Ohio Statesman 33, 55
Ohio University 221
Olds, Chauncey N. 197
Olmsted, C. H. 202
O'Neill, John 159
O'Reilly, James K. 190
Orr, J. H. 209
Otis, W. F. 185
Ottawa, IL 33
Ould, ___ 230
Oviatt, O. M. 128, 186
Paddock, ___ 129
Page, E. D. 182
Paine, Robert F. 103, 105, 106, 107, 185
Paine, Mrs. R. F. 189
Painesville, OH 103, 131, 219
Painter, J. V. 185
Palmer, C. W. 183
Palmer, J. D. 184
Palo Alto, Mexico 13
Parnell, James 184
Parrott, Edwin A. 98–99, 122
Parsons, Frank W. 184
Parsons, George M. 33, 94, 96, 197
Parsons, R. C. 183
Patrick, D. C. 210
Patterson, James 199
Paul the apostle 136, 174
Payne, O. H. 190, 191
Payne, Henry B. 172, 183, 184
Peck, E. M. 185
Peixotto, B. F. 184, 191
Pelton, F. W. 184
Pendleton, George H. 31, 159, 222
Pendry, ___ 114
Pennsylvania, Lincoln's visits 140
Perkins, E. R. 184
Perkins, J. M. 185
Perkins, Joseph 185
Perry, ___ 195
Perrysburg, OH 102
Pettingell, Charles 184
Pfau, ___ 114
Philadelphia, PA 20, 107, 140, 148

Philadelphia Public Ledger 59
Pierce, Franklin 104
Pierce, Henry 66
Pierce, L. A. 183
Piqua, OH 216
Pitkin, L. M. 184
Pittsburgh, PA 127, 223
Platt, Augustus 199
Pleasant Valley, OH 215
Plutarch 89
Polk, James K. 13
Pomeroy, OH 102
Portage County, OH 220
Portsmouth, OH 102
Potomac River 139
Potter, M. D. 66
Powell, ___ 209
Preble County, OH 95
Prentiss, F. J. 185
Presly, George 184
Preston, ___ 108
Price, David 184
Price, Henry 66
Price, Joseph 227
Pryor, Roger A. 77
Pugh, George E. 31, 171, 222
Purdy, Nelson 184
Purron, Mrs. ___ 216
Quayle, Thomas 185
Quebec, Canada 170
Quinn, Arthur 185
Quito, Ecuador 226
Race, Seymour 191
Radebaugh, Jno. 199, 201
Ramage, A. C. 95
Ramsey, Amos S. 199
Randerson, Joseph 185
Randolph, ___ 46
Ranney, Rufus P. 25, 150, 172, 220
Ravenna, OH 103, 107, 128
Raymond, ___ 118
Raymond, H. N. 184
Read, C. A. 185
Redding, OH 102
Reddington, J. A. 185
Reinhard, J. 199
Renick, Jonathan 102, 106
Republican Party, founding of 14, 27, 28, 29, 63, 104, 220, 226
Rettberg, A. 185

Reynolds, ___ 97–98
Reynolds, H. K. 184
Rhode Island, Lincoln's visit 97
Rice, ___ 129
Rice, Harvey, 184
Richardson, W. P. 201
Richmond *Enquirer* 77
Richmond, IN 217
Richmond Junction, OH 216
Richmond, VA 212, 230
Riley, Joseph H. 122
Rio Grande River 26, 139
Roberts, Ansel 183, 184
Robinson, ___ 195
Robinson, J. P. 185, 186
Robinson, J. V., Jr. 102, 106
Rock Island Bridge Company 18–19, 21
Rockwell, E. 184
Roeder, P. 185
Rogers, C. C. 184
Root, E. S. 184
Rosecrans, William S. 143, 150
Ross, ___ 198
Ross, John P. 184, 191
Ross, T. 184
Rover Guards 114
Rower, ___ 195
Ruggles, H. D. 184
Runyan, George N. 66
Russell, Addison Peale 64, 95, 222
Russell, C. L. 128, 184
Russell, W. S. 95
Ryan, Daniel J. 7, 11, 12, 224, 226
Sackrider, E. W. 185
Sage, J. C. 183
St. Clair, J. E. 198, 199
St. Louis, MO 19
St. Paris, OH 216
Sands, A. C. 102, 105, 106
Sandusky Commercial Register 92, 93
Sandusky County, OH 95
Sandusky, OH 227
Sanford, A. S. 183, 184
Saturday Evening Post (Philadelphia) 107
Scarrett, Charles 199, 201
Scarritt, J. A. 211

Schaeffer, Louis 159
Schenck, Robert C. 144, 147
Schroeder, Jacob 185
Schuyler, P. N. 102, 105, 106
Scott County, IN 220
Scott, Dred 36, 43, 47–54, 75, 76, 95
Scott, J. 122
Scott, Winfield 135
Scoville, O. C. 185
Senter, George B. 128, 182, 183, 186
Seward, William 93, 134, 135, 175, 193
  assessment of Lincoln 141, 174
  cabinet member 173, 174
  and "popular sovereignty" 37, 38, 39
  and slavery 67, 77
  presidential aspirations 97, 99–100, 103, 105, 108, 109, 110
Sexton, D. B. 183
Seymore, B. 184
Shannon, T. B. 211
Sheridan, Philip 143
Sherman, John 31, 110, 143, 182, 186, 221
Sherman, William T. 143
Shillito, George 66
Shultz, H. 66
Sidney, OH 102
Simmons, ___ 129
Simms, E. 184
Simpson, ___ 182, 194, 195, 211
Skeels, O. N. 184
Skiles, John W. 198, 199, 201, 203
Slater, William 215
Smith, Anson 95
Smith, B. E. 215
Smith, Richard 66
Smith, W. F. 196
Smith, William J. 185
Smith, William Henry 118–120, 178, 225
Smithknight, Louis 185
Sommer, ___ 114
South Carolina, secession of 132, 133, 135, 139, 227

Spangler, B. L. 184, 191
Spaulding, ___ 184
Spaulding, Rufus P. 29, 183, 184, 186
Spencer, Erastus 95
Spooner, Thomas 66, 101, 102, 105, 106, 107
Sprague, A. N. 66
Sprague, William 177
Spriggs, Mrs. ___ 14
Springfield, IL 19, 93
  funeral honors 181, 182, 190, 196, 215
  Lincoln's hometown 30, 32, 96, 97, 99, 100, 111, 122, 113, 122, 135, 136, 140, 175
  Lincoln's speeches 92, 96, 140
Spring Grove Cemetery 22
Stager, Anson 183, 184
Standard, N. M. 185
Stanley, David 143
Stanley, George A. 185
Stanberry, Henry 25, 221
Stanton, Edwin M. 20, 21, 143, 220
Starkweather, Samuel 183, 184
Steadman, B. 185
Steedman, James 143
Steel, John 66
Steese, Isaac 103, 105, 106, 107
Sterling, E. 184
Sterling, John M. 184
Stephan, Daniel 184
Stephens, Alexander H. 52, 133
Sternburg, ___ 195
Steuben Artillery 114
Steubenville, OH 103, 220
  Lincoln's speech 127
Stevenson, Job E. 211
  oration of 211–214
Stewart, F. 199
Stivers, ___ 209
Stokely, Samuel 103, 105, 106
Stone, A. B. 184, 192
Stone, Jr., Amasa 183, 184
Stone, A. P. 95
Storer, Bellamy 22
Strong, S. M. 185

Sturges, Joseph 183, 184
Sullivant, S. 199, 209
Summit County, OH 95
Sumner, Charles 93, 173
Sutliffe, Milton 103, 105, 106, 107
Swan, Joseph R. 28, 29, 30, 31, 97–98, 199
Swartz, Leonard 66
Swasey, A. E. 66
Swasey, Moses 66
Swayne, Wager 143, 201, 208
Swett, Leonard 92
Swigart, D. W. 102, 105, 106
Swords, ___ 182, 195, 211
Taney, Roger 179
Taylor, ___ 182, 195, 211
Taylor, ___ 199
Taylor, David 102, 105, 106, 107
Taylor, V. C. 184
Taylor, Zachary 20, 100, 104, 221
Terry, T. W. 211
Texas, secession of 132
Thatcher, Peter 184, 185
Thayer, Eli 136
Thayer, Proctor 184
Thieme, Augustus 185
Thomas, Nicholas N. 66
Thorman, S. 184
Thrall, W. B. 95, 199
Throckmorton, Eliza 216
Thurman, Allen G. 25, 31, 110, 220, 222
Tibbitts, ___ 195
Tiffin, OH 102
Tilden, D. R. 186
Tod, David 149, 183, 184, 186
Todhunter, ___ 60
Townsend, ___ 211
Townsend, Amos 182, 183, 184, 190, 191
Townshend, Norton S. 105, 106, 107, 224
Tracy, James J. 184
Trimble, J. M. 197
Trounstine, Joseph 66
Truscott, W. H. 183
Troy, OH 102, 216
Uhrichsville, OH 127
Underground Railroad 15

Unionville, OH 215
Upham, J. J. 195
Urbana, OH 102, 215
Usher, J. P. 226
Vallandigham, Clement L. 11, 222, 227–228, 229, 230, 231
  banishment issue 149–170
  gubernatorial run 150–151, 170–172, 231
  opposes war efforts 145, 147, 148
  on secession 145, 146
  on slavery 148
Van Camp, C. 196
Van Camp, E. 196
Van Voorhees, N. H. 102, 105, 106
Van Voost, James 200, 201
Vermont, Lincoln's visit 97
Vicksburg, siege of 170, 172
Villard, ___ 215
Vincennes, IN 100
Voges, ___ 195
Waddle, John 95
Wade, Benjamin 29, 31, 33, 93, 103, 144
Walcutt, John M. 199
Walker, ___ 209
Wallace, F. T. 184, 185
Wallace, William 103, 105, 106
Walnut Hills, OH 22
Wands, H. P. 209
Warner, John F. 185
Warner, Willard 102, 105, 106
Warren, OH 103
Warren County, OH 95, 122
Washburne, E. B. 135, 136
Washington County, OH 95

Washington Dragoons 114
Washington, George 30, 79, 115, 117, 133, 203, 206, 212
Wassenick, E. 66
Waters, Octavius 182
Weasner, T. H. 66
Weaver's Station, OH 217
Webber, ___ 200
Weber, G. C. E. 184
Webster, Daniel 14, 110, 175, 223
Weekly Dayton Journal 57
Weitzel, Godfrey 143
Welles, Gideon 231
Wellhouse, W. 185
Wellington, OH 27, 29
Wellsville, OH 127
Welsh, John 122
Wenham, A. J. 184
West, George 196
West, J. E. 66
West, W. H. 102, 105, 106
West Liberty, VA 221
Westville Station, OH 216
Wheeler, John A. 184
Whetstone, Thomas H. 66
Whitaker, Charles 184
Whitcom, ___ 114
Whitcomb, George 66
White, C. A. 159
White, J. W. 159
Whiting, ___ 60
Whittlesey, Charles 184
Wickliffe, OH 182
Wiggens, Samuel 66
Wikoff, A. T. 209
Wilcox, ___ 201, 205
Wilcox, J. A. 209

Wiley's Station, OH 217
Wilkinson, M. C. 203
Willard, E. S. 185
Willey, George 184
William Case (locomotive) 182
Williams, Caleb A. 103, 105, 106
Williams, Mrs. Milo G. 216
Williamson, S. 95, 183
Willich, August 66
Wilmington, OH 222
Willoughby, OH 131
Willson, H. V. 183, 184
Wilson, Henry 201
Wilson, J. D. 210
Windsor, Canada 170
Wing, J. 202
Winslow, R. K. 184
Wise, Henry 78
Witt, Stillman 183, 184
Wolcott, C. P. 95, 103
Woodford, Seth 95
Woodstock, OH 215
Woodworth, George W. 184
Wooster, OH 102
Worswick, James 184
Wright, G. B. 66
Wright, F. M. 95
Wright, Nathaniel 66
Xenia, OH 102
Yale University 219
Younglove, M. C. 185
Zaleski, OH 102
Zanesville, OH 103, 221, 222
Zinn, Peter 32, 63, 64, 66

Please visit our web site

www.oldhundredthpress.com

for details on other unique and hard-to-find books relating to Ohio and the Civil War.

For more information on Ohio Historical Society programs, go to

www.ohiohistory.org